Memories of a Hyphenated Man

Memories
of a
Hyphenated
Man

Ramón Eduardo Ruiz Urueta

The University of Arizona Press
Tucson

The University of Arizona Press
© 2003 The Arizona Board of Regents
First printing
All rights reserved
∞ This book is printed on acid-free, archival-quality paper.
Manufactured in the United States of America

08 07 06 05 04 03   6 5 4 3 2 1

Library of Congress Cataloging-in-Publication Data
Ruiz, Ramón Eduardo.
Memories of a hyphenated man / Ramón Eduardo Ruiz Urueta.
p. cm.
ISBN 0-8165-2332-0 (acid-free paper)
1. Ruiz, Ramón Eduardo. 2. Historians—United States—Biography.
3. Mexican Americans—Biography. 4. Mexican Americans—Ethnic
identity. 5. United States—Relations—Mexico. 6. Mexico—
relations—United States. 7. Pacific Beach (San Diego, Calif.)—
Biography. 10. San Diego (Calif.)—Biography. 1. Title.
E175.5.R85 A3 2003
973'.0468'0092—dc21
2003001851

British Library Cataloguing-in-Publication Data
A catalogue record for this book is available from the British Library.

Hay una creencia literaria . . . de que escribir es eso,
que por eso la gente tiene necesidad de contar su historia,
porque es lo que les da identidad, contar para ser.
—Federico Campbell, *La máquina de escribir*

━━━━

No sabes si vale la pena recordarlo.
Sólo quisiera recordar . . . lo que va a suceder:
no quieres prever lo que ya sucedió. En tu penumbre,
los ojos ven hacia adelante, no saben adivinar el pasado.
—Carlos Fuentes, *La muerte de Artemio Cruz*

Contents

Preface   ix

1. The Home Town   3

2. Euphoric Days   24

3. Ambivalent Times   49

4. The Halls of Ivy   69

5. The Dogs of War   92

6. The Graduate Student   116

7. The Holy Grail   141

8. Marvelous Journey   158

9. Smith   173

10. Exile's Return   196

11. Epilogue   220

Preface

This journal is about my life in the United States as the son of Mexicans, about the days in Mexico when natives took a dim view of kin born across the border, and about my uphill climb to win acclaim as a historian of Mexico. I am of the generation that was born in the United States and came of age on the eve of World War II; until then, Mexicans (that is, those born in Mexico), our parents, had ruled the roost, small as it was. Mine was largely an apolitical generation, though occasionally, as recent scholars remind us, bold men and women rose up against exploitative bosses in mines and fields. Nor, exceptions granted, did my generation give much thought to questions of identity; to believe that this matter troubled the sleep of most was to whistle in the dark. Because many of this generation did not speak Spanish or spoke it poorly and took no pride in their ancestral roots, haughty Mexicans referred to them as *pochos,* "brown outside but white inside."

By birth, I am an American, but by culture, thanks to my parents and to the upbringing they gave me, I am also Mexican. I know the country of their birth, its people and its culture, as well as I know my own. I have made my life studying Mexicans and writing about them. That Hobson's choice was actually a life jacket when I was young and vulnerable; knowing my ancestral roots helped me to keep my head above water when phobic neighbors would have let me drown. To forget where you come from not only discourages pride in your culture but, more to the point, means a loss of your self.

The tale unfolds on a stage where the odds were long, at a time when whites in the South made the lynching of black men into a public spectacle and when in San Diego neighborhoods bigots would not rent to working-class Mexicans. In cities and towns of the Southwest, Anglos fenced off public swimming pools to Mexicans, told them to sit in the balconies of movie theaters, and placed their children in segregated schools. In the so-called integrated towns of San Diego's hinterland, as sociologist Paul Taylor documented, the hazing of Mexican children by Anglo classmates was not uncommon, nor was grouping them in the back of school busses, away from other students who were unwilling to associate with them. Teachers had white faces, and the pages of U.S. textbooks were bare of Mexicans or their historical deeds. Given these circumstances, it is no wonder that Mexican children could be highly sensitive, feel socially ostracized, and drop out of school. And, so far as I know, no one of my ancestry taught Mexican history in a university in this land of the fair.

It is said all too frequently that we live in an age of testimonials, when many feel the urge to tell a story drawn from their own experience. Yet we who write history know that people have always exhumed their past. The personal narrative, moreover, may be the true coin of ethnic expression. My Mexican ancestors even developed a special form to write about themselves and, concomitantly, to strengthen national bonds: *cuadros de costumbre* (writings about everyday life). Guillermo Prieto, one of its progenitors, wrote the much-read *Memorias de mis tiempos,* which looks back nostalgically on the *tertulias* (soirees) of his student days at the Academia de San Juan de Letrán, where every Wednesday he heard poetry readings by luminaries at a time of horrendous economic woes and political chicanery.

Who am I? How did I become what I am? That is what I am trying to explain, a singular task because by ethnic ancestry and culture I am hardly your typical American, although what is typical is changing rapidly. And as a skeptical Virginia Woolf once asked: "How many people have succeeded in drawing themselves with a pen?" Writing digs up memories long forgotten or relegated to the dust bin of history. At times, I lie awake at night, struggling to recall the past, troubled by events of yesteryear.

Two cultures, I will say again and again, brought me into being. Born of Mexican parents, one *el color de la tierra* (the color of the earth) and the other fair, I am hardly blond, a cross one bears in a country where color, like chancres on the social body, poisons class differences and largely frames one's existence and dictates how one is regarded. I stand out in a crowd. Yet I was born in this country and went to school here, and by that fact alone I am an American, even though Anglos of my generation looked upon me as a Mexican. The days when companions saw me day in and day out at school but kept to themselves out of school are difficult to set aside, no matter how circumstances may have changed.

From the start, I have confronted two choices: endeavor to be like others, impossible because of ethnic ancestry and the prejudice of neighbors, or stand up for my own identity. The first option, as I perceive it, is that of the *lacayo,* the lackey; the second is the only way to preserve one's sense of self-worth. By choice, I am a university professor, but by accident I am an American; I did not choose to be born here. In the land of the stars and stripes, I am both at ease and troubled, rarely in accord with the prevailing Yankee view of the world. At times, I feel like a fish out of water, a foreigner in my country, unable to understand or speak the official language. I have spent virtually an entire life teaching and writing, occupations that in reality have become my real home. As for Mexico, the land of my parents, I have paradoxical feelings; when there, I feel at home, and at times I regret returning to the land of Washington and Lincoln, but were I to live there, I would miss the security that the surroundings here in the United States provide.

"When you are forty," to quote a truth, "half of you belongs to the past. And when you are seventy, nearly all of you." I recall that adage because I am no longer young; *"ya voy para viejo"* as Mexicans are wont to say. I no longer can be certain that the part of my brain safeguarding secrets from yesteryear will not betray me. At times, nostalgia more than likely dictates what I recollect. Memory, after all, is a maddening thing, blinding us when we're trying desperately to remember, as if a tent were collapsing on us. Mark Twain said it well: "It isn't so astonishing, the number of things that I can remember, as the number of things I can remember that aren't so."

A professor's life, as distinct from that of presidents who make decisions for millions of people or of generals who lead armies into battle, may seem calm and boring. Unkind critics say that historians feast on the lives of others, which makes them dull subjects. I nonetheless may have something of value to convey, a story for those who study what is unique in the American experience. I chose to become a historian at a time when just a handful of us, Mexicans by ancestry, walked through the portals of a college and when even fewer went on to graduate school. As my credentials testify, I have enjoyed a fruitful career, with a few detours along the way. While writing this testimonial, I have thought of others of my flesh and blood, men and women who want to stand tall. This memoir is in part for them, to tell them what I put up with and how I coped, the cost of achieving some success and surviving with dignity. I write this story, too, as a testimonial to my parents and to my wife, Natalia, who with love and devotion accompanied me on my journey.

When I set out to write this chronicle, a few fellow scholars—practitioners of the craft of history, as I am—helped me recall events of the past or set the record straight when I wandered off the beaten path and thus made this memoir more complete. For their suggestions and advice, I am grateful to Mario T. García, Rodolfo Acuña, Félix Almaraz, David Gutiérrez, Richard C. Atkinson, Patrick Ledden, and Arnoldo de León.

Memories of a Hyphenated Man

I

The Home Town

———

It was no easy ride growing up when every Tom, Dick, and Harry was a Podunk politico, village storekeeper, church deacon, or schoolteacher, but every Tomás, Ricardo, and María—men and women of my flesh and blood—were the hewers of wood and drawers of water.

This story, which I undertake with a skeptic's reticence, unfolds at Sessions Ranch, a place in southern California thirty miles from Mexico and half that distance to San Diego, which, in 1921, the year I was born, had fewer than 75,000 inhabitants.

It was a long, long time ago, when the *San Diego Union,* the one newspaper in town, referred to the Japanese as "Japs" and once in a while said something about a visiting Mexican dignitary in Tijuana but nary a word about Mexicans in San Diego. A new Ford roadster cost 556 dollars; women's house dresses were 98 cents; you could eat prime rib au jus at Bergman's, an upscale restaurant on Broadway, for 48 cents; Logan Heights was not yet a Mexican barrio; and you could still buy a Reo or Cleveland motor car. You watched vaudeville at the Spreckels Theatre or saw movies at the Casino and Cabrillo, and partygoers raised hell in night clubs in Tijuana, where orchestras played American jazz. Today, what was Sessions Ranch lies in the bosom of Pacific Beach, itself a sprawling suburb of San Diego; the wealthy enclave La Jolla, a resort renown for its beaches and tennis clubs, sits on its northern fringe.

My travails, that of a man of Mexican ancestry born in the United States, start with Papá, the *patrón* of our family dynasty who, with Mamá keeping watch, tailored my identity. You cannot know me unless you know him. Papá set foot in San Diego early in the twentieth century; he hailed from Mazatlán, a port town on the Pacific Ocean. He had been a sailor in the navy of Porfirio Díaz, the master of Mexico for thirty years, but had abandoned his country before the advent of the Revolution of 1910, which cost Díaz his job and turned the economy topsy-turvy. As to why he left Mexico, I can only wonder because he never threw light on the subject. He had been to Ensenada, a port sixty miles south of San Diego and in fact may have visited the U.S. city.

Born in Altata, a mining town not far from Mazatlán, he had spent most of his young life near the sea, so, not illogically, San Diego, a port on the Pacific Ocean, beckoned him, and there as a bachelor he found lodging among the Mexicans on the waterfront. For the first years, he tried his hand at commercial fishing, sailing a small boat and, alone, casting his lines off the Coronado Islands, part of the Mexican Republic but just a few miles beyond San Diego's harbor. When he gave that up, he became a deck hand on the lumber schooners plying Pacific ports from San Francisco to San Diego and then as a stevedore joined the Industrial Workers of the World.

In 1910, according to census statistics, Papá was one of 220,000 Mexicans in the United States, although scholars assure us that many others entered illegally. A rule of thumb, among those who claimed to be in the know, was that for every Mexican who entered legally, three came across illegally. Crossing the border was no sooner said than done because much of it was unguarded, and the Rio Grande, miles of it shallow, was forded easily. A decade later there were more or less 500,000 Mexicans in the United States. Texas had the largest number, followed by California. Aside from Los Angeles, a city in California that drew Mexicans like bees to honey, the biggest Mexican settlements were in San Antonio and El Paso, Texas, the latter with a population more than 60 percent Mexican. Because San Diego was a small city, unconnected by railroads to population centers in Mexico, and not an industrial hub where jobs were plentiful, few Mexicans settled there. My father, an early immigrant, was one of a tiny band. There were also California-born Mexicans, whom Papá referred to as "Chicanos" and who, according to him, kept to themselves even when working alongside Mexicans, thinking themselves superior because they spoke English.

Most Mexicans, driven by the nature of their jobs, put roots down in the countryside, doing seasonal farmwork or laboring in the mines of Arizona at Morenci and Clifton, in Colorado at Las Animas and Ludlow, and in New Mexico, or tending sheep and cattle in out-of-the-way ranches. All western railroads employed them to build the road beds, repair tracks, and put down wooden ties for iron rails. Bright and early, if you drove through the countryside, you might see "a section gang" of twenty or so, sledge hammers in their hands, backs bent over, pounding steel spikes into wooden ties under the watchful eye of an Anglo boss. Railroad officials admitted they could not get along without Mexican workers. That acknowledged, the Santa Fe Railroad, a major employer, thought of itself as "owning them body and soul [and] . . . treat[ed] them like caged animals," editorialized *El Cosmopolita,* a Mexican newspaper in the rail hub of Kansas City. Either as farm hands, cowboys on cattle ranches, fruit pickers, copper miners, or railroad workers, they lived among their countrymen. This was not surprising because this choice replicated a mode of life in Mexico, where, though they might be peons, *labradores* (laborers), or *ejidatarios* (farmers on communal farms), Mexicans stayed together in villages.

Others became urban dwellers but were segregated from Anglo neighbors. In cities such as Los Angeles, they settled in old communities, where residents had been citizens of Spain and Mexico; they spoke Spanish and shared similar customs, making it easier for the newcomers to adjust to life in a foreign land. Occasionally immigrants left the inner city for its outskirts, where they established barrios of another type. At other times, they set up households outside of city limits, *colonias* eventually swallowed up by urban sprawl. Mexicans also could be found in small towns, clusters of families congregating on the "wrong" side of the railroad tracks. In 1928, they dwelt in tens of hundreds of communities of a thousand or more inhabitants. Here and there one stumbled across Mexicans in lonely railroad junctures, where, beyond the big house for the American boss and next to the tracks, they lived in "section houses," freight and passenger trains roaring by each day and night. There were dusty farm camps, where Mexicans huddled in wretched shacks without running water and, no matter how cold the day or night, used outdoor privies, a life that exacted a brutal toll in sweat and tears.

Almost always Mexicans were hired to do the dirty, back-breaking labor, chiefly in agriculture and for paltry pay. In the Imperial Valley, just over the mountains from San Diego, Mexicans picked tons of raisins, tons of walnuts, countless boxes of lemons, and even more boxes of oranges. They tended vineyards and melon fields elsewhere in California, picked cotton in Arizona and Texas, and dug sugar beets out of the soil in Colorado, Wyoming, and Montana. In the hot day sun, Mexicans wielded picks and shovels for city streets and for ditches for water pipes; mixed sand, gravel, and cement for bridges; and in San Diego poured concrete for the Coronado Hotel across the bay.

True, others had different occupations. A handful of Mexicans, by dint of hard work and a bit of luck, ran small grocery stores, always in Mexican barrios, where they sold tortillas, *chorizo* (spicy pork sausage), and other Mexican foods. A few earned their keep as musicians, playing at Mexican dances and festivals, and occasionally one encountered a physician or lawyer sporting a degree from a Mexican university and serving the Mexican community. They were what there was of a Mexican bourgeoisie. Yet, as historian Mario García aptly points out in *Mexican Americans,* even Mexicans who had achieved a sort of upward mobility, barring exceptions, remained "economically vulnerable due to their dependence on a poor Mexican community and clientele."

Papá sprang from that milieu but went his solitary way. There was something out of the ordinary about him. Unlike most Mexicans who ventured north, he brought no wife or children. He was a solitary man, shorn of family ties. He was singular, too, because of where he established his household: he lived off the beaten track, apart from other Mexicans. When once I asked why he had not settled among his *paisanos,* his reply was that he did not want his family in shabby housing or his children shunted off to segregated schools, then the rule. He knew of what he spoke. Urban Mexicans were hardly better off than Mexicans who planted and harvested the crops, most of them calling slums home and enduring below-standard living conditions. By chance, Papá stumbled on Kate Sessions's nursery in the hills above Pacific Beach, where he received the promise of a fine job and a good house and where empty land stretched for miles, the sky was clear, and peace and quiet had the run of the day.

Miss Sessions, as she was known, was on her way to becoming San Diego's legendary horticulturist, as a statue of her in Balboa Park testifies. She had arrived from San Francisco, where she had been a schoolteacher. When she asked the city for a lease of thirty acres to start a nursery in Balboa Park, it was granted on condition that she plant trees: she is now remembered as one of the architects of the famous park. Later she moved her business to the hills above Pacific Beach, at a place baptized Sessions Ranch, where my father saw her. They must have hit it off from the start because he stayed. Under Miss Sessions's watchful eye, he spent years learning to care for flowers, plants, and trees. When he married my mother, a young Mexican woman, he brought her to Sessions Ranch. The house where I was born, though much changed, still stands.

I remember Kate Sessions, especially because of her clothes. She dressed in the fashion of the late 1890s, a blouse and jacket over a skirt that covered black, high-top shoes, and a hat that she pulled down over her ears. When she walked, the skirt nearly touched the ground. She walked rapidly and talked with a rasping, whining voice common to some old women. After Papá had his own nursery, she would come by to see what he was up to, annoying him because she loved to give advice. Whatever the reception, she went right on dropping by to say hello and to tell "Ramón" what he should do. When she saw my mother, she would ask, "How are you, Mrs. Ruiz?" Miss Sessions never learned to drive, so she would come by with a chauffeur. I also remember her because, as I grew older, she kept asking my father to allow me to drive for her. That was one request that riled him: "*Nunca* (never)," he would tell me.

Eventually Papá began dreaming of owning his own nursery and of being free of Kate Sessions. As a *San Diego Union* column written about our family explains, he "had emigrated to this country and went to work . . . in a large nursery. In a few years he had learned [enough] to strike out on his own." The "prejudices some Californians hold against Mexicans were only a challenge for him to work all the harder." No other Mexican in San Diego had a flower business; grocery stores, yes, but little else. When Papá attended the yearly meetings of nurserymen in San Diego, he was the sole Mexican—that I know because he would take me along to interpret what he did not understand. His knowledge of the English language, although acceptable, was not perfect. When Pascual Ortiz Rubio, once president of Mexico, stopped by because he saw Mexicans at work in the nursery, he told Papá: "You must not just say you are a Mexicano; you must trumpet it."

Pacific Beach was quintessential small-town America, a somnolent village, largely of Protestant men and women as white as Norman Rockwell's picket fences, whose frame houses with their wide porches Rockwell could have drawn for the cover of the *Saturday Evening Post*. Lots for the house builder sold for seventy dollars, ten down and five a month, and there were few takers. These were the "roaring twenties," the days of Warren G. Harding and Calvin Coolidge, when Americans voted to outlaw demon rum but drank bootleg booze, and so it was in our town, bare of saloons but not of bootleggers.

It is said that landscape helps shape the character of an individual, so let me tell you a bit about that of my home town. On a map, Pacific Beach resembled a tortilla, water and flour studiously mixed but with sloppy results, as though done by unpracticed hands, not by Mexican women, whose mothers over centuries taught them how to tug and pull the dough into shape. Ragged on its flanks, Pacific Beach, an alluvial plain, stretched for three miles along the southern slopes of Soledad Mountain and fronted on the ocean and Mission Bay, an estuary of mudflats. Rain was usually a novelty during the winter, short of duration and rarely cold. Residents had their houses on the meadows where wild cattle and sheep had roamed earlier but now were planted to lemon groves as well as to guavas and loquats. Empty lots yielded tons of hay, and coyotes, jackrabbits, and rattlesnakes had the run of the place, so much so that teachers had to warn students, some of whom walked barefooted to school, to keep their eyes peeled for snakes. Paved streets overran the land only here and there, and weeds, sagebrush, and chaparral climbed the hills beyond or stopped at the Pacific Ocean's edge, where great waves crashed onto the shore and the sand swept up to barren cliffs eroded into crevices and deep cracks by winter storms.

My memories of Pacific Beach, a seaside village of perhaps fifteen hundred inhabitants, date from the late 1920s, when we lived in a big house on Hornblend in the heart of town. The house, which harkened back to the Victorian era, stood a block south of Garnet, a dirt road that ran from east to west and linked San Diego to La Jolla. Aside from Papá and Mamá, there were five of us: I was the eldest, Roberto a year younger, and then Berta, Emma, and Eva followed. The house of clapboard and porches belonged to the next-door Presbyterian church; a dirt alleyway separated the two, both buildings two stories high, with fading gray paint on their wooden sides. Grant Wood could have used either one for the backdrop of his *American Gothic*. The church dated from the turn of the century, when only an occasional building broke the monotony of the barren countryside. Our home was both ancient and modern. We had a telephone, housed in a wooden box with a crank, which hung on a wall of the kitchen, but had to use an outhouse; not till later was an indoor toilet added. To bathe us, Mamá filled a large, metal tub with hot water and set it in the kitchen or outside during the summer, when she heated the water over a wood fire.

Luckily for me, the house had an attic with books on the glories of ancient Egypt lying in jumbled heaps on the floor; though Mamá told us to stay out of the attic for fear we might damage the books, I would climb up there when she was not home, open the books, and stare at drawings of pitched battles waged by Egyptian soldiers armed with spears and shields. That was my initial brush with the study of history.

On the west side, a half-mile or so from the Pacific Ocean, was Sam Dunaway's pharmacy, the most impressive building in town and one of two soda fountains. A dour Anglo, Dunaway was the unofficial mayor, who also made the first milkshake I ever tasted. Try as I may to ransack my memory, I recall little of him except that I thought him rather cold. Favel's Meat Market, a one-man butcher shop, occupied one side of the Dunaway building. Across the street was a Texaco station, with a garage and an auto mechanic, and a hamburger joint. Where the ocean tides lapped the beaches, speculators from Los Angeles built the Crystal Pier and Ballroom.

At the opposite end of town, Mike Whelan, a tall, gregarious man, unambitious and ordinary, ran the other soda bar. Most of his customers walked over from the San Diego Army and Navy Academy, a private school for boys that referred to itself as the West Point of the West. The cadets, one the son of a Mexican general, wore blue-gray uniforms and on Sunday marched in parades open to the public. On some nights during the summer, the academy band played under a band shell, and residents of Pacific Beach, our parents among them, listened to the concerts, seated in their cars. We called the Pacific Beach girls who dated cadets "academy bait." One was Margaret Whelan, Mike's pretty, sassy daughter, older than I and regarded as the sexiest girl in town. She and Rene Scrum, one of the other girls in the sixth grade, were the flappers of the day: at school parties, they put on high heels, painted their lips red, and smoked Chesterfield cigarettes.

My schoolmates were, with rare exception, Anglos, among them Betty Ravenscroft, who never wanted classmates to see her walking to school with me; as we approached, she would ask me to stay behind. Was it because she was shy and did not wish for classmates to see her with a boy, or, I asked myself, was it because I was a Mexican? I remember Betty because her parents had a grocery store kitty-corner to our house, where Mamá did her food shopping. The family lived in an apartment above the store, so we saw them daily. Like their neighbors, the Ravenscrofts, father and son in suits and ties and mother and daughter in fancy dresses, went to Sunday service at the church across the alley. Nearly all local residents were working class; no one went to college. To speak of class divisions in Pacific Beach would be a mistake: my parents, along with one or two other families, had a bit more than the others, but the rich were prominent by their absence.

Papá's nursery sat on the edge of the northern foothills, a half-mile or so from the ocean; at night, one could hear the rumble of the sea. Only a handful of homes were within sight. Just beyond us were the Yamashitas, one of two Japanese families in Pacific Beach. My brother and sisters and I played together. Roberto and I shot marbles, hopscotched with our sisters, and romped around as cowboys and Indians in the open spaces. Our horses were made of lath—thin, flat, wooden sticks four feet long on which we strapped burlap to serve as saddles. We rode them yelling "Gid-dap, gid-dap," shouts that resonated up and down the paths we carved out with our feet between tangles of sagebrush. Once in a while we put up the kind of large umbrella people carry to the beach, draped burlap on its sides, and held a circus; Roberto and our sisters became clowns, elephants, and tigers, and I the ring-master. At the evening performance, when Papá arrived home from work, our parents were the audience.

Mamá also shopped at Hill's Market, a mile or so south of us facing Dunaway's—run by a former marine, a bit doltish, Mamá would say, but friendly—and at Favel's Meats, where she bought round steaks, the cheapest cut. Favel, the butcher, wore a long white coat over his shirt and trousers, testimony to his cleanliness, I guess. It was a truism in our home that eating beef kept you healthy, a routine broken on Fridays, when as Catholics we had fish, purchased from Mr. Newall, an English fish peddler who sold his catch from a Model T truck. The fish was rock cod, which our mother prepared in a spicy stew or pan fried. I looked forward to the stew, cooked with tomatoes, green chilies, and onions. We ate the fish with flour tortillas Mamá cooked daily at three in the afternoon, using her hands to fashion the dough into balls, then putting the balls in a bowl, and covering them with a cloth. Two hours later, with a wooden rolling pin, she rolled them flat and cooked them on a hot griddle.

By the standards of big-city folk, Pacific Beach was Hicksville, and in many ways it was. Not far from our old house on Hornblend, there was a goat dairy, to which, until Papá learned it was not cow's milk he was drinking, Mamá dispatched us pail in hand for the milk we were to drink at breakfast and dinner. We walked or rode bicycles to school, our footsteps forging paths from school to home across empty, weed-filled lots; during the summer months, after the semesters had ended, we took off our shoes and went barefoot. By September, the soles of our feet were as tough as cowhide. At school, we wore denim pants and shoes made of canvas with rubber soles that we called tennis shoes, but that actually were brown or black high tops. When Roberto and I wore out the knees of our pants, as we always did, Mamá cut out the torn fabric and replaced it with a cloth patch of the same material.

Life was simple. We went to bed with the chickens and got up with the roosters. After Roberto and I were in high school, we congregated at Snyder's gasoline station, a rickety wooden structure on Garnet. In the early evening, everyone was there: men with "souped up" cars; others on Harley Davidson and Indian motorcycles; and idlers with nothing else to do, among them Roberto and I. Mr. Snyder and his family, one of whom was my classmate Roy, lived in an apartment behind the station, where tall, cylindrical gasoline pumps, which you emptied by pulling a long handle back and forth, were filled with Eagle, Gilmore, and sundry brands of gasoline that cost from nine to eleven cents a gallon. Mr. Snyder, a dour man who seldom uttered a word, never made any effort to keep his business spic-and-span; he just sat there and waited for cars to drive up the gravel entrance, which he never raked. One reason for his inactivity, aside from the fact that he preferred rest to work, was that, according to rumors, he had a fondness for whiskey. He had dexterous hands, however; he made the best wooden clocks in town. When he died, Roy took over the business, and Bud, the older brother and the spitting image of his father, set up shop as the garage mechanic. There was nothing on a car that he could not fix. At first, Roy tried to alter the image of the service station, raking the gravel path, wiping the windshields of cars and checking the air in the tires. That did not last long; soon everything returned to normal.

On racial matters, Pacific Beach was neither a liberal stronghold nor a sinkhole of bigotry. It was possible to be friends with Anglos, but when we least expected it, we had to put up with racial slurs. These were bigoted times, the heyday of eugenics, when Anglos dreamed of "improving" the racial stock by selective breeding. Progressives and retrogrades, scientists as well as humanists, jumped on the bandwagon, among them Margaret Sanger and Charles Eliot, Harvard's president, as well as Paul Popinoe, a self-taught biologist whose books I read in college. Not until the Nazis sullied its credibility did the "science" of eugenics fall on its face. The bilge exemplified Anglo fears of unwelcome Jews, Italians and others from southern Europe, and—among the unholy—Mexicans. As late as 1928, racists in the Southwest lynched Mexicans.

Still, in Pacific Beach you could live where you wanted so long as you had the money to buy property. As far as I know, no one bothered Mr. Tate and his family, the sole blacks in town. On almost any day, Mr. Tate, who swept the streets for the city of San Diego, could be seen pushing his two-wheel cart. His daughter Edna, a big girl who took no guff from any of the boys in school, was in my grade, and Frank, always courteous, was one of my sister Berta's classmates. Yet, by choice or design, the Tates lived on the west end of Diamond Street, far from any neighbors.

As Ruth Tuck points out in *Not with the Fist,* however, we were "lumped together under the blanket term Mexican." The title *American,* as Tuck says, was "very seldom used" for us; we were condemned to "remain Mexican generation after generation." Some Anglos, to pour salt into the wound, used *Mexican* as a pejorative, an insult. In the sixth grade, for instance, James Harvey and I got into a fight; when I got the better of it, he called me a "dirty Mexican." He was much too young to arrive at that conclusion on his own, so he must have heard that snide remark from his parents, neighbors, or classmates. Nor will I forget how I felt specifically targeted when Miss Drury, the fifth-grade teacher, labeled as cowardly and cruel the Mexicans who killed the defenders of the Alamo during the Texas rebellion against Mexico. I can even describe how she looked on that day. A dull blond, tall and thin, her skin the color of sunlight, she had on a long-sleeved blouse tucked into a pencil-thin skirt that fell below her knees, and tan shoes with leather tongues, the kind women wore on golf courses.

One day when our father was looking at the land he had just bought for our new home, a smartly dressed Anglo woman, friendly on the surface, drove up in a new car. She explained that she lived in the house just down the street, the only one between our property and the ocean. She wanted to know if our father would sell her the land. "I know why you want to buy it," he replied; "you think that because I am a Mexican that I am going to build a shack, don't you? Well, let me tell you, I am going to build a house better than yours." And he did!

On a street corner to the south of us, Roy Crawford, a red-faced man in a green uniform and black bow tie, ran the Texaco service station where our parents stopped for gasoline. Crawford was always courteous, referring to our parents as Mr. and Mrs. Ruiz. But one day, when my brother Roberto was playing football for La Jolla High, we stopped for gasoline, and Crawford, seeing Roberto in the back seat, paid tribute to his football prowess and averred to Papá that someday his son would be a fine coach, but only in an "Indian school."

The two Japanese families were truck farmers who raised vegetables and flowers for the markets of San Diego. The Yamaguchis were dirt poor; Yateo, the father, had arrived in Pacific Beach in 1915; Manuel and Sammy, two of the boys in the family, went to school with us, one a year ahead of Roberto and the other a class behind. Sammy talked all of the time, but Manuel kept his thoughts to himself. Their homestead, which Mr. Yamaguchi rented, sat north of Garnet in the rolling countryside. The Yamashitas were entirely different. Toshitaro, the father, also had settled in Pacific Beach just before World War I; he and Yateo were old-timers. The Yamashitas farmed land at the foot of Soledad Mountain, less than half a mile from our home, and employed a half-dozen or so men, all of whom, except for Raimundo, a hard-drinking Mexican, were Japanese.

By comparison to his Anglo-American neighbors, Mr. Yamashita was well-off. During the 1930s, the years of the Great Depression, he purchased a new Buick sedan, which no one else in Pacific Beach could do. We knew Shigeru, the second eldest sibling, and Shizu and Kiku, his sisters, who played hide and seek or jumped rope with us. Kiku, the youngest, would bring fresh flowers, grown by her father, to school. Shigeru was our paperboy and on Sundays sometimes went to the movies with us. Older, he attended La Jolla High and completed his schooling at the University of California at Berkeley, a feat accomplished by no one else in Pacific Beach and by few in San Diego at that time. Mr. Yamashita and our father, a truck farmer and a nurseryman, were among the better-off in town. Though my father did not buy Buicks, by 1937, when his business began to pick up, he could buy new Chevrolet pickup trucks. When he bought the first of them, Anglo-American neighbors in the vicinity, one my school teacher, stopped by to marvel at the new truck.

Those accomplishments did not stop World War II Washington from shipping the Yamashitas and the Yamaguchis off to concentration camps, euphemistically titled relocation centers. On February 19, 1942, President Roosevelt—who, like many bigoted Americans, believed Japanese immigrants unassimilable and unworthy of property rights and equal citizenship because of racial traits—ordered the internment of 120,000 residents of Japanese ancestry, more than half of them U.S. citizens; there were no hearings and no appeals. One day the Yamashitas were our neighbors; the next day they were gone, or so it seemed to us. I remember vividly the paper flyers tacked on telephone poles in the wake of the bombing of Pearl Harbor by Imperial Japan, warning persons of Japanese ancestry to stay off the streets after a certain hour, and then the disappearance of Shigeru, Shizu, and Kiku, whom we never saw again.

Roosevelt's reprehensible belief that the Japanese in this country represented a potential source of fifth columnists cost the Yamashitas and the Yamaguchis everything they had built up over many years. According to our neighbors' mean-spirited gossip, the Japanese were slant-eyed traitors; Papá even heard that Mr. Yamashita had a long-range radio transmitter in his home, which he used to send messages to Japan. These were lies, as were the reasons that authorities used to justify the unprecedented roundup and relocation of Japanese Americans. Some bigots, however, were less dishonest: the Grower-Shipper Vegetable Association of that day, a California group of Anglo-Americans, claimed, "We've been charged with wanting to get rid of the Japs for selfish reasons. We might as well be honest. We do." I recall the days of this crime against good neighbors and wonder how we would have fared if Mexico had deemed it wise to recapture its lost territories, especially considering that both our father and mother remained citizens of Mexico until their deaths. And that was the long and the short of it in Pacific Beach, a tiny slice of the national pigmentocracy.

Anglo neighbors aside, our family was very Mexican. Its head, at least in theory, was our father, as we acknowledged every day at dinner. Monday through Saturday, at approximately six in the evening, we ate when he sat down at the head of the kitchen table, where Mamá served him first and then the rest of us. On Sundays, Papá presided over a more formal dinner and the heady talk in the dining room. On his good days, he was a very good father, but on other occasions a stern taskmaster who shared the biblical axiom "spare the rod and spoil the child." When Roberto and I misbehaved, he would take us outside, take off his belt, and give us a whipping, until one day my brother grabbed the belt away and told him to stop it. From that day on, the whippings ended.

Our father, whom other Mexicans addressed as Don Ramón, was a self-made man. "Maturity," says a sage, "is the capacity to endure uncertainty," and that Papá certainly had. For him, I later represented what he aspired to have been but never could because of circumstances beyond his power to control. In our home, he represented power and authority, discipline and repressed emotion, all of which shaped us. He set out to inculcate in me, the eldest son, a relentless drive to achieve success, to do things properly and on time, and to be disciplined. As Mexicans in the United States, he would tell us, we "had to work twice as hard as Americans in order to get ahead." Leisure and relaxation were alien concepts to him. One of the "old school," he rarely rested; there was always something else to do. In all the years we knew him, he never took a day off and certainly not a vacation. That was both his strength and his weakness.

There were moments of pleasure with our father. On Sunday mornings, when my brother, sisters, and I were quite young, we climbed into bed with him once Mamá had gone to the kitchen to cook breakfast and argued over which one of us would lie next to him. He also took us to the beach, where he taught Roberto and me to swim. On Sunday afternoons, Roberto and I went to the movies with him, driving to San Diego to the Casino and Aztec Theaters on Fifth Street, where for fifteen cents we watched two Westerns, starring Tom Mix, Buck Jones, or Ken Maynard, the reigning cowboys of Hollywood; a short comedy, perhaps with Laurel and Hardy; and Movietone News. After the movies, our father might take us to eat at the Nanking, a Chinese restaurant on Island Street, a hop, skip, and jump away from the film palaces and home to the Leroy Rooms, a whorehouse patronized by sailors. I still remember the aroma of cigars, which Papá smoked on occasion, and the pungent-smelling tobacco of his pipe, Prince Albert or Tuxedo.

Given the unpredictability of the future, Papá would admonish us, "One needs a skill to fall back on if one's luck should turn sour." That skill was nursery work. Roberto and I had daily chores to do. We learned the botanical names of plants, how they grew, and how to care for and feed them. We were taught how to make "cuttings" from which new plants spring, how to sow seeds in flats and then transfer the seedlings to other flats, how to prune rose bushes, planted in bare roots in the spring, and how to use good old cow manure. Fuschias and begonias required shade and acid food. Some plants rejoiced in the full sun; others withered away. Roberto and I helped build lath houses to shade potted plants, hauled top soil on a dump truck, and drove into the nearby mountains to gather the rotting leaves of live-oak trees, called leaf mold, and tried not to stumble across poison oak.

My brother, sisters, and I lived a Jekyll-and-Hyde life. In school, we spent our time with Anglo-Americans, *bolillos* our father called them. He seldom referred to his neighbors as *gringos,* a term open to sundry meanings. His use of the term *bolillo* came from the fact that Anglo-Americans—unlike Mexicans, who preferred tortillas—loved to eat bread, in particular the small baker's loaf with a nipple on each end and a curl of crust between, known in Mexico as a *bolillo.* Our home was a Mexican home, though, a Spanish-language haven. We spoke only Spanish to our parents, though our father understood and spoke English, and they spoke only Spanish to us. I do not remember when this rule was broken; never did I utter a word of English to either of our parents or, as a matter of fact, to either of our two maternal aunts, whom we saw from time to time. We were told to speak only Spanish among ourselves, a rule we broke the moment we learned English in school, to our parents' chagrin. Because our father and I shared identical first names, our parents called me El Rey, the king, in part because I was the eldest of the siblings. Roberto was Beto. I learned to hate "El Rey" because American classmates and teachers insisted on calling me Raymond or Ray, names I detested.

By and large, Americans love to anglicize foreign names; you have to fight to prevent their bastardization. Our parents, moreover, always told me that I should insist that others call me Ramón; our mother, for her part, lamented that I did not use Eduardo, my middle name. Even now in my retirement years, I occasionally get calls on the telephone from someone, usually a stockbroker, who thinks it smart to call me not only by my first name but Raymond. That riles me because I learned long ago from our mother, a stickler for manners, that you "never *tutear,* refer to older people by the informal tú, but by *usted,*" the formal address, which has disappeared from the English language but not from the Mexican one. My wife, who is of Hispanic parentage and speaks Spanish fluently, and I drummed into our two daughters, both bilingual, the importance of the use of *usted.* I take pride that I have upheld our parents' teachings, though familiarity rules in today's southern California. That goes for the traditional handshake as well, which, although a must in Mexican society, even among youngsters, is largely forgotten here.

All of this has to do with the daily battle to conserve our identity, to keep ourselves from being forced into a suffocating conformity, where we supposedly would be like all other Americans. As Günther Grass admonished, if one abandons one's own traditions, one abandons oneself. Still, when we were growing up, conforming was highly unlikely. We were different; unless we had a suit of armor, we suffered wounds almost daily. We were Mexicans and thus—with the exception of Eva, the youngest of my sisters—were dark of skin, a legacy from our father. Whether we liked it or not, we did not look American (meaning "white"), and unkind classmates almost always reminded us of this difference. In the California of our day, the inescapable fact was that whiteness of skin conferred social acceptance. Loyalty to one's Mexican "racial" ancestry, therefore, was not merely an act of pride, *orgullo* in Papá's words, but also of courage.

Our parents lived an isolated life, broken only by periodic visits by Tía María, also known as Nina Chávez, for as our mother's sister she was our aunt but also my godmother because she and her husband baptized me. When our parents built their home on the northern side of town, Nina Chávez had to walk nearly two miles to visit her sister. She was a lonely woman, for she never had children of her own; Terencio, her half-Mexican and half-Italian husband, hailed from the mining enclave of Cananea in the border state of Sonora. When his Italian father abandoned his mother, Terencio adopted the name Chávez, his mother's maiden name, for himself. Terencio had fought on the side of the revolutionaries in Sonora and, according to those who knew him then, had wantonly killed his enemies. As one man from Sonora told our father,

Terencio could never go home. Nor was he a good husband; from time to time, he would get drunk and stay out all night. Early the next morning Nina Chávez would be at our doorstep to get Roberto or me to go looking for Terencio; one time we found him in La Jolla getting over a bout of binge drinking in the company of a floozy. We brought him home unrepentant and smelling of cheap booze.

Our mother also had a younger sister in San Diego whom we saw from time to time. In her youth, Tía Aurora had been pretty, but through a series of bad companions, starting with a handsome yokel named Salvador, who dumped her and returned to Mexico, she lost all vestiges of her former beauty. The last of the scoundrels was Jesús, a tall, stupid drinker and wastrel. After Aurora's death, he became a bum; Roberto, who saw him last, says Jesús was sweeping up leaves from the lawn of the San Diego City Jail, where, most likely, he was serving time for being drunk in a public place. From a broken heart, perhaps, Tía Aurora had taken to drink, which in its turn took its toll on her body and soul. When sober, however, she was a wonderful person, always ready to help her sister.

Now and then neighbors participated in our daily life. We saw them at the store, bought gasoline from them, and sat next to them at school functions, which our mother attended religiously. Our mother spoke English haltingly at best, so language may have been a barrier. Yet our parents had little in common with their neighbors. By culture, language, and cuisine, those neighbors were miles apart, though Mamá exchanged local gossip with them at the nursery or the grocery store. Not once, however, did our father ever stop dreaming of a return to the homeland; all he needed, he would say, was a nest egg. That was the Rosetta stone of his existence. He never wanted to die in the United States. Our mother, on the other hand, far more sociable than her husband, gave scant credence to that dream. She was happy where she was, a reality made the more inevitable because her children had been born on this side of the border. As immigration scholars note, when a Mexican woman has children in the United States, she is there to stay.

One consolation for our father, idiosyncratic in some ways, was Tijuana, the Mexican town just south of San Diego. In the 1920s, Tijuana was a border town of ill repute, a place where Americans came to whore, gamble, and drink. Revolución, its main street, had more bars and night clubs than reputable places of business, all owned by Americans who also ran the racetrack, where Americans came to bet on the horses. On weekends, crowds of Americans made fools of themselves on Revolución, where few Mexicans were seen. Drinking went on until the wee hours of the morning; so drunk were some Americans that they were unable to drive the long distance back home to Los Angeles, thus encouraging the settlement of San Ysidro, California, a tiny community just across the border from Tijuana that became replete with auto courts catering to late-night revelers away from home. What turned Tijuana awry and, yes, perverted it—along with its sister cities Ciudad Juárez, Nuevo Laredo, and Matamoros on the Gulf of Mexico— was the Volstead Act of 1919, better known as Prohibition. This bit of puritanical mischief banned the manufacture and sale of alcoholic beverages in the United States. From that time on, the American fancy for booze and the Tartuffery required to give the lie to it set the course of the border drama. Lines from *The Jester's Plea* aptly epitomize what transpired for a decade or more on the Mexican side of the border: "The World's as ugly, ay, as Sin,—And Almost as delightful."

For our father, Tijuana, though a border town and certainly not the land he remembered, was Mexico nonetheless, a place to recharge his Mexican soul. So he visited Tijuana, sometimes with his family in tow and sometimes alone. But the Tijuana he visited had little to do with the Tijuana of American tourists, though he would stop to drink a bottle of Mexicali beer at the Long Bar, the biggest in town. Once in a while he would have dinner there, the Mexican food he loved so well. He enjoyed telling us again and again how on one occasion he drove over in his work clothes, walked into the best restaurant in town, and sat down for lunch; a waiter, who obviously thought that our father had lost his way, walked over and suggested that he had better leave because the food was expensive. Our mother, who usually took care that her husband looked presentable, never thought the story funny.

Over the years, our parents made friends in Tijuana. The homes of the Mexicans our parents visited were on the edge of town, far from the activities of tourists, or around the Plaza del Teniente Guerrero, where locals gathered on Sunday afternoons. On his way home, our father would stop at a drugstore to buy Mexico City newspapers, usually the Sunday edition of *El Universal;* we came to know its comics quite well, many of them simply Spanish-language reproductions of American ones, such as "Mutt and Jeff" or "Bringing Up Father," the tale of a domineering wife, a philandering husband, and an unmarried daughter. But there were also Mexican comics, one of them about the fat *charro* or gentleman cowboy who was always getting into trouble, in part based on "Bringing Up Father." One time Papá brought back Mexican school texts, which we had to study under his tutelage. That was how I first learned to read Spanish.

Our parents also returned with records to play on the Victrola. Our mother preferred the music she remembered from her youth, songs such "Júrame" by María Grever and "Morir soñando." At work in the kitchen, she would hum them to herself, unaware that we were listening. For his part, our father loved martial airs, the marches played by Mexican military bands: "Zacatecas," "Torreón a Lerdo," "El Cañón de Bachimba," and, of course, the "Himno nacional mexicano," the national anthem of Mexico. One of the rare moments I enjoyed while a U.S. Army Air Force cadet was marching behind a band playing "Zacatecas," led by a Mexican American sergeant.

Our mother, her father and mother, her grandparents, and all the patriarchs before them were born and nurtured on the outskirts of Parral, a mining town in the border province of Chihuahua that dates from the seventeenth century, where most of them also were overtaken by death. Our mother and two of her sisters, María and Aurora, were the exceptions. Tía Chayo, a nickname for Rosario, another sister and resident of Ciudad Juárez for decades, is buried in that city. For my part, excluding time spent flying aircraft in the army during World War II and years teaching in Massachusetts, I have spent most of my life within hailing distance of the Mexican border, at one time or another calling Texas, New Mexico, Arizona, and California home. El Paso and Ciudad Juárez and the two Nogaleses I know from my youth, a long, long time ago, in the days of train travel to Mexico City by way of those ports of entry. When I was in my early twenties, Tijuana was also a place to meet girls, at the *tardiadas,* the Sunday evening dances at the Palacio Municipal, where mothers kept a watchful eye on their daughters' virtue. In the 1960s, when my family and I had a home in northern Mexico, we passed through Nuevo Laredo countless times, as well as through Piedras Negras, Ciudad Acuña, and Matamoros. The Mexican border is an integral part of my life, as it was for my father.

In this cultural hodgepodge, I was happy both at home and in the world outside of our parents' abode. I had friends at school, earned good grades, and spoke English. I inhabited two worlds—one with my parents, brother, and sisters and the other with the offspring of the Anglos who dwelt in Pacific Beach. This divided life was emphasized particularly when I went on to junior high school, also in Pacific Beach. By then, our parents had built our new home, designed in the Spanish California style, white stucco walls and a red-tile roof, and had established their nursery. The house was not large, but it was one of the better ones in the village. Our parents had paid three thousand dollars for an acre of land and taken out a mortgage of five thousand dollars, with an interest rate of 1 percent on the house, which was a half-mile or so from the junior high; open land separated the two. Yet no sooner were we ensconced in our new abode than the national economy collapsed.

2

Euphoric Days

The early 1930s were the best and the worst of times. Euphoric times for me, some of the happiest of my life, but for our parents they brought hardships in their wake. Economic downturns had hit earlier, as recently as 1920, when the postwar boom collapsed, but they had not endured for long. By 1923, life was back to "normalcy," pontificated Warren G. Harding, all but for farmers. The short-lived downturn, however, had led to congressional passage of immigration quotas, the first limiting the number of immigrants in a year to 3 percent of each nationality according to the census of 1910 and the second to 2 percent on the basis of the census of 1890, blatantly discriminating against Italians, Jews, and Slavs. At the behest of employers of cheap labor, Mexicans were exempted, but not entirely. Congress included persons "likely to become a public charge," and the Border Patrol, set up to stop the illegal flow of Mexicans across the border, dates from that year.

For nearly a decade, the Great Depression ravaged the economy. The ranks of the jobless multiplied by leaps and bounds. By 1930, some 4.4 million were looking for work, a figure that three years later skyrocketed to almost 13 million. Not only were workers out on the streets, but those with jobs had their wages and their hours cut. One year later 17 million persons were on public relief. "White folks," wrote Carey McWilliams, got a taste of the bitter tea Mexicans knew only too well.

By 1933, nearly 2.5 workers were available for every farm job in California, and Anglos, who previously had scorned such jobs, began to compete with Mexicans for them. To exacerbate matters, the poor from Oklahoma, Arkansas, and Texas—jobless and destitute "Okies"—began to flood the labor market; estimates place their numbers at just under 1 million. The windfall of workers led the legislature in Sacramento to pass an ordinance requiring that labor on public works be done by U.S. citizens, a measure designed to bar Mexicans from construction jobs, while at the same time private contractors refused to hire them. So desperate were Mexicans that they did stoop labor, the worst kind, for thirteen cents an hour, an all-time low, and their average annual income in California agriculture fell to 289 dollars, at a time when the Roosevelt administration thought that 780 dollars barely covered minimum necessities.

The economy of San Diego, a city of not more than 150,000 inhabitants, relied on the U.S. Navy as well as on fishing and canning for its income. San Diego was an open-shop city; labor unions did not disturb its calm, which encouraged municipal spokesmen, among them the *San Diego Union,* to believe that the Depression would not be felt strongly. Well, they were wrong. By 1933, economic woes were on everyone's mind. Unemployed men, now considered hoboes, were seen walking the railroad tracks or riding freight cars; others stopped by homes, hat in hand, to beg for a bite to eat. At almost any hour of the day, they would knock at our back door to say that they would work for food. They were neither blacks nor Mexicans, but Anglos. So many San Diegans were unemployed that the *Union,* a staunch supporter of Herbert Hoover's laissez-faire policies, urged women of "independent means" who had jobs to relinquish them. Others called for unemployment relief, a cry endorsed by the conservative American Federation of Labor, which asked for higher taxes on the rich as well as a redistribution of wealth.

The city council of San Diego, where conservatives stood watch, was ready to spend 35,000 dollars on public works, a jobs project. Relief for the unemployed was the sole concern of the San Diego Unemployment Council, organized to find ways to alleviate it. And it should have because San Diegans were in deep trouble.

Foreclosures were no longer a novelty because home owners, jobless and unable to pay either mortgages or taxes, simply walked away. One could buy an abandoned lot simply by paying back taxes on it, as our parents did for a lot adjoining our property. Some San Diegans were hungry; one, turned burglar, was caught hiding under the drainboard of a restaurant because, as he said, "I am hungry and out of work, that's all I can say." Fearful that their life savings might go up in smoke, San Diegans decried rumors of bank insolvency, a topic of growing concern. "In these modern times," wrote a reader to the *Union,* "when all our money is kept in banks, our happiness depends on the safety of our banks because the bank is almost like a house pantry."

Hard times exacerbated racial bigotry. In 1932, San Diego's board of supervisors hired a police officer to patrol the San Ysidro port of entry to keep "unescorted girls" from visiting "Tijuana, stay[ing] for dinner and [having] no means of getting back to the United States." He was also to stop "indigent Mexicans from coming to this side for the express purpose of landing in the county hospital." The National Club of America, headquartered in San Diego, kept a record of the cost of aid given to "aliens," largely Mexicans; it concluded that the state had wasted millions of dollars and asked counties to keep tabs on the money they spent, statistics to be used to exert pressure on politicos in Washington to deny assistance to immigrants. Declared an editorial in the *San Diego Union:* "Let it be admitted before all the world that the old American tradition of hospitality to the troubled and oppressed of all nations has proved a failure and must be abandoned." The *Union* was not alone in this opinion. The *Saturday Evening Post* had already published articles pressing Washington to limit Mexican immigration, one of them alleging that in Los Angeles "one can see the endless streets crowded with shacks of illiterate, diseased, pauperized Mexicans . . . bringing countless numbers of American citizens into the world with the reckless prodigality of rabbits."

In 1930, Congress again took up the matter of immigration. New arguments were heard, which boiled down to two: Mexicans took jobs away from Americans, and Mexicans were racially undesirable. A report prepared by a professor from Duke University for John Box, a congressman from Texas, claimed that Mexicans were not much more advanced than animals, and a medical doctor from the Los Angeles suburb Pasadena assured other congressmen that Mexicans were like smart dogs.

In 1931, more than 35,000 families were on the welfare rolls in Los Angeles County, and the numbers spiraled upwards. Six years later, according to the *New York Times*, 2 million of the 2.5 million Mexican workers in the United States had no jobs. Amazingly, however, just a fraction of families on the dole were Mexicans. Nevertheless, as welfare rolls ballooned, city fathers in Los Angeles turned a blind eye to these statistics, blamed Mexicans, and asked for their deportation. To quiet the clamor, the Hoover administration launched a campaign to rid the country of "illegal aliens," who, it asserted, took jobs from Americans, and dispatched agents to Los Angeles to start the ball rolling.

Politicos and the press hailed the deportation plan that, along with hard times, drove thousands of Mexicans out of southern California. Legal residents, too, were encouraged to return to Mexico, a process labeled "voluntary deportation." If a Mexican agreed to be *repatriated,* the euphemistic term that was employed, authorities paid his fare and food to the border. Between 500,000 and 600,000 Mexicans, among them children born in the United States, were sent packing. I remember this shameful episode because I accompanied Papá on his visit to a Mexican coastal freighter, the *Progreso,* that docked in the harbor of San Diego to carry Mexicans back home. It weighed anchor with 800 on board. A consulate official never forgot the screams of a woman passenger as the ship left its birth: "Let us off. . . . I am just going to die. [I have] no money, no one knows me in that town in Mexico."

In Lemon Grove, a hamlet of citrus groves on the outskirts of San Diego, racism and the Depression led to efforts to segregate Mexican schoolchildren. As a supporter of the efforts said, he wanted to "segregate these greasers." Yet most of the students' parents had been in Lemon Grove for years, and the children themselves were first-generation Americans; seventy-five of them attended the Lemon Grove Elementary School, almost half of the student body. On January 5, 1931, the principal, at the behest of the school trustees, stood at the door of the school, barred Mexican children from entering, and sent them off to an old two-room building. This was school segregation plain and simple, new to Lemon Grove but not to California, where enrollments in sixty-four schools in eight counties were 90 to 100 percent Mexican. To the trustees' surprise, Mexican parents kept their children home and, with the help of the Mexican consulate, hired a lawyer and took the matter to court. A San Diego Superior Court judge ruled in their favor, telling the school board that it had no legal basis to segregate the children. This ruling antedated the 1954 Supreme Court case *Brown v. the Topeka School Board* by two and one-half decades.

Back home, as the Depression deepened, matters went from bad to worse. Sales of trees and shrubs, hardly everyday necessities, dropped so that my father's landscape business nearly went broke. The number of men who labored for Papá fell from six to one—in the face of competition from jobless Anglos ready to labor for a pittance. *"Estos carajos,"* Papá would say, "work for twenty-five cents an hour," strong language given that, aside from *carajo* and *cabrón* (bastard), Papá seldom indulged in obscenities. There was a mortgage to pay off, as well as the upkeep of a large family. I would hear Papá and Mamá trying to find ways to cut household expenses, to buy three bottles of milk instead of four, or to put off the purchase of clothes and postpone household repairs. Mamá improvised miracles in the kitchen; we ate more tortillas and beans, potatoes, and rice dishes, and skimped on meat. I can't remember how often we had *fideo* (vermicelli) for lunch. Mamá patched together our clothes, which we wore for longer periods, and Papá cut our hair and put half-soles on our shoes.

I often wonder how Papá and Mamá kept the household afloat, never once having to turn to relief agencies for help. Papá's strength in the face of adversity, I suspect, came from his pride in being Mexican, knowing that he could not *manchar el pabellón,* dishonor himself or his country by accepting defeat. He might bend, but he never gave up. From those days, I store in my heart a cardinal truth that over the years has served me royally. Success, as Papá asserted time and again, begins by taking pride in who you are. When he said that I was a Mexicano and that I should be proud of my heritage, I never doubted him. My childhood heroes, the ones Papá talked about, emerged out of Mexican history. How often did I not hear the call to arms of the "Himno nacional mexicano" and listen to the heroic deeds of Father Miguel Hidalgo, the patriot priest hailed for his efforts to free colonial New Spain from the Spanish yoke? On September 16, we accompanied our parents to San Diego to hear the Mexican consul give the "Grito de Dolores," Hidalgo's cry for independence.

Those parental truths go to the core of my identity. From that time on, I knew that although I was born in the United States, I was a polar opposite to Anglos not simply because of ethnic differences but also because of cultural differences. This helps explain why, although I was never raised in a barrio, I can feel in my bones the anger and dreams of Mexican Americans, whose blood runs in my veins. I may not always march in tune with them, but I know how they feel, unlike many Anglos who speak for dissimilar verities. Nonetheless, to say that I had to go through a process of acculturation misleads. From the first grade on, I grew up with Anglo kids—freckle-faced neighbors burned red by the summer sun, a redness hidden by swabs of Noxzema cream on nose and cheeks—and with the smell of their peanut-butter-and-jelly sandwiches and the boys' annoying habit of flexing their biceps.

Today, now that our father is long dead, I occasionally ponder the reasons for his exalted nationalism. Some are obvious. He was uprooted, wrenched away from his country, unprepared by training to accept an alien world, and in exile accepted no other frame of reference. He was raised a Mexican and always spoke Spanish, a custom broken only with Anglo-Americans. Life meant hanging on to things Mexican. One was music. We never missed a performance of the touring Orquesta Típica de México when it stopped in San Diego. From Mexico and under Miguel Lerdo de Tejada or Fernando Torre Blanca, this orchestra of *salterios,* violins, cellos, and the harp played *música mexicana*. At that time, music, as much as mural art, embodied the strident nationalism of the Revolution of 1910, giving birth to what critics refer to as *música mexicana*, a music as yet untouched by the rhythms of Cuba: the boleros, *danzones,* and rumbas that captured the hearts of Mexicans starting in the late 1930s. One of the leading composers of this school of music was Ignacio Esperón, whose "Nunca, nunca, nunca" tells of a man unable to believe his good fortune: the woman he adores loves him.

On Sunday mornings, our parents listened to Spanish-language radio from Los Angeles. Pedro J. González and his trio of guitarists, Los Madrugadores, came on at the break of dawn each day of the week, so early that Mamá in jest would say, "If you listen carefully, you can hear roosters crow." His music did not greatly appeal to her, so they heard him only now and then; she preferred the music of Ramón B. Arnaiz, a former general in the Mexican army who, owing to a botched military coup, had fled the country. Arnaiz spoke an elegant Spanish and had an orchestra that played *música mexicana,* waltzes, and *paso dobles,* melodies from the early years of the century, when our mother was a young woman and looked forward to the dances in Parral. She would explain how excited she and her sisters were, describe the clothes they wore, and talk about the journey by horse and cart from the ranch in El Valle de Allende, some thirty kilometers away, to their home in Parral.

El Valle de Allende, the oldest Basque colony in the Western Hemisphere and the first Spanish settlement in Chihuahua, was where our maternal grandparents had their ranch. Our grandfather was Eduardo Urueta, a Basque name, the son of an hacendado from Cordero who in the custom of the day had once been listed on the civic roles as a mestizo, a person of Spanish and Indian ancestry, but soon became a Spaniard as he grew wealthy. Teresa Maldonado was our maternal grandmother. They were married on February 26, 1870, "in a solemn mass," according to the record, in the Church of Nuestra Señora de Guadalupe in Parral, Chihuahua, having previously gone through all of the anticipatory rituals required for a formal Catholic wedding. Later photographs of the pair show a tall, thin man with deep-seated eyes standing next to a smaller, slender woman, hair combed in a *molote* (bun) and stern of character. Whatever their racial lineage, our maternal grandparents looked Spanish, and their clothes denoted social standing in the community.

Our mother, Dolores Urueta de Ruiz, called Lola by her friends, was one of eleven siblings. Small and slender, she had short, dark hair that she combed away from her face and that turned gray as she aged. She wore eye glasses, the granny kind with thin-wire temples that curled around her ears. Though she was fair of skin, the rays of the sun had tanned her face; neighbors mistook her for an Italian or a Spaniard. She walked with a jaunty step and was never intrusive, never complaining and never hypochondriacal, a wonderful mother, tender and solicitous.

Yet she was also a child of her society and of the values of her age. She prized whiteness of skin, though she never spoke of that. During the summer, when we spent every hour outdoors, she would tell us to wear hats and wrap scarfs around our necks to keep the sun's rays from turning our skin darker. For complex historical and psychological reasons, most Mexicans, it must not be forgotten, tend to favor fair skins, a bigotry that pervades all classes, especially the well-off. Some *burgueses* (bourgeoisie) go to great lengths to keep their family "white," especially in the border states, where—until the recent influx of central and southern Mexicans, usually swarthy, Indian types—local inhabitants tended to have Spanish features. In her zeal to protect us from the sun, our mother was simply behaving in the Mexican manner. All Urueta siblings completed six years of primary schooling, remarkable for nineteenth-century Mexico. Our mother wrote Spanish quite well, far better than our father.

Mamá was subordinate to her husband, who on the surface ran the show, but she played a lively part in it. That I know something of manners, the social gentilities so prized by women who follow the dictates of the Emily Posts of the world, I owe to our mother. She made certain that we spoke when spoken to, that we behaved in the company of others, that we obeyed our father. She disliked loud, boisterous behavior, whether among Mexicans or Anglos. Table manners were her forte, and she made certain that no one picked up a fork until Papá, who always sat at the head of table, began to eat. For occasions when she drove me to San Diego after school to see a physician about my sinuses, she brought me a suit and tie to wear along with a clean white shirt and polished shoes. She sheltered her three daughters, who were her special responsibility, as Roberto and I were our father's. As our sisters began to grow into womanhood, Mamá cast jaundiced eyes on the soldiers from foxholes who began to appear in every vacant lot after World War II broke out. She could be caustic on the subject of her daughters, unafraid to tell the world that the last thing she wanted was for them to marry a man *"que no tiene ni donde caerse muerto"* (without a penny to his name).

Mamá was a widow when she married our father. We know almost nothing about her first husband except that his name was Victor Bravo. Until after her death, no one in the family knew that she had been married previously; it was Tía María who told us. Mamá was a self-reliant person. She had learned to drive a car, a novelty for Mexican women of the 1920s. Raised on a ranch in Mexico, she had been a good equestrian, willing to ride the most skittish of horses. She bought the groceries, kept the financial records, and, after we had the nursery, spent days in the potting shed, cared for plants, and helped with sales. Customers often sought her out. She did the comparison shopping, visiting other nurseries to check prices. When our father was busy, she would go shopping for suits and ties for Roberto and me, usually ignoring our pleas for clothes she thought inappropriate. She spent wisely; that skill she had in common with our father, who, according to Tía María, watched his pennies *(agarrado)*. However, it was always best for us to buy clothes with Papá because, though careful with his pennies, he did not hesitate to shop at the better stores in San Diego—Lion's haberdashery, the best in town, for one.

A devout Catholic, Mamá put up an altar in her bedroom every December in honor of La Virgen de Guadalupe, the brown virgin and national saint of most Mexicans. All of us were baptized in the Catholic faith, made our first communion, and were confirmed. On Saturdays, because Pacific Beach had no church, she drove us to Mary Star of the Sea, the Catholic church in La Jolla, for catechism, then confession, and on Sunday to mass. Later, she was one of the founders of the local church. Yet, though she went to mass every Sunday and raised us Catholic, she was not intolerant. When I began to study philosophy in college, courses taught by a self-confessed atheist, and told her that there was no proof of an Almighty God, she would smile and say that "experience would teach me differently." When at age twelve Roberto and I were confirmed, and Papá declared that we "could now decide whether we wanted to go to church," the two of us said no, but our mother did not object. She was not going to impose her opinions on us. Like a good Mexican male, our father, who claimed to be a believer and a Catholic, attended church only once a year, on December 12, the day of La Virgen de Guadalupe. Our father would tell us not to trust priests: "they were just men," with their private agendas and their prejudices. They were *curas* in his vocabulary. In the years I knew him, I never saw him genuflect, go to confession, or take holy communion.

Nuestra Señora de Guadalupe stood in Logan Heights, the Mexican barrio in San Diego; it was an adventure for us to travel to San Diego because it was unknown territory. December 12 meant a high mass, with a monsignor presiding and priests and altar boys at his side; the mass went on for hours, or so it seemed to my brother and me, who, along with our father, wore our Sunday suits and ties. What I recall of those masses were the number of times we had to kneel, then stand up, before we could sit down. However, when my brother and I went off to war, Papá returned briefly to the fold of the church, joining our mother on her Sunday pilgrimages to mass. When we returned safe and sound, he stopped going. Our mother, despite altars to La Virgen de Guadalupe, worshiped a different saint, La Virgen de la Soledad, whose church stands in Parral's old plaza.

Our father could not have been more different. He came from

a background poles apart. Not terribly tall but neither short of stature by comparison with his countrymen, he was heavy through the chest, with coarse, black hair that took on a salt-and-pepper color as he grew older. Because he was swarthy of skin, no one mistook him for a European. Photographs show a young man clearly of Indian descent, though there was nothing Asiatic about his face, a common characteristic of Mexican Indians; the older he got, the less Indian he looked. Though he lived alongside Anglo-Americans, his dark skin never bothered him. I remember calling him from Utah during my first days in the army to tell him that my skin had turned dark after days in the sun. "Be proud," he replied, for "*el color moreno* (the dark color) is beautiful."

Socially he came from the bottom of the class ladder. Emiliano, his father, who arrived in San Diego some time after 1910, had been a soldier in the Mexican army during the Porfiriato (1876–1911), a victim of the *leva,* the Mexican version of the draft. Though he served off and on for a good many years, he never got beyond the rank of corporal. He sold marijuana to his buddies in the army and drank heavily. He may not even have been Papá's father because Papa's birth certificate says *padre desconocido*, "father unknown." Yet Papá, who had nothing in common with this man, always referred to him kindly. On El Día de los Muertos (the Day of the Dead), we drove to the Catholic cemetery in San Diego where Emiliano lay buried, a man we never knew. Emiliano rested in a pauper's grave with just a small wooden cross on it—why, I will never understand. "Some day," our father averred, "we must put a headstone on it." He never did, though he never lacked for money; a year before Emiliano died, Papá had purchased a new Ford truck. Not until our father died did Emiliano's grave have a headstone. My brother and sisters and I paid for it.

Papá never knew his mother, for she died soon after his birth. An only child, without relatives of any kind, he was raised by a stepmother, whom he recalled fondly, but she too died when he was a boy. Until then, the two, Papá and his stepmother, mostly followed the troops from town to town. His stepmother was a *soldadera,* a camp follower.

Papá spoke of journeys with his father to Acaponeta, Santiago Ixcuintla, San Blas, and, of course, Mazatlán and its Olas Altas, the sea wall and promenade around its bay, which he called home. Mazatlán was a port city, where *mozos*—men wearing a burlap sack, which served as a hood for the head and a cape for the back—unloaded sailing ships and steamers at the wharf. The Plaza de las Armas, with its *kiosko,* slender steel columns holding up a cupola at its center, was the heart of the city; a regimental band gave concerts there. La Cervecería del Pacífico, which made beer, and a cigarette factory were the local industry.

A spell-binding storyteller, Papá concocted spooky tales to entertain us; one that I remember vividly was about La Llorona, the legendary woman who drowned her children in a river and then, as punishment by the Almighty, spent her afterlife wandering over Mexico looking for them. Stories of the hereafter, of spirits that protected buried (usually ill-gotten) treasures, and of the cemetery dead who came to life after nightfall were among his favorites. But, in a more realistic vein, he also spoke of the campfires of his youth, of "watching his stepmother cook tortillas on a *comal* (grill) over a wood fire and eating them with only beans or salt." Yet Papá spoke with pride of his early upbringing, never lamenting the weaknesses of the man he called his father.

Sometimes, too, if we begged hard enough, he recalled his days in the Mexican navy, an experience, we learned early, about which he preferred not to talk. Soldiering was never his cup of tea. When he did talk, however, he would explain how ambivalent he felt when men twice his age had to salute him and about the time his ship had transported federal troops, among them his father, to Guaymas, Sonora, to battle the Yaqui Indians, who were defending their lands from voracious speculators. When we asked why he had not made a career of the military, he would remind us that rebels had sunk every one of the ships he had served on during the Revolution of 1910. Still, he showed us how to tie square knots, a figure eight, and a stevedore knot, among others, a skill only old-timers on sailing ships mastered; in the navy of Don Porfirio, Papá had served on antiquated warships that plowed the seas under both sail and steam.

Amazingly, Papá spent just three years in a primary school; that was the extent of his formal education. He was, however, very bright, ambitious, disciplined, and hardworking. Had he been formally educated, he would have gone far in Mexico. Like most human beings, Papá had his quirks. He prized his *Encyclopedia médica del hogar,* a guide to home medicine, more than six hundred pages long, which offered remedies for everything from a common cold to stomach ills. When one of us fell sick, Papá consulted the book and prescribed a cure. One of them, however, was hardly dulcet. I will never forget every December of my boyhood because of a certain ritual he followed. Convinced that we must cleanse our stomachs of impurities, Papá would line us up in the kitchen and feed us spoonfuls of castor oil, a foul-tasting liquid. We spent the rest of the morning rushing off to the toilet.

Despite only a semblance of formal schooling, Papá was quite literate in Spanish and had, as I indicated earlier, a fairly good knowledge of English. In the small library in the living room, there were reference books on horticulture, including L. H. Bailey's three-volume *Cyclopedia of American Horticulture,* which he consulted from time to time. He read every evening, usually the *San Diego Evening Tribune,* so he kept up with events in the United States. He thought Calvin Coolidge a good president because his business prospered. He made money during those years of Republican prosperity, but, conversely, he heaped scorn on Herbert Hoover, who, he believed, had brought the economy to its knees. The Roosevelt administration was an enigma to him. On the one hand, he thought it good that something be done to end the Depression and get men back to work. A staunch advocate of "do it yourself," however, he had unkind words for the Works Progress Administration (WPA) and other make-work programs of the New Deal. He thought it a blot on a Mexican's pride *(amor propio)* to accept a job from the WPA or any other handout, as he called such assistance, from American rulers.

Our mother, for her part, did not object to her husband's version of the world. As long as she had her children, she was happy. Events in Mexico, whether historical or not, did not trouble her.

Though she had enjoyed a sheltered life in Mexico, she was not eager to return to the country of her birth. By the time we were born, her parents had died, and many of her ten sisters and brothers thereafter. One document in my collection of family records is the announcement, a white sheet of paper with black edging, of the death of her mother, Teresa Maldonado de Urueta, widow of Eduardo Urueta, in Parral on March 21, 1916. What a blow this must have been for our mother, who was then living in the United States. Of course, I was not around to see this particular announcement, but later, from time to time, a letter would arrive from Parral, telling of a death in the family. One I remember clearly came in 1928, when our mother learned of the death of Cevera (she was Tía Ita to us), an older sister who a few months earlier had come to visit us. I can still see our mother sobbing at the kitchen table, head in her arms, and our father pacing the floor.

Aside from their children and the business they managed together, our parents had one thing in common. Both felt deeply about the importance of education. Bad report cards meant bad times at home for us, a scolding from Mamá and a bigger one when Papá arrived home from work. Our report cards were never bad, but now and then a grade in class was not up to what was expected. We were told to study, obey teachers, and bring home good grades. Anything less than a B grade was unacceptable. During our elementary years, our mother was a frequent visitor to class, where she would discuss our work and behavior with the teacher as best she could and then sit through a class or two to see how we were doing. That evening she would report to our father what the teachers had said, whether our grades were up to our capacity, and whether we behaved properly. Emma, for example, loved to chatter in class, and that was a topic of concern at home. As a result our mother's involvement, most of our teachers came to know "Mrs. Ruiz." On the day of our report cards, we stood in line, with me at its head, in front of Papá, who sat in one of the big chairs in the living room; after studying carefully each one, he either congratulated us or, if a grade were lower than wanted, asked why that was so. He made clear that he wanted improvement by the next semester.

Why this ardent faith in schooling? I can't explain it; I don't have a good answer, although I have asked myself this question many times. For Mamá, perhaps, it was a bit of a class issue. She wanted her children to learn, but she also may have held education aloft because of snobbery: standing in the community, which went hand in glove with a title, required schooling. For Papá, however, the matter was more complicated. As he said again and again, he regretted having had so little schooling, which had held him back, he would tell us. "If only I had *más escuela*" (more years of schooling), he would lament, "I could do more." Education would give us what he had been unable to achieve: the prestige of a degree in medicine or law, rewarded by a fat income and the esteem of both Americans and Mexicans. As a Mexican, he wanted us not to be seen as dunces by Anglo-Americans, which would bring shame on his people and, heaven forbid, lead to our doing manual labor for *bolillos.*

More than Papá, our mother coveted the teachers' respect. She highly esteemed their opinions. So it was that two incidents turned our household topsy-turvy, although when I look back at them, I can see they were inconsequential. One day Eva, the youngest of the siblings, came home to report that when her teacher asked the class what they ate at home, she replied that it was "beans." When our mother heard this, she was deeply embarrassed: How could Eva have said this when it was just not true and when, to make things worse, beans were the staple of the Mexican poor? On another occasion, the school nurse sent Eva home because she had lice in her hair. When our mother learned this, she was at her wit's end. What would school authorities think of her? The lice had arrived by way of a young Mexican girl who at that time did the housework. She had gone home to see her family and apparently came back with the lice. That afternoon our mother washed Eva's and the cleaning girl's hair again and again with hot water and soap and combed it repeatedly until she was certain the lice had been exterminated.

Another less-formal side of schooling were our parents' *consejos,* as Juan de Dios Peza, a Mexican poet, dubbed them in

Cantos del hogar, exhortations for his children. "Old people like to give good advice as solace for no longer being able to provide bad examples" goes an old moral maxim. Among Papá's was "study, learn, and aspire to get ahead." Usually around the dinner table after we had eaten, when I was left alone with our parents because Roberto and my sisters fled the dining-room table when they finished their meal, Papá, Mamá, and I talked, but more often than not I listened to Papá's counsel. The subject of our future often came up. "What do you plan to do with your life?" Papá would ask, and before I could answer, he would tell me what he expected. I would be "a physician and Roberto a lawyer." Whatever we chose to do, Papá stressed, he wanted us to do more than he had; that was the goal, which, as I think about it now, sounds terribly bourgeois. For Papá, our success was what mattered, not whether we stayed close to home, which was a very Mexican family ideal. "I will be happy," he would say, "no matter how far away you are, so long as you are a success in life." For her part, Mamá would nod in agreement but from time to time voice doubts; all things being equal, she wanted her children nearby.

For some reason, too, our parents wanted us to take music lessons. So there I was learning to play the violin, a most cantankerous instrument, while Roberto had a trumpet and Emma a piano. As I look back at that tragicomedy, which lasted three years, I can say honestly that I had no ear for music and certainly not for the violin. I remember having to practice five days a week, taking the violin out of its case, tightening the bowstring, placing the notes on a music stand, and then—to the dismay of the teacher who appeared once a week—filling the room with awful sounds. I got only so far as the "Glow Worm" before, to my delight, Mamá put a stop to the charade.

The early 1930s, as I said earlier, were on the whole good to me. I enjoyed living at home and being with my parents, brother, and sisters, and at the same time I got along well with Anglos my age and never felt like an outsider. I looked forward to the opening of the school year, especially when I was in the junior high. I had always been a good student, even skipping part of the third year in the elementary school, but only after a thoroughly unpleasant experience never completely forgotten. When our mother took me to school for the first grade, I knew not a word of English. We spoke only Spanish at home. When very young, my brother, sisters, and I, to the extent that we spoke much of anything, spoke Spanish among ourselves. So on that first day at Pacific Beach Elementary, no more than a short walk from the house, there I was seated among Anglo-Americans I had never seen and who spoke a strange tongue. The teacher had nothing to say because I did not understand a word. To my later embarrassment, no sooner had Mamá deposited me in her care than I ran out the french doors of the classroom and was on the way home. When Mamá arrived, I was waiting for her. She took me back and this time sat there through the rest of the class day. No other mother had to do this. Because of my ignorance of the English language, I had to repeat a semester and watch classmates move on to the next grade. *Stunned* is not the word to describe how I felt when this happened; I was ashamed. Thankfully for my wounded ego, I made up for this derailment in the course of time.

I came into my own when I entered junior high. Those three years were the happiest of my youth. To start with, I had good classmates. But during the summer months Roberto and I spent every day in the nursery or working in La Jolla, so we seldom saw them, days they spent lying on the beach and getting a tan. When school opened in the fall, I looked forward to seeing them and renewing friendly ties, especially with Roy Snyder and James Harvey, the two classmates I knew best, who had spent their time together on the beach. I knew both quite well, James especially because Roy eventually dropped out of high school in the tenth grade. Though Roy tried hard on occasion, his star never shone brightly. He began to smoke and to ditch school and, as we saw it, to "hang out" with the wrong crowd. On the other hand, James—whose mother, by the way, kept his clothes spotless—and I not only went from elementary school through high school together, but also took every course together.

I met James when he, Mary Sue McIntyre, Olive Underwood,

and I skipped a grade into the fourth-year class taught by Artha Tyler, a young woman just out of college, with whom I developed a special relationship over the years. James, the son of a carpenter, was as Anglo as one can be, blond and blue-eyed. He played the banjo, and his older brother Ken, no less Anglo, played the violin in the best Western-music style: they loved to sing "Frankie and Johnny," a risqué song for the time. Lonnie McAlister, one more classmate, was a Christian Scientist; on more than one occasion, he tried to convince me to abandon my Catholic upbringing and talked about the folly of relying on physicians.

Another of my classmates was Jesse Peavey, the youngest brother of a ranching clan in Rose Canyon, some three miles east of the Pacific Ocean. A runty fourteen-year-old so near-sighted that he had to wear thick glasses, Jesse rode horses and drove a caterpillar tractor on the ranch run by his father and older brothers, who raised soybeans and ran cattle. His mother had died some years earlier. Jesse loved to sing cowboy ballads, which he did during homeroom, songs such as "When the Work's All Done This Fall" and the popular "Chisholm Trail." When he sang "I've Got No Use for the Women," he would blurt out that "today's women only know how to cook out of tin cans and paper sacks." With this remark, modern feminists, I am certain, would have run him out of town. He would climb out of his desk, walk to the front of the class, and start to sing—a cappella. He taught me the difference between Levi pants, which he always wore, and just denim pants. The men who rode horses and worked on ranches wore Levis, he preached, the authentic brand; the others were drugstore cowboys. During our junior high school days, when WPA orchestras—a piano, violin, saxophone, and drum—played for dances on Wednesday evenings in the auditorium of the elementary school, Jesse, his older brother Charles, and his pretty sister Mary would arrive in a pickup truck in Levis, cowboy boots, and big Western hats.

The school had its share of country bumpkins. One I recall vividly was Kenney. His parents were as poor as a dirt farmer on a concrete parking lot; he went without shoes, and his clothes were tattered more often than not; if he took a bath, it was infrequently.

Tall and lanky, blond and blue-eyed, he walked slightly bent over and, off campus, often had a cigarette in his mouth. In the year I knew him, I never saw him open a book. But he was a cutup and a joker, as funny as can be. Kenney arrived on the scene in the seventh grade and for a year was the nemesis of teachers and principal because of his antics. He rode a donkey to school, his long legs dangling on both sides. And until H. Horton Blair, the principal, caught him doing it, he rode it onto school grounds; when told not to do it, he tied up the animal in a nearby pasture. Kenney, who seldom paid attention to his teachers, kept classmates in an uproar much of the time because of his silly behavior, and usually he was sent to Mr. Blair's office for a scolding. If you giggled, you went with him. Once, when I laughed, I was sent along with him. On that occasion, Kenney and I had to wait in the anteroom until Mr. Blair had time to see us. While we waited, Kenney unbuttoned his pants, pulled out his penis, and began to play with it. Although I confess that I watched in wonder, I was more astonished than frightened that Mr. Blair might suddenly open the door to his inner sanctum and catch Kenney with his penis in his hand and me watching him.

Pacific Beach Junior High was small; it consisted of two upstairs rooms and three below. Assemblies were held in the library, and there was no gym. We took physical education on dirt fields in our street clothes during sixth period, the last of the school day so that we could go home to shower. Some teachers, I learned later, "wondered how many of us actually showered when we got home." Without a cafeteria, students brought lunches from home and ate them sitting on outdoor bleachers. The school had a bit more than a hundred students, our graduating class only fifteen. There were seven teachers. One or two of them taught English, usually Cornelia Wright, a motherly type; the others taught math, social studies, or general science, where Walter Lott held forth, spraying us with saliva when he spoke. One man, Richard Boronda, taught boys' physical education, math, and Spanish. Mr. Blair, a tall man and bald as an egg, would put us to sleep with his occasional rendition of "Asleep in the Deep." He was the one who meted out punishment, sometimes the corporal kind, a rap with a stick on the knuckles or on the buttocks. He had a fatherly side to him, though—to that I can testify. One day after I had dropped a pair of pliers in the transmission of a Model T Ford truck, I persuaded Pete Rader, a fellow student, to come home for lunch and stay over to help recover the pliers. This meant ditching the rest of the school day. We had begun to dismantle the transmission when we heard a man's voice say that was the wrong way to fix the problem. It was Mr. Blair, who had come for us but stayed around long enough to explain the correct way to do it.

Now and then when I think of my days at Pacific Beach Junior High, with a bit of childish nostalgia I confess, I know that I learned a good bit. It may have been located in Hicksville, a haven for kids of working-class families, but it was a fine school, staffed by teachers who cared and blessed with high student morale. From time to time, for instance, to help us country yokels be comfortable with girls in a social setting, they set up half hours of dancing to record music at lunch breaks, when I would trip the light fantastic, or so I thought, with Olive Underwood, a classmate who still remembers "dancing" with me. Also, as I learned eventually, the school turned out a surprisingly large percentage of successful graduates, among them architects who went on to win fame in San Diego and San Francisco, one later becoming a leading regional artist.

I will never forget Miss Tyler, a teacher who over the years became a friend and mentor. I met her in the fourth grade during the first semester. She was short, pert, and lively. After a honeymoon in Mexico, she came back as Mrs. Barbour, eager to tell us about the wonderful country she had seen for the first time. Memories of those days are shaky, but I know that I learned to do long division under her tutelage. We met again when I transferred to junior high; to my surprise, she had joined its faculty. She taught English, social studies, and even Spanish, which was not her forte. During my years in junior high, she showed me how to dance, the "one, two, three step," during which, no matter how hard I tried, one foot kept getting in the way of the other. Regardless of what she taught, she was always my teacher, the best I ever had in all of my years of schooling.

To my delight, she came to believe that I showed promise as a student. Olive wrote to me recently that "Our dearest teacher, Artha Tyler Barbour . . . recognized you had great potential and nurtured these qualities in you from the beginning." In the eighth grade, when Artha—as I know her now—taught English, she began to work on my grammar, taking time to jot down on sheets of paper words that I misused and to correct the slang popular among classmates, words such as *guy* and *ain't*. I would study them, working hard to master what she had written. From that time on, my use of English began to improve, and I started to avoid grammatical errors, such as the use of the double negative, so much a part of the Spanish language. In social studies, when time was running short and we were attempting to complete a verbal assignment, which required that everyone in class read out loud a part of the essay, Artha would ask me to read past my time because I was a fast reader. But that was only a start. She drove from San Diego to Pacific Beach and on her way home would stop at the public library for books to give to the more advanced students. That is how I read Stuart Chase's *Mexico: A Study of Two Americas,* a study by a famous economist; H. G. Welles's *Outline of History;* and Richard Halliburton's lively tales of adventures. This was my initial venture into the grown-up prose of adults. The book by Chase, terribly mistaken as I now realize, was especially relevant, for I already had an interest in Mexico.

As I look back on those days, I realize that Artha saw me as a budding college student. How else to explain her eagerness for me to get to know San Diego State College? Along with one or two others, she would take me to watch light operas put on by the drama department. I remember vividly *The Merry Widow,* Franz Lehar's operetta, with the haughty and wealthy Hanna, who must be persuaded to marry the dashing Count Danilo so that her money will replenish the coffers of Ponteverdo. When Artha's husband returned from studying for a doctorate at Yale, they took me to see San Diego State's football team play rivals. One of its stars was Frank Galindo, a Mexican American.

Those were also the years when I started to become aware of world events. I knew from conversations at home that Germany under Adolf Hitler had begun to challenge the hegemony of Britain and France. But these were also the years of Lázaro Cárdenas in Mexico, when land reform, that forgotten promise of the Revolution of 1910, had taken on new life under the leadership of this remarkable man, who nationalized the country's petroleum industry, telling Standard Oil and Royal Dutch Shell to pack up and leave when their spokesmen rejected labor's just demands for higher wages and recognition of their union. No wonder, therefore, that Mexican events took precedence over European ones in discussions at home. In Artha's social science class, however, the talk centered on events reported in San Diego newspapers, and, aside from scathing criticism of Franklin D. Roosevelt and the New Deal so common to these conservative journals, most stories focused on Europe. They told of the Spanish Civil War, the rise of Nazi Germany and Fascist Italy, and the help given Francisco Franco by the two dictators of these countries. In class, we reported on what we read in the newspapers and argued among ourselves, especially over whether or not the United States should take sides. I was a firm believer in neutrality, as were most of my classmates.

Each year Artha directed a school play, the highlight of the semester, staged at the elementary school auditorium, one performance on Friday afternoon for students and the next night for the community. Tryouts for the plays were by faculty invitation, and only second-semester eighth as well as ninth graders were eligible to compete. Stage crews were organized among the students, who used shop classes to build the sets, and volunteers handled arrangements. A good bit of social prestige went with participation as an actor or actress in the plays.

I was not unaware of the plays, but it had never occurred to me to try out; after all, why would they want a swarthy Mexican in a role written for lily-white Anglos? Yes, I had adapted to the Anglo world, but that did not mean I was unaware that I was different. I was too young to know about the importance of cultural differences but not too young to know that I was hardly blond and blue-eyed, that I was the son of Mexican parents, and that our food and language were different. When I was young, people often accused me of being shy, but there were reasons for that shyness; one of them, if not the main one, was my being a Mexican. When young, one wants to be part of the herd; I could not because of my skin color. I stood out like a sore thumb, whether sitting in class or in a school photograph. Always, there I was, the one conspicuous person, set apart because of color. Anglos, by contrast, were very much at home because they looked like everyone else; they could go anywhere and not risk meeting cruel rebuffs, but I had to move warily. As a result, I became tongue-tied when trying to speak to Anglo girls. Superpatriots, of which there are scads in this country, will retort that this difference was all in my head, that I was an American because I was born here. True enough, but hardly realistic.

I also learned early on that my relations with boys were quite different from those with girls, all of whom were Anglos. In elementary school, these girls never had crushes on me; I never saw a girl in class with my initials written on the back of her hand, a common practice by the sixth grade. True, probably owing to my academic success, I was treated a bit differently in junior high, but not entirely so. Girls sought me out for help with class work, and I could dance with them at school dances and at the WPA weekly dances at the elementary school, but none ever asked to walk home with me after school or to see me on the beach during summer vacations. Boys might boast about kissing a girl at the beach, but that was not my bliss.

It was Artha who urged me to try out for the school play. To my surprise, I was given a part, one of the better ones. The boy and girl leads were taken by second-semester ninth graders, veterans of previous plays. During the last three semesters at school, I was in every play—*The Taming of Tuffy, Crooks for a Month,* and *Campus Quarantine*—the last time as the lead opposite Mary Sue McIntyre, a girl I had a crush on. Every evening from Monday through Friday, Artha would come by in her car to pick up cast members and take them to the elementary school auditorium to rehearse, just like professional actors. During the final play I did, Artha would take me home last and, while sitting in the car, talk at length about school and life in general. Our mother used to wonder what we were up to because during these conversations, at times with the engine of the car running, the minutes dragged on to become half hours and more.

The highlight of the semester was the evening performance, but I had mixed feelings about it. True, it was a wonderful feeling to see our mother and father in the audience and to know that they were proud of me, but at the same time I knew that the performance meant the end of rehearsals and the wonderful times I shared with Artha and my companions.

The biggest satisfaction was yet to come, however. Each year there was an election to pick the student-body president. I don't remember who asked me to run for the office, but I did, never expecting to be elected. The previous president had been Peter Clark, as Anglo as one could be and simply one of many others who had held that office. Mary Sue, pretty and popular as well as a good student, also chose to run. Frankly, I never had hopes of being elected, although I knew I could count on some classmates, my brother for one, to vote for me. He later told me that he had campaigned actively for me. But I thought Mary Sue would surely win because she was one of the cast in the school plays and one of Artha's favorites, until Artha told me that I should not be surprised if I did. The election proved her a prophet, for I became school president.

Not as important, but also rewarding was my job as the sports editor of the *Beach Log,* the school newspaper, which was published once a month; I would write the article, and Artha would type it and reproduce copies on a mimeograph machine.

As I look back, the years I spent as a student at Pacific Beach Junior High School were euphoric ones. I was class president and then later captain of the football and basketball teams, the top handball player, and a stalwart of the track squad.

That euphoria was soon to end, however. To my sorrow, there was no high school in town. One had two options: if one lived south of Garnet Street, one went to Point Loma High, a school in the suburbs of San Diego, where many Portuguese families lived, most of them tuna fishermen; if one lived north of Garnet, one went to La Jolla High, and that was my misfortune.

3

Ambivalent Times

———

I came of age in the turbulent and contentious years between 1940 and 1950, when the number of people of Mexican ancestry in the United States more than doubled, with between two and three million born in those years. Scholars employ the term *generation* to describe these people because nearly all shared similar experiences, one being anti-Mexican bigotry. This in no way denies the importance of class, race, and gender, which Mario García, the author of *Mexican Americans,* says "are the motor forces of history." Mostly employed as cheap labor, Mexicans were part and parcel of the working class, albeit more of them no longer toiled in agriculture but in industrial and service occupations.

Mexicans of an earlier era, those born in Mexico, one being my father, shared a comparable but distinct experience. Fleeing from the turmoil of the Mexican Revolution and the poverty and despair of the Porfiriato, they trekked north in search of brighter horizons. Most concluded they were better off in the United States, although exploited and shunted aside by Anglo bigotry, a relationship that Rodolfo Acuña, a patron of ethnic studies, describes as "internal colonialism." Yet they were of two minds: yes, economically they were better off, but, on the other hand, they were treated as outcasts, far from the customs of their native land. Filled with nostalgia, they dreamed of a return to the *madre patria* (mother country) once they had acquired a nest egg. Life in the United States was temporary.

These Mexicans enjoyed one huge advantage over children born in the United States. They never lost sight of who they were:

Mexicanos. That in part may explain why they tolerated Anglo prejudice—segregation in barrios, for example. These annoyances were merely temporary, to be endured until they could return home. Not so for those born in the United States, who went to school there and spoke English, but were raised by Mexican parents who spoke Spanish and worshiped Mexican gods. Consigned to the sidelines of society by Anglos, many of this new generation developed problems of identity.

Various Chicano scholars, perhaps best described as a third wave of Mexican ancestry, have dealt harshly with the older generation, which they indict as an "accommodationist" generation— bluntly put, *pocho* or "brown on the outside, white on the inside." Nirvana was shedding the ethnic heritage, moving out of the barrio. The Mexican American, troubled by his connection to Anglos, who never ceased thinking themselves superior, frequently cut himself off from his own language and culture in order to escape Anglo bigotry. Manuel Servín, a university scholar and himself a Mexican American, even indulged in a bit of self-flagellation, asserting in *An Awakened Minority* that the Mexican American generation had over the years gone from bad to worse, especially during the Chicano era: Why, he asked, were there only a few more professors of history of Mexican ancestry "than [there were] . . . in the 1930s?" And, he added, "they are not in the same class as the older group," referring to George I. Sánchez, a pedagogue, and Carlos Castañeda, a historian in Texas. A staunch conservative, Servín let his politics interfere with his judgment, attributing the lack of excellence in higher education to Chicanos who "waste more time in political activity than in scholarly endeavor." Well, he was dead wrong, but that is another story.

In 1937, the town of La Jolla, four miles up the coast from Pacific Beach, was a bifurcated, white community with essentially two kinds of residents: the wealthy, who dwelt in palatial homes on the edge of the Pacific Ocean or on Hillside Drive, which circled the slopes above the town, or on the Muirlands, where the Country Club was located; the others, who ensconced themselves on the rocky shores of South La Jolla, where high tides swept the beaches of sand. A middle class of shopkeepers and clerks aped the lifestyle of the rich. The rest of the inhabitants were carpenters, house painters, plumbers, masons, and store clerks. During summer, the rich and the pretentious wore white buckskin shoes, blue blazers, and white trousers or skirts or knickers for playing golf, along with tennis, a standard pastime. Convertible cars were the vogue—Pierce Arrows, Packards, and Lincolns—and older women tooled electric cars up and down the streets. The wealthy swam at the Cove or at the La Jolla Beach and Tennis Club, closed to outsiders. The Valencia Hotel, which overlooked the Cove, was a watering hole for the well-to-do. One or two shops, a plumbing store, a hardware store, and the Bank of Italy made up the tiny business district.

Not everyone attended La Jolla High School. Many of the wealthy enrolled their daughters in the Bishop School, an Episcopal institution of Spanish-Moorish buildings behind high walls. La Jolla High lay on the gentle slope of the town, where most of the workers and their families had homes. One or two African American families made up a tiny enclave near the electric plant, and a mile or so beyond was the heart of the village of La Jolla, as locals referred to it. A majority of the students hailed from the working class, but there were enough children of the wealthy to give La Jolla High the reputation of being an enclave of rich snobs. No more than two or three African Americans attended, one a stalwart of every athletic team. He was the star running back on the football team, a high scorer in basketball, the swiftest in track, and a heavy hitter in baseball. I was one of two Mexicans, though a girl who was two grades ahead was of similar ancestry but light of skin and pretty as well as haughty, but she never claimed her Mexican ancestry. Her mother and grandmother occasionally would visit our mother, and at times this girl would tag along, but at school or at Sunday mass she gave no sign of recognition.

I use the term *Mexican* fully aware that because most of the people like me were born in the United States, they were Americans by nationality and usually by culture and language. Yet prewar United States, to hark on this point again, was hardly a racial paradise, and certainly La Jolla was not. No Anglo-American spoke glowingly of bicultural values, and university academics, in particular scholars of U.S. history and society, deplored hyphenated Americans, whom they deemed unpatriotic. These were the heralded days of the hypocritical "melting pot," when "self-conscious racial diversity" was condemned. As Theodore Roosevelt, a jingoist of the first order, once said, "there is no room in this country for hyphenated Americanism . . . the only absolute way of bringing this nation to ruin."

In La Jolla, even more than in Pacific Beach, to look Mexican was enough for Anglo-Americans to denigrate you. No wonder that some Mexicans felt shame in their ethnic background; *Mexican* was a pejorative term. Our father thought these turncoats *pochos,* bastard Mexicans, and, when he was angry, *gringos de nalgas prietas,* "brown-ass gringos." In the 1930s, bigots dubbed a Mexican, no matter whether Mexican by birth or *pocho,* as a "Mex" and in parts of Texas as a "Spic."

I arrived at this Anglo school with high hopes. I had been successful at Pacific Beach Junior High, which was equally white, so why not at La Jolla? I was in for a rude awakening. As time went on, the school became a precarious equilibrium between withdrawal into my private world and flashes of hard acerbity. The first semester went well. Miss Moore, the algebra teacher, resembled that tall, dour teacher in one of the murals that José Clemente Orozco, the famous Mexican artist, painted on the walls of the Baker Library at Dartmouth College; she was an old spinster, with all of the stereotypical characteristics of that breed. She gave an exam to each entering class and assigned students by rows according to the results. I ended up in the A row, which was next to the windows, and spent the rest of the semester fearing I would be demoted to a row in the back of the room. Her brother, who was married but who resembled his sister in more ways than one, taught geometry, like algebra a required subject for the college major. Geometry was my Waterloo, and Mr. Moore a puzzle. He was so unlike my father, and I doubt that he had ever taken the trouble to know anything about Mexicans. The social studies teacher, a Mr. Barber, was a former football player, tall and handsome according to the girls, who spent every class hour tapping the podium with a ring he wore on his finger and reading from the textbook we had already studied. When the semester ended, I had better than a B average in his class, but he gave me a C. When I spoke to him about the error and used my exam papers to prove it, he acknowledged his mistake and promised to change the final grade but never did, as I learned when I saw my transcript when applying for college.

I remember other teachers, too. Mr. Skinner, the Spanish teacher, wore thick glasses and could not see past his nose, so students did everything but listen, including tossing spitballs when he turned to write on the blackboard. I did acceptably well in the course but learned nothing. Yet he was the one teacher who welcomed me because I could speak Spanish. In the English class, Mr. Ferguson, a bald, red-faced man, spent most of the time on grammar, though we also read Walter Scott's *Ivanhoe.* What I remember is that I learned much about the use of the comma and the meaning of *metamorphosis* from reading *Silas Marner* by George Eliot. Still, consciously or not, no teacher encouraged me to join the debate team, try out for the drama club, look forward to being a member of the honor society, or write for the school newspaper. Left out of what was trendy on campus, I felt like a marginal human being. From that semester on, things went from bad to worse, largely because the school forgot me. The La Jolla High I attended was hardly a receptive abode for a Mexican kid from Pacific Beach. Were it not for my parents, I suspect that I might have come to perceive a relationship between racial identity and what I could do academically.

As I mentioned earlier, I was an athlete in junior high. The editors of the *Beach Log,* the school annual, even predicted that I would end up as football coach at Santa Clara, a Catholic college with a big-time football schedule. This history did not help me at La Jolla, though during the first semester I made my letter in track as a long-distance runner—one of the best in San Diego County, I like to boast. I made the football team but not the first string;

during spring practice, I thought I had, but when I returned for the fall semester, to my chagrin the former coach was now the vice principal, and I had to prove myself to another coach, who concluded that my talents needed seasoning. That fall during football season, I played sparingly as a substitute, a role I had never encountered previously. That was bad enough, but to make matters worse some on the football team were arrogant s.o.b.s who made no effort to welcome me. It was a clan closed to outsiders. When I tackled one of them during a scrimmage, he voiced loudly his disdain for Mexicans. When I met them in the halls, they gave no sign of recognition. I was not one of the crowd. Eventually I concluded that football was not for me. What a jolt that was because I had my heart set on being a footfall star. That more or less concluded my athletic career, though I made another letter in track.

More trouble loomed ahead. When I came to La Jolla, I was at that awkward, adolescent age when girls were becoming important. Yes, I had noticed them earlier, especially Mary Sue in junior high, who to my anguish had her eyes set on someone else. In Pacific Beach, I had never had much time to spend on girls outside of school hours. None, moreover, lived nearby; their parents had homes across town. During the summer and after school, my brother and I worked in the nursery or with the landscape crew in La Jolla. I had arrived at La Jolla during the spring semester, my sole good time in school, mainly because I met Mary Lou, who I thought liked me. Well, I was wrong. Her heart belonged to James Harvey's fiddle-playing older brother, which left me wandering about, friendless and forlorn. I was saved further embarrassment because when I returned for the fall semester, I learned that the object of my affection had moved to Missouri. No other girl was bowled over by either my looks or my mind. I learned quickly that Anglo-American girls at La Jolla were no different than the boys: they dated only their own. As Roberto, later a football luminary at La Jolla, explained it, they might "hug you if you played on the first team but, just the same, would not date you." Yet my brother was luckier than I because when he came out for football, the worst of the rednecks had graduated. For my part, I decided to complete my schooling as quickly as possible; by taking heavy course loads, I graduated in two and one-half years at the ripe old age of seventeen.

In the years I spent in this Anglo bastion, I was not once invited to a beach party, a school dance, or any other social event. When Friday came, I simply went home to await Monday. What occurred on weekends I never found out because no one ever told me. I saw boys and girls in the halls talk and laugh together and heard them go over the good times enjoyed on weekends. As for my companions from Pacific Beach, they went their own way: Jesse Peavy and Roy Snyder dropped out of school, and the rest of them, including Olive, went off to Point Loma High. Mary Sue, to my horror, began to smoke cigarettes, paint her face, and date army and navy academy cadets. When the La Jolla High School annual appeared, with pictures of graduating seniors and their plans for the future, I learned, to my astonishment, that I wanted a job, although no one had taken the trouble to ask me what I hoped to do. What a contrast with the *Beach Log,* where my bio was the biggest of the bunch.

As I look back on these years, I shudder, thinking about how I was tottering on the edge of an emotional precipice. That I kept my feet planted firmly on the ground I owe to Papá and Mamá, whose love and devotion never faltered, and to the time they spent inculcating in us a pride in being Mexican. I always knew who I was. Despite being cut off from the school's social life, I never saw myself as inferior because of ethnic ancestry or class. My father was not a common laborer, and Mamá was not just a housewife. In Pacific Beach, they were, relatively speaking, persons of some standing. Yes, I ran afoul of the offspring of wealthy families at La Jolla High, who paid scant attention to me, a new experience because I had not crossed paths with them in Pacific Beach. But most students at La Jolla were sons and daughters of working families, the type of people I had known all along.

Until La Jolla High, I had spent my youth among blond and blue-eyed Anglos. Only at home did I interact with Mexicans, aside from the men who worked for Papá. Rarely had I shared class time with someone of my ethnic background. These moments were mostly disappointing, even embarrassing. The few ethnically similar students I had known were the offspring of Mexicans who worked in the brickyard of Rose Canyon, a housing slum, or occasionally of working-class families in Old Town, where the Spaniards had built the first of the California missions. Never were there more than a handful of them and rarely one in my class. They seldom did their homework and usually paid scant attention to the teacher. When asked a question, the answer to which they should have known had they done their homework, they sat silent, *con los brazos crusados* (arms folded), to quote our mother. One episode from the start of the fall semester in seventh grade lingers in my mind. In the back of the classroom sat a plump, unattractive Mexican American girl who never spoke and never opened a book. Her last name, to my despair, turned out to be Ruiz. The teacher, a big woman with short, dark hair who rarely moved from where she sat behind her desk, assumed that we were brother and sister. I am sorry to admit that I made haste to disabuse her of that idea.

Incredibly, many of the teachers, largely the entire staff, had distorted misconceptions about Mexican students, the name they applied to all of us. When it came to math, English, or social studies, we were said to be slow learners. These subjects were supposedly beyond our grasp. That same cockeyed view held that we were good at working with our hands, at times artistic, and excelled especially in art and music. I have no idea how these people arrived at these conclusions because they certainly did not fit the Ruiz mold. None of us were terribly artistic, though Roberto usually did quite well in art, and both of us were stalwarts of wood shop. However, both classes included Anglo-Americans who were at least as talented. As for the other Mexican kids, they were hardly brilliant in any subject and surely not in art, so far as I could tell. Most of them were mediocre, often with poor attendance records; they might come to school an entire week and then be absent for days on end.

Today, after years of study, I understand that the home environment plays a key role in the intellectual development of students. If father and mother are uneducated, perhaps even illiterate, if they take no interest in the academic achievements of their offspring, if homes are barren of books and newspapers and the neighbors are of similar bent, and if teachers do not care, it does not take much insight to predict that students will do poorly in school. But then I was young and unschooled, and I believed everything Papá held aloft, mainly that one merely had to work hard to get ahead. However, the values school, so dear to American conservatives, is more myth than fact. Aspirations for a better way of life derive from helpful parents and, equally important, from available opportunities, as the psychologist Mortimer Adler wrote; one needs models whose hard work and study have yielded personal success.

When I began the fall semester at La Jolla High, my life abruptly changed out of school as well, but not necessarily for the better. For this turn of events, I owe the men who worked for my father, one in particular. Marcelino, just twenty-one, was squat and beefy, easy-going, and fond of company, with a Cheshire cat smile on his face, though my father could have done without it because Marcelino spent more time laughing and talking than working hard and thus was more a replacement than a member of the work crew; Papá relied on him when he needed extra help, so, to my regret, Marcelino was not always around. Marcelino and his brother Salomón, an employee Papá prized, along with Daniel and Miguel, belonged to the second group of workers Papá hired after he started his business. Daniel, at twenty-eight, was the oldest of the crew, and Marcelino the youngest. They hailed from Old Town and were the sons of Mexicans and spoke Spanish, whereas the crew of the 1920s and early 1930s—the Acostas, Castros, Agustíns, and Corderos—were Mexican born, more or less Papá's age, with whom on Saturday afternoons, the day of *la raya* (pay day), he would reminisce about old times in Mexico. To Salomón and the Old Town crew, younger than the Mexicans, he would proffer advice: "Don't waste your money on fiestas, don't drink too much *cerveza* (beer)," and so forth, to which Salomón and the others would swear that they were leading an exemplary life. During the

summer months, Roberto and I looked forward to laboring alongside Marcelino because he always had amusing stories to tell, including what he did when just married, which was, as he boasted,
to fornicate with his wife on the kitchen floor the moment he got
home. There was no waiting to shower or eat supper; he rushed in
with an erection.

One day when Roberto and I were transplanting potted plants
into larger containers, Marcelino, who was helping, told us of a
wedding reception to be held in San Diego at the Eagles Hall. "Why
don't you go," he suggested, promising to get us an invitation. So
we went, though we knew neither the groom nor the bride nor
anyone else. It was quite a party, the groom in a tux and the bride
in an elegant white gown. The occasion disclosed a new world for
me. The crowd was entirely Mexican, even the orchestra, which
played both American and Mexican pieces. And the girls, at least
some of them, were gorgeous. Nearly all of them, I learned, lived
in Logan Heights, the southeast district of San Diego, and attended
San Diego High School. Until then, my only contact with this
colony had been through the yearly pilgrimages with Papá to worship the Virgin of Guadalupe on December 12. At the ripe old age
of sixteen or so, I was introduced to the life of barrio Mexicans.

At the wedding reception, I was smitten by a young woman
whom I asked to dance again and again. Berta Saínz—not a raving
beauty but, to quote the old saying, "beautiful if you love them"—
was two years older than I but yet a junior at San Diego High School;
that troubled me not, though it should have set off an alarm. At
that age, why was she still a junior in high school? Though I had
Berta on my mind, months went by before I saw her again, this
time at a neighborhood dance just a block from where she lived.

Logan Heights, a haven for the working class, was a one-of-a-
kind experience, poles apart from the snobbish La Jolla I knew and
even from Pacific Beach. Unlike these Anglo boroughs, Logan
Heights was Mexican from first to last, nearly all of the older folk
hailing from Mexico, although their offspring were American
born. It was urban, part of the greater San Diego and, by comparison with the aseptic beach towns, had the feel and smell of age.

The boundaries of Logan Heights, not terribly big, lay within Southeast San Diego, between Sixteenth Street and Thirtieth and from Imperial Avenue to the bay. The community dated from 1905 and was named after John A. Logan, a Union army general turned railroad promoter. Logan Heights rode the ups and downs of the wheel of fortune, starting out as a haven for the better-off and ending up as refuge for the poor. The harbinger of settlement in the area had come with the establishment of downtown San Diego in 1867; soon adjacent subdivisions sprang up, one eventually being Logan Heights. In the beginning, it had rural charm, fertile soil, and a view of the bay, and it was close to downtown. It boasted a good school, first named East School and then Logan School; among its graduates were mayors of the city, councilmen, and a police chief. Some of the early residents, who dwelt in spacious homes built in the Victorian gingerbread style, were among San Diego's most prominent families.

Its heyday did not last long. By 1907, the advent of the San Diego and Arizona Railway line to the Imperial Valley, which cut through Logan Heights, already had ushered in land-use changes, opening up the area to business and industry. First came the California Iron Works, then San Diego Marine Construction Company, followed by tuna canneries and, in 1919, by the Naval Docking and Fleet Repair Base. By the end of World War I, many of the older homes were showing signs of wear, and, more important perhaps, the automobile had made its debut, opening areas of San Diego previously inaccessible. That and the growth of industry, with its noise, odors, and traffic, made Logan Heights a less-desirable place to live. By 1920, the prominent families had left for Mission Hills, Kensington, and East San Diego. As they departed, Mexicans began to replace them; by the late 1920s, Logan Heights had become a Mexican neighborhood, with African Americans living on its fringes. Mexicans settled there for obvious reasons: the lower cost of housing and rents; bigoted real estate agents' unwillingness to show Mexicans any homes in other parts of San Diego; the existence of racial covenants; and, surely, Mexicans' preference to live among others of their nationality.

When I arrived on the scene in the late 1930s, Logan Heights had fallen on hard times. Most of its residents were Mexicans who had come between 1917 and 1930 and who early on worked for the San Diego and Arizona Railroad, many now employed as manual laborers by the gas and water municipal utilities, a work week that stretched from Monday to Saturday noon. On the edges of Logan Heights, signs of decay were starkly visible; houses were old and dilapidated, the paint on their exterior walls cracking and peeling and, according to the Federal Writers' Project of 1937, a slum; however, that term has the whiff of class bias. Moreover, the heart of Logan Heights, where Mexicans of another sort had homes, was a reputable neighborhood. On weekends, residents put on their Sunday best and attended mass at Nuestra Señora de Guadalupe, the one stucco building in the neighborhood. These Mexicans took care of their homes, tended lawns and shrubs, planted red geraniums in flower pots, and kept their yards spic-and-span. In the late 1920s or early 1930s, there was even a parade with floats on September 16, Mexican Independence Day, presided over by a beauty queen.

The principal streets, National and Logan, which ran west and east, had what there was of commerce—Mike Amador's grocery store and, half a block away on Newton, the Campos family's store, plus El Carrito, a restaurant for Mexican food, and La Victoria, where women made tortillas by hand. Mike Amador's two sons, because they were a businessman's children, were highly sought after by girls of the "better" families. The grocery sat not far from the one drugstore in the neighborhood, owned and operated by Juan Doria, whose brother was the sole Mexican physician in San Diego, the one who took out my tonsils. I won't forget him because he did it in his office and put me to sleep with chloroform; for the rest of the day, I bled and was sick as a dog.

Nuestra Señora de Guadalupe, the Catholic church, stood on Kearney, a block north of Logan, a white, California Spanish–style building with the rectory to one side. Kearney was one of the better streets in the barrio. The church had been built in 1931 by the Spanish Augustinian Recollects. Now, though Mexicans made up the congregation, the priests were Irish Americans, thanks to Charles F. Buddy, named bishop of the newly created Roman Catholic Diocese of San Diego in 1936. Bishop Buddy—who saw his Mexican Catholics as a "burden" on his diocese because of their poverty and, as he charged, their lack of religious instruction— wanted priests of his own ethnic ancestry. So that "these misguided people be taught their place," Bishop Buddy told Father Damián Gobeo, a gentle and much-loved priest at the parish since 1932, that he was being replaced by Father Matthew Thompson, an Irishman from Imperial Valley.

The Mexican faithful were of the opinion that an injustice had occurred, so fifteen hundred of them signed a petition asking that Father Damián be retained because he "fosters and maintains the devotion of Our Lady of Guadalupe" and "speaks our language." Bishop Buddy, however, would not hear of it and asked the district attorney's office in San Diego to investigate what he dubbed was a "rebellion among the Mexicans of Our Lady of Guadalupe parish." An angry laity asked Rome to countermand Buddy's order, point- ing out that their sole crime was being Mexicans whose "only two loves were to fill their heart with religion and their native land." When Pius XII, to whom the letter was addressed, turned a deaf ear, the parishioners retaliated by crossing the border into Tijuana for marriages, baptisms, and confirmations and by removing fur- nishings and household items, kitchen utensils and bedding in- cluded, from the parish house.

Both schools in the area, Logan Elementary and Memorial Jun- ior High, were heavily Mexican. Two movie houses, the Coronet and the Metro—both the property of a Mr. Fink, who lived out- side the neighborhood—were the only ones in San Diego to show Mexican movies, enormously popular with adults. Just to see a Mexican film, our parents would drive from Pacific Beach without even knowing what was playing. When invited, I went along, as did my sisters, so we came to know the film stars of Mexico: Sara García, who always cried when she played the role of the *madre sufrida,* the suffering mother of Mexican families; *los hermanos* Soler, middle-aged gentlemen in coats and ties; Joaquín Pardavé,

the actor and composer of "Varita de Nardo," a country music classic; Roberto Soto, *el panzón* (big belly); and, of course, Jorge Negrete,
the singing *charro,* and Gloria Marín, a film beauty he later married. Negrete was the idol of the women, particularly after he made
the film *Ay Jalisco no te rajes* and made famous its theme song. He
was tall, dark, and handsome, sported a mustache, and sang. His
films featured swaggering *charros,* men on horseback who rode
hard, drank tequila, and died a tragic death at the hands of their
rivals, usually over the love of a woman. Unlike Americans, who
prefer their movies to end on a happy note, with lovers united and
obstacles conquered, Mexicans love tragedies, where death comes
to the hero or sometimes to his lover. The greater the tragedy and
the more tears flow from both actors and audiences, the more
popular the film.

On Sunday mornings, however, Nuestra Señora de Guadalupe,
the Catholic church, drew the biggest crowds, in particular the late-
morning mass. They were mostly gatherings of women because
men, as was the habit in Mexico, seldom attended church. Older
women could be seen dressed in black, the sign of mourning,
shawls covering their heads. They took seriously both their religious devotion and, if accompanied by their daughters, the business of watching that no man seduce them. The end of the high
mass drew the biggest crowds, for that was when the young men,
suitors or hopefuls, arrived to watch the girls in their Sunday
dresses, high heels, and fancy hats. The men would flirt with the
girls, and if all went well, they might take one of them home or, if
very lucky, for a ride—that is, if by chance they had a car and there
was no mother around to say no.

Rivaling the Catholic church in importance was the Neighborhood House on the corner of National Avenue and Newton. La
Escuelita, the name given it by local Mexicans, tended to young
and old. It was largely a settlement house for immigrants, akin to
Hull House in Chicago; it offered something to nearly everyone.
The building was two stories high, longer on Newton than on National, and painted a drab beige.

Over this neighborhood, a fetid smell fell from Monday to Friday during certain seasons of the year. Only on weekends was it free of that stench. The odor, which crept in around windows and under doors and fowled the air, came from the fish canneries on the waterfront, on the south side of Main Street. On some days, it seemed worse than on others. The Van Camp cannery was the biggest. At the docks, fishermen unloaded their catch from boats, mainly tuna but also albacore; in the canneries (called *canerías* in *pocho* Spanish), the fish were deboned, cleaned, and packed in cans. Women, nearly all Mexicans, young and old alike, did the work. Early in the morning and in the evening, they could be seen going to work on Newton and then coming home, their bodies and clothes smelling of fish. On Fridays, when the young women who labored at the canneries went to the monthly dances at the Neighborhood House, their hair stank of fish if not washed again and again with boiling water and soap.

It was into this neighborhood I went when I began to socialize with the young men I met at the wedding reception. All were Mexican Americans and attended San Diego High—Andy Castro, Ernie Barrios, and Joe and Henry Carvajal, whom I knew best. On weekends, I would drive to Logan Heights to see them, at first mostly Andy and then Henry and Joe, two of a large clan of brothers who lived next door to the Catholic church. An older brother-in-law supported the family household; no father was visible, and the mother enjoyed the good life. Joe and Henry helped out by caddying on weekends on the golf courses of San Diego. Andy was the son of a railroad worker who never gave me any sign of recognition and whose wife never failed to say hello. What I recall about Andy, shy and likeable, was that he spent hours on end talking of the sexual prowess of his buddy Ernie; he was wasting his time, for no one boasted of his conquests more than Ernie—famous, Andy claimed, for his gigantic penis, so big that even the prostitutes at the Molino Rojo, the biggest whorehouse in Tijuana, would not take him on. Womanizing led Ernie into trouble: though he was "going steady," he got a seventeen-year-old girl whom he hardly knew pregnant and had to marry her, a mistake he corrected by leaving her after their child was born.

Life in the barrio of Logan Heights was life with Mexicans. In the year or two I spent visiting friends there, I never saw one Anglo of our age. If the homes had been designed and built in the Mexican style, I might just as well have been in Mexico, albeit the language of my new companions was English. With Andy and Ernie, whose parents I saw only once, I came to know more of life in Logan Heights: *kermeses* (bazaars that served Mexican delicacies), gab fests on Sunday afternoon at the Carvajals, dances, movies, as well as the weekly prize fights at the Coliseum Athletic Club. I especially remember watching Johnny "the Bandit" Romero, a native of Logan Heights, beat the young Archie Moore in a much ballyhooed prizefight that had the local and heavily Mexican crowd on its feet for all ten rounds. Lamentably, Romero, who showed so much promise, died a destitute alcoholic, like so many washed-up prize fighters.

To my astonishment, in 1939 or thereabouts, some of the young men of Logan Heights, among them Ernie and Andy, underwent a fashion metamorphosis. They let their hair grow long and began to wear coats that reached down to their knees, pants that came up to their chests, and wide-brimmed hats. To Andy and his pals, these outfits were "zoot suits." Where this fad originated is uncertain, though some scholars give credit to El Paso, Texas, or Los Angeles. So far as I could tell, for Logan Heights it was Los Angeles because Andy and his friends began to pal around with Angeleno fashion cohorts. Older Mexicans, who looked down on their peculiar clothes, labeled them *pachucos,* a pejorative term.

In recent years, pundits have made much of these young men, seeing them as rebels, precursors of the Chicano movement, as Luis Valdez, the playwright depicts them, or as lost souls, to paraphrase Octavio Paz's dubious portrait in *Labyrinth of Solitude.* Yet whatever their identity elsewhere, in Logan Heights, from what I could tell, their sole concerns were a hankering for clothes and the use of argot, a peculiar vocabulary. Not once did I ever hear any of them discuss politics, social injustices, or questions of ethnic identity. As for Mexico and its culture, they could not have cared less.

To my surprise and delight, Berta Saínz, about whom I had been thinking since the wedding reception, was at the first neighborhood dance I attended in Logan Heights, and she had come alone. "This is my big chance," I told myself, "it's now or never." After tripping the light fantastic with her, or so I thought, I walked her home, just a block or two from the festivities, and asked to see her again. When she said "yes," I wanted to jump for joy. That was the beginning of my great love affair, the first of my life. It was to endure for nearly two years, in the beginning at times painful because, as I learned quickly, I was not her first beau. Until she decided that we would "go steady," she led me a merry chase.

Berta's mother was Doña Porfiria, a native of Cananea, a mining town in northern Sonora, and a woman in her early fifties whom I never came to know well; aside from greetings, I don't think I ever had a real conversation with her. She was a single mom, although men visitors appeared from time to time. She had been divorced more than once or at least had lived with a number of men because Berta and her siblings did not have the same fathers. Berta had an older brother, who was in the Civilian Conservation Corps (CCC) camps and who came home occasionally, and a younger sister and brother. I heard more about Doña Porfiria from Terencio, Tía María's husband, who had known her in Cananea; according to him, she had been a flirt, widely popular among the young men.

Whether Terencio, who was something of a rake, spoke the truth I don't know, but when it came to her daughter, Doña Porfiria was a prude; she hovered over Berta like a hawk. Her daughter's virginity was uppermost on her mind. After I had known Berta for some time, I gave her a book on marriage I had read because I thought it useful for a couple "going steady." She promised to read it, but because she never seemed ready to discuss it, I began to suspect that she had simply set it aside. When I asked why the delay, she told me that she had to read it when her mother was not around because "it discussed sex." Berta was a very proper young lady who, even after I got to know her, was allowed out of the house only on Saturday nights. When I saw her during the week, it was on Wednesday evening, when we sat in the parlor and held hands while Doña Porfiria kept a close watch from the kitchen. My big moment with Berta was escorting her to the senior prom of San Diego High. She wore a formal gown; I put on my best dark suit and washed and polished my 1930 Chevy coupe, dark blue with bright-yellow wheels, a gift from my parents and an inducement to study hard in school. Owning a car set me apart from almost everyone my age—from Roy, James, and Lonnie in Pacific Beach, none of whom could afford one, as well as from Andy, Ernie, and the Carvajals in Logan Heights. It also provided the transportation to see Berta; after all, our home was miles from Logan Heights.

The late 1930s, when this turn in my social life occurred, saw the coming of the big bands of Glen Miller, Tommy Dorsey, Duke Ellington, Count Basie, and Jimmie Lunceford. There were also Mexican orchestras that played boleros, rumbas, and *paso dobles* for dancing—"Mala noche" and "Lagrimas de sangre" of Agustín Lara, among them—not just in Tijuana but also in San Diego. La Clave Azul held forth at El Castillo, a nightclub on the outskirts of Tijuana, popular with the young of Logan Heights, who were part and parcel of the swing era, when jitterbugging was the fad.

All this was normal for the kids from Logan Heights, except no one ever talked about school or mentioned teachers. I don't remember that any of them did homework, at least not in my presence, or studied for a test. On weekends, they might carry textbooks home but, so far as I could tell, left them unopened until Monday's classes. Teachers and counselors at San Diego High School, their alma mater, disproportionately relegated them to activities perceived as marginal—that is, nonacademic classes: wood and metal shop, typing, and home economics. Strangely, my newfound companions simply accepted their fate because none aspired to a college degree. For a while, I fell into this pattern, and, most logically, not only did my grades suffer, but to compound matters I found myself even more isolated from classmates at La Jolla High.

This behavior also brought me into conflict with my parents, both of whom had their minds set on their sons' attending college. Well, so did I, until I could think of nothing else but Berta.

When I think back on that juvenile caper, I can recall little about her except that I was smitten. Actually, we had little in common beyond the Spanish language, a taste for Mexican food, and "Two Sleepy People," a song we made our own. Things went from bad to worse when, as I was about to graduate from high school, I asked Berta to marry me and she accepted. Elated, I rushed home to tell my parents but also worried because deep in my soul I knew that they would not care for the news. Was I right! They were angry. "What about college," they asked, and the "dreams of a professional career, of becoming a doctor or a lawyer?" When I insisted that I wanted to get married, Papá blew his top. "If you marry this girl," he told me, "you will not be welcomed in this home." I was angry and hurt but stubbornly refused to cede ground. It was Mamá who saved the day, pleading with my father to bend a little. "All right," he said, "if you will work for me for one year before you marry, you will be welcomed again."

The job was manual labor on the landscape crew, at a salary of fifteen dollars a week, seven of which I had to give to my mother to pay for room and board. Each day I labored alongside men who, married and with families, had no aspirations beyond buying a better automobile and whose conversations revolved around drinking beer with their buddies. It took just three months of this labor for me to come to my senses, as Papá and Mamá surely hoped. Somehow, to Berta's unhappiness, I got up the courage to postpone the wedding and permit time to do its duty, and then I applied for college. As the months went by, no more was said of getting married. No one was angrier than Doña Porfiria, but Papá and Mamá, although they said nothing, knew it was the right thing to do.

Now, when I feel age like an icicle down my back, troubled by missteps of the past but unable to resist retracing those steps, I recall this moment when events seemed seductive, yet deep down I sensed that I had lost my way but chose instead to throw up my hands and let fate take its course. What torment I must have inflicted on Papá and Mamá! Where would I be today, I ask myself again and again, if they had not put their feet down? That I can look back on years of college and university teaching, on books and articles published, I owe to them. What saved me was the up-bringing they gave me, a home where love went hand in glove with old-fashioned discipline, a respect for one's identity, and aspirations for a better future.

4

The Halls of Ivy

In the fall of 1940, life at San Diego State had an up as well as a down side. We were young and full of life, and the Great Depression was over, but a war ravaged Europe. When I stepped on the campus, the Germans, French, and British were again in a dogfight, just twenty years after the slaughter of World War I; trench warfare, the scourge of that earlier bloodbath, was no longer in vogue, but bombers rained death from above, not just on soldiers but on women and children.

However, there was peace at home. Consumption of goods remained high; one could buy anything at Marston's or for less at the Dollar Store, at a time when domestic rearmament and aid to Britain and the Allies had become a major goal of Roosevelt's administration. As John Galbraith noted in *The Affluent Society,* this consumption could not go on for long without subjecting military supply to serious delays. But no one wanted to cut back in the production of consumer goods; as Galbraith wrote, "the ultimate fact [was] that people wanted goods, regarded them as important, and . . . the men who made the goods shared the latter conviction and wanted to supply them." It may appear supremely odd, but Americans were convinced that a high standard of living was central to their way of life; it would be paradoxical to abandon that standard in order to prepare to fight a war to preserve it.

Yet no matter how much Americans might want to bury their heads in the sand, there was a war, and whether they liked it or not, their government was becoming increasingly involved in its outcome. Roosevelt and his supporters were talking more and more as though the survival of the American way of life depended on an Allied victory. Given the anti-German propaganda, much of it from Washington and from radio and newspapers, American opinion began to tilt toward the Allies. Even so, Americans went on buying cars, shopping for clothes, and in San Diego going to the beach on weekends as though nothing was happening in the outside world. No different were the Mexicans of Logan Heights. Some were trying to complete high school; others had gone off to the CCC camps; and the older ones began looking for work. Few talked about the war, and few saw dark clouds looming on the horizon.

The reality was something else. If one took the time to look, the writing was on the wall, in bold, stark letters. The bloody conflict was thousands of miles away, however, and I, like most young men, shut my eyes and pushed the danger to the back of my mind; I was nineteen years old and just then becoming aware of the scope of the trouble overseas. Our parents had started to worry that the war would surely engulf the United States and, most likely, their two sons. They had ample reason because not only did they oppose the war, but at President Roosevelt's prodding, Congress soon passed the Conscription Act; from then on, young men older than twenty-one were subject to a military draft.

State, the name by which San Diego State was known, was a small college of less than two thousand students. Those from Pacific Beach formed a tiny minority, virtually all men; even La Jolla High was poorly represented. The campus stood east of San Diego, off to one side of the highway to Arizona. State was San Diego's version of the halls of ivy. It was not just the academic heart but the cultural soul of the city. Local lore had it that if you went to State, you were accomplishing something terrific. Graduates got jobs in business, and nearly all public-school teachers had studied there. In the 1920s, it had been a normal school, then a teachers' college, and finally a state college. Yet even as late as 1932, the freshman football team, which the *San Diego Union* touted as one with the "most potential in history," was still playing high school teams. For most of us, there was no other school, but, as writer George Atlas would put it, this was not a place for people "whose fathers had given them a set of Gibbon's *Decline and Fall of the Roman Empire* for their twelfth birthday."

The campus nestled among barren hills, its tower and walls resembling a kind of fortress monastery built in the Spanish California mold, white stucco walls and red-clay tiles. Most of the classrooms fronted on a central quad, where on sunny days the less diligent napped. State's mascot was Moctezuma, a squat, stone sculpture that sat in the middle of the quad, its name taken from an Aztec emperor of pre-Columbian Mexico. The college fight song was "Fight on, Fight on, You Aztec Men," a rousing chant one heard at football games.

State was a commuter college, from Pacific Beach a half-hour drive, through Old Town and then by way of Mission Valley, the channel for the San Diego River, where dairy cows grazed on both sides of a two-lane road. We pooled rides, driving our cars on some days or riding with others. One year I exchanged rides with Dick D'Vincent, who turned topsy-turvy a stereotypical Anglo prejudice at State in that he enjoyed visiting Tijuana, by himself or in my company. The redheaded, adventurous, and usually jolly D'Vincent was a maverick; he spoke no Spanish but had fallen in love with Tijuana and Mexican movies and never ceased to talk about his adventures in the border town and the film *Ay Jalisco no te rajes*. The names Jorge Negrete and Gloria Marín, the stars of the film, were constantly on his lips. He was a premed student, walking around campus with a slide rule on his belt and talking about physics and chemistry classes, which I detested. Thanks to D'Vincent, I got through college physics; although eager to leave the campus, he would stop by the laboratory class and help me finish the assignment that was turning my hair prematurely gray and keeping him from going home.

D'Vincent's name calls up an annoying bit of racist buffoonery I had to stomach. From time to time, the two of us had talked about getting a part-time job, so when D'Vincent told me that United Parcel Service was hiring college students to drive its delivery trucks and asked if I were interested, I replied, "Of course." The next day we drove over to the company's office, where a gruff man met us. Yes, he said, there were openings, but I noted that he gave me the cold shoulder. When we left, I had a gut feeling that something was amiss, but D'Vincent told me not to fret. We had the jobs: "You're overly sensitive, Ruiz." The next day he went to work for United Parcel, but I never did.

At State, I got down to business—that is, to being a student, an inclination absent in me since the early days at La Jolla High, though my first semester was hardly memorable. Determined to make up for quitting football in high school, I played on the freshman team and, though not on the first squad, earned a letter, a black sweater with the number forty-four, my class year. Then, near the close of that semester, I came to my senses: I had not gone to college to play games. The next semester I received As and began to awaken to the need to write lucidly, thanks to a professor who taught a writing class; good English prose, she would say, was more a skill than a body of acquired knowledge. You learn by teaching yourself how to write a simple sentence. Of course, there were guidelines: replace superfluous adverbs with dynamic verbs; use precise nouns over weak adjectives; and, by rearranging the syntax, turn the passive sentence into an active one.

Professors at State were more teachers than scholars. One such person was Alvena Storm, a tall and physically formidable geographer who turned me on. During the earlier male-dominated era, professors at the University of California (UC) at Berkeley, where Mrs. Storm earned her bachelor's degree, had told her that women should not be doing a Ph.D. and advised her to teach, which brought her to the old Normal School in San Diego in 1926 at a salary of thirty-eight dollars a week. What I remember about her is that she made discussions an intimate part of her class, lecturing only to explore what she thought the textbook had left out.

A very different sort was Abraham P. Nasatir. Short and dumpy, Abe, as his colleagues referred to him, walked around campus in a dark, double-breasted suit, a cigar in his mouth and a fedora on his head. He was the cock of the walk wherever he went but was hardly a happy man, believing that because of his publications he deserved to be in a university. Like so many professors at State, Abe had done his graduate work at UC Berkeley: his mentor was Herbert E. Bolton, father of the borderlands school, who wrote about Spanish explorers who traversed the Southwest. Bolton's best-known book was on Father Eusebio Kino, one of the missionaries who helped spread Catholicism among the Indians. He called it *The Rim of Christendom*. The weakness of Bolton's school was that it was short of ideas. He simply wrote about explorers and friars who walked from here to there over unchartered territories, often the home of hostile Indians, and tried to make Catholics out of pagans.

Abe looked up to Bolton. Why? I don't know. During Bolton's long tenure as chair of the Berkeley history department, no Jew was ever hired. This implication about Bolton bothered Abe, yet perhaps because Bolton was his mentor, he did not speak ill of him. Some colleagues at State, however, made little effort to hide their own anti-Semitism from Abe, an Orthodox Jew. Yet, paradoxically, Abe's own social conscience seemed to be flabby at best. One time an Anglo student told me that Abe had asked him to be the reader in his course but he had refused; he suggested that I ask Abe if I might do it, so I sought Abe out. "I am not looking for a reader," he told me.

Abe wrote in an obfuscated prose about French fur traders in the upper Mississippi Valley in the seventeenth and eighteenth centuries. In his rambling lectures for his course "History of the Americas," in which he read from yellow paper frayed on the edges from years of usage, he loved to talk about the traders but unfortunately left out intellectual content, as Bolton had. When Abe spoke of the Spaniards, we heard him talk about Coronado, Cabeza de Vaca, and other intrepid adventurers who wandered over uncharted lands to establish presidios and missions. I wrote my senior thesis, then a requirement for graduation from State, under Abe, calling it "For God and Country." The topic was the Santa Fe Trail, the coming of American merchants into Spanish New Mexico in the 1820s. Abe let me use archival material he had culled from the Archivo de las Indias in Sevilla, Spain. This was my first exposure to documents of this kind—reports and letters by colonial Spaniards, often in nearly illegible handwriting. Whether Abe thought that I had done a good job or not I never knew, yet years later, after I had reworked this senior paper for my master's thesis, he borrowed a copy to find some obscure information he needed for a book he was writing.

I decided early on that I wanted to teach history. That goal dates from San Diego State; however, my fascination with history began with Papá, who spoke eloquently and frequently about the past. I would teach history despite its unimportance to most Americans, who frequently used the phrase "that's history" to dismiss something irrelevant to current concerns. My initial aspiration had been to teach in a high school, marry, have children, and live in San Diego. That changed the day I took a class in the history of modern Europe. The professor was Lewis B. Lesley, a wiry, nervous man who outside of class paid scant attention to students. He wore granny glasses and squinted when he spoke to someone. I never liked him as a person, though I admired his lectures. Doubts about French and English innocence in the European conflict never furrowed his brow. His eagerness to get us into the war spilled over into his lectures, which riled those who had no wish to soldier. One time when Lesley was haranguing the class, telling us that it was our duty to volunteer for military service, almost implying that we were cowards for not doing it, a student got up and asked him why he did not join the army if he felt so strongly. At this retort, Lesley slammed shut his notes and walked angrily out of the classroom.

What field of history would I teach? Thoughts of European history crossed my mind or perhaps U.S. history, largely because of Charles Leonard, a gruff, cynical man who scoffed at every patriotic myth; to hear him speak was to believe that he was an iconoclast. Yet he enrolled his daughter in the Bishops School, where tradition and religion held sway. He was tall and heavy, spoke with a guttural voice, and tinkered constantly with the buttons on his vest. He belittled colleagues' attempts to publish—barbs, I suspected, directed at Abe. He took pride in never telling us what outside books we should read for exams, but he was a provocative teacher.

Mexico and its history, thanks to Papá, were uppermost on my mind. I kept recalling stories he told about the struggles for Mexican independence, Benito Juárez and Don Porfirio, and the Revolution of 1910. At times, I would wonder about the veracity of the stories, until one day in my first semester at State I began to explore the library, where I found books on Mexico that verified, more or less, what Papá had said, though written in English and from an American point of view. Two of them caught my attention: Frank Tannenbaum's *Peace by Revolution,* a glorification of the upheaval of 1910 by an expert on penal justice, and *Mexico and Its Heritage,* a realistic view of the 1920s, when graft and political chicanery prevailed, by Ernest Gruening, the editor of *The Nation,* a respected left-wing journal. "If I don't steal now when I can," Gruening quotes a state governor, "when will I be able to do it?" Viewed from historical hindsight, Gruening's book, far less flattering to Mexico, holds up much better.

My exploration of library stacks was not limited to books on Mexico, not after I chanced upon a shelf holding a handful of books about Mexicans in the United States. This was the first time I had come across such studies. I would sit for hours in the aisles between stacks, book in hand, reading and looking at photographs of persons who looked like me. I was then just a young man and hardly an expert on the travails of Mexicans and their offspring in this country, so my reaction to what I read, I admit, was not what it would be today. I grew up among Anglos, where questions of ethnicity were never explored in school. Yes, I came from a Mexican home, but my parents rarely talked about Mexicans in the United States, though Papá, a fierce do-it-yourselfer, would tell us, when he felt like it, how he had run afoul of Anglo bigotry.

So there I was reading books about people of my ancestry, at a time when racial bigotry spread over the land like the stench of a garbage dump. They surely made an impression on me because I still recall, at times strikingly, the names of authors and titles. When I began to write this memoir, I went back to the library to look at them and upon turning their pages felt like a schoolboy again. I emerged with egg on my face: I found their authors, whom I had looked up to decades ago, earnest and well meaning but myopic at times and often grossly mistaken. As Josh Billings once quipped, "The trouble ain't that people are ignorant; it's that they know so much that ain't so."

In my youth, scholars rarely wrote about Mexicans in the United States; that was left to others. I chanced upon books, mere pamphlets if measured by their size, by Protestant ministers more dedicated to Bible study than to scholarly research. All spoke highly of Mexicans, heaping praise, but nonetheless their negative comments put those views to rout. One book I recall because of its catchy title, *That Mexican! As He Really Is, North and South of the Rio Grande,* by Robert N. McLean. He spoke Spanish—at least he claimed to do so, although his spelling was atrocious—and admired the Mexican, in part because, he wrote, "worn by the toil of the day, and oppressed by the pangs of hunger, he has found happiness in the treasures of the soul." The Mexican child, McLean explained, had "artistic tastes"; music was "in his soul." Almost before he began to talk, he had "learned to hum little tunes . . . when the average American child is interested only in tops and dolls."

The Mexican suffered from ills of sundry sorts, one being an "inferiority complex." He brought with him "his inherited ignorance, his superstition, his habits of poor housing," but "with his abiding love of beauty." McLean told of visiting a railroad worker and his family in a "dilapidated red box car": when "I knocked at the door, I chanced upon them at their evening meal eating *frijoles.*" The man "was very glad to have steady work with the railroad, although at heart he was a rover," here one day and gone the next. Nor did the Mexican save for a rainy day, even "though his way of living may make him a pauper tomorrow." Yet, McLean wrote, given an opportunity, the Mexican began to "better his own living conditions" if helped by "efficient health services." Unfortunately, "the poorest representatives of the Mexican race" had come to America; those "who have initiative, who have acquired property" stayed home.

Vernon McCombs, another of these Protestants, swore in *From over the Border* that he "had never met a more responsive or delightsome people than the Mexicans." On the race question, he acknowledged, the "approach to Mexicans is blocked when reference is made to white folks"; however, "even if [they] . . . did have color, it is external which a tactful, experienced servant of God . . . learns to forget." On the subject of school segregation, some Anglos, he pointed out, "[think] that segregation is better for the Mexican children themselves . . . while others believed in segregation because the Mexican children may bring dirt, disease, and vermin into the schools." McCombs expressed no misgivings about the practice, so long as "it is a matter of condition, rather than of race, there is probably little peril in it."

Emory Bogardus, a university professor and author of *The Mexican in the United States,* conceded that not all Mexicans were "low-grade illiterates"; some were "broadly cultured." Nor did he lump together all Mexicans. In one category, he placed "native-born Mexicans," old inhabitants of the Southwest, many "largely of Indian origin": citizens of the United States by birth, but "Mexican and Indian by culture," in Texas called "Tejanos." In the second category was the elite of "aristocratic Spanish families, descendants of . . . leaders in the Southwest in early days," and symbols of "the fading glory of a ruling past." Partially related by class were wealthy Mexicans who were fleeing from upheavals but who longed to return to their homeland.

Then came unskilled Mexicans, nearly everyone a recent arrival, who occupy most of Bogardus's book. Mexican fathers, Bogardus was convinced, viewed carelessly large numbers of children, in part because of a "primitive attitude." If the children proved burdensome, fathers might desert the family. For a mother, if a baby died, it was God's will; "there is one less mouth to feed; there will be another one along soon." The working-class Mexican had "not been trained" to assume "responsibility . . . he has not been taught to save . . . thrift has not entered his vocabulary." When the harvest ended, children were taken out of school because Mexican parents opposed "the education of their children." When the lower-class Mexican, "with his paternalistic and communal culture[,] has come into contact with American individualism, he has tottered."

During my second year, I enrolled in a class on Mexican history taught by Abe Nasatir. Although I was a gung-ho student and time and time again attempted to stir up discussions, Abe, who spoke no Spanish, was a disappointment to me. He was not interested in Mexicans; he spoke about the Spanish Conquest and ran through the independence struggle without saying much about the patriot fathers. But when I read the class textbook—Henry B. Parkes's *The History of Mexico,* a brief summary of Mexican history written by an Englishman—I knew immediately that I wanted to teach and write Mexican history.

There was another reason, too, why I turned to Mexican history, to the study of my ancestors, and to the memories of a childhood in the bosom of a Mexican home and of altars fashioned in December to honor La Virgen de Guadalupe. The study of Mexico meant knowing more about myself, who I was, where I had come from; knowing Mexicans and their cultural contributions was crucial to me because I lived among persons who almost always were ignorant of the history of Mexicans and disdainful of their achievements. In school, nothing was ever said about Mexico, its heroes or its writers, poets, and artists. In textbooks, it was as though they had never existed. Teachers, every one an Anglo, cared nothing about Mexico. In all of my years in public schools, I never had a teacher of Mexican descent, nor did I ever hear of one. Not until I was at State did I meet one at a gathering of El Club Azteca, where Spanish majors met once a semester. Rodolfo Morales, a 1936 graduate of State with a major in Spanish, was teaching typing at San Diego High; he had been unable to find a job teaching Spanish— an occupation, from what I could tell, reserved for Anglos who spoke the language poorly.

As I embarked on this quest, I began to understand the complexity of Mexican history, a product of two remarkable societies. The racial makeup of Mexicans was mestizo, the offspring of the Spanish conquerors and the natives of a "new world." They were scions of a medieval Spain—one of the military powers of Europe, intolerant of faiths not Catholic but basking in a Golden Age of Cervantes, Lópe de Vega, and El Greco—and of a pre-Columbian people who carved huge stone sculptures, built great cities, worshiped a panoply of gods, and, in the case of the gifted Maya of Yucatán, were one of three civilizations in the world to develop writing of their own independently.

The Spaniards, it became obvious, were autocrats, intolerant of others' beliefs and, like all European conquerors, eager to impose their beliefs on their victims. Although the native peoples resisted, both actively and passively, they had no chance—to quote Aldous Huxley's essay on Atitlán, "no more chance than a rock against a sledge hammer." Yes, "the Indian rock was a very large one, but the hammer, though small, was wielded with terrific force. Under its quick reiterated blows, the strangely sculptured monolith of American civilization broke into fragments." Huxley knew of what he spoke. Because of the brutality of the Conquest, Mexico's culture was *criollo*—that is, of Spanish origin, though racially most Mexicans were mestizos. After all, what was pre-Columbian about the Catholic Church, Roman law, and the Spanish language, bulwarks of Mexican society?

My major was history, with a minor in Spanish. Every semester I took a course either on Spanish grammar or literature, which in the manner of those days meant reading *El Lazarillo de Tormes,* a Spanish picaresque novel, and spending an entire semester on Cervantes's *Don Quixote,* which left little time for Spanish American literature. Professors joked about the windmills that Don Quixote tilted and about his Dulcinea, the woman he loved who turned out to be an oaf, and stressed the importance of Sancho Panza, the simple and, yes, wise companion to the errant knight. Reading Cervantes, one of the great masters of literature, was a learning experience, but it came at the expense of what really interested me. If I remember correctly, I also read *Los de abajo* by Mariano Azuelo and the novel *Doña Bárbara* by Rómulo Gallegos, the Venezuelan writer.

Walter Philips and Leslie Brown, the professors who taught these courses, spoke Spanish poorly, and Brown had a Castilian lisp. Neither could carry a conversation in the language, though Philips believed himself to be an expert on what he called "proper

Spanish." When he asked me in class what was the Spanish word for *money,* I hesitated, not knowing whether to say *dinero* or *moneda;* foolishly I chose *moneda,* which Philips used to illustrate how Mexicans in this country corrupted Spanish. Yet, though *dinero* was the more correct word, *moneda* was commonly used, especially along the Mexican border. Philips had been to Mexico, but Spain was Brown's sole love.

They were, moreover, old-fashioned language teachers. Their idea of teaching Spanish literature was to translate every Spanish word into English. For each class meeting, we were assigned certain pages to translate from the novel we were reading, *Don Quixote* for example; then, during class, the professor, who taught the class in English, asked each student to translate a paragraph or two. The semester grade was the average of these performances, never mind how poorly a student spoke Spanish. By the end of the semester, my abbreviated *Don Quixote,* which some professor in a major university had written for classroom use, had two texts on each page, one in Spanish and the English translation.

Worse still were the first-year Spanish classes, which focused exclusively on grammar, never strongly emphasized in Mexico. We spent our time learning verb conjugations, all twenty-two forms, the use of the subjunctive, and the *tú* and *usted* forms of address, which I had always known. The word *boring* is not strong enough to describe these classes, which many students took because they believed that Spanish was easier to learn than French and because a foreign language was required for graduation. Despite this, I minored in Spanish: if one is to know Mexico, one must know how to speak, read, and write its language.

My social life at State was only slightly better than it was at La Jolla, though most students were friendly. There were never more than six or seven of Mexican descent, mostly men. But then, I was so accustomed to being the only one that it never occurred to me to think something awry. This was normality, I had concluded long ago. Not until a year after I enrolled at State did I become aware that two women of Mexican descent were on campus, one from Old Town, but just as I got up nerve to speak to her, she left school.

State gave me the first opportunity I had to discuss history and literature with persons of my racial background. These Mexican Americans aspired to a better life, most dreaming of teaching in the public schools, but fully aware that these were racist times, when Mexicans found it difficult to find a teaching job. In an article about Roberto and me in the "Parents' Corner," a weekly column for the *San Diego Union,* Richmond Barbour, Artha's husband and a school administrator, had acknowledged "that [Ramón] might have a little trouble getting a job . . . [so] we have encouraged him to go ahead and get his Ph.D." and teach in a college.

One of the Mexican students at State was Frank Verduzco, who sang classic arias and popular Mexican songs, "Morena linda" in particular, and beat me every time we played handball, though I had been handball champion of Pacific Beach Junior High. Frank was working his way through college; late in the afternoons, if I were still around, I would find him, brooms and mops in hand, cleaning rooms, exchanging janitorial services for the chance to attend college. There was also Leonard Fierro, a resident of Logan Heights who loved to wrestle and was majoring in history, and Paul Arriola, whose parents were natives of Mexico and who was majoring in Spanish and wanted to become a university professor. Then there was Frank Galindo, older than the rest of us, a football player who had dropped out of State because of illness and had returned to complete his degree. One of my favorites was Hope Pedroarena, whose father owned a ranch outside Tecate, a Mexican village east of Tijuana. She was two years ahead of me and looked upon me as too young for her. I dated her, went dancing and to the movies with her, but she never took me seriously. What social life I enjoyed came from the semester reunions of the Club Azteca, where I met Hope. Yet in the years I was at State, just once did I take a class with another Mexican American, a javelin thrower from Santa Ana who was more interested in telling me how far he could throw the spear and how he had fared on his dates than in discussing his studies.

That said, campus social life was reserved for Anglo students. African Americans were nearly invisible, with no more than three of them, and Jews, a small minority, went their separate ways. But there were sororities and fraternities, and social activities for many Anglo students revolved around them. One Greek I knew was Frank Roach, son of a chief petty officer in the navy. He was a gentle soul, gregarious and kind, until one discussed the Japanese navy. It would take just one day for the U.S. navy to sink the Rising Sun of Japan, he would argue. When he arrived on campus, he would come looking for me, usually in the library, virtually the student center on State's campus. I came early to the library because tardiness might deprive me of a chair at one of the tables used to study.

One day Frank was excited because one of the fraternities, off-limits to Mexicans, had pledged him. From that moment on, his conversations dwelt on fraternity life and, a year later, on a girl he had met at a sorority. In the two years I knew Frank, it never occurred to him to ask me to join his fraternity or to realize that his talk of good times in a fraternity closed to Mexicans might offend me. Knowing what the frat system was like, I had no interest in joining one, but it would have been gratifying to know that I could have. Frank was not the only insensitive student, but he was supposedly a friend.

So, as previously, I had most of my social life with girls from Logan Heights. None, so far as I could tell, aspired to a college education, but they spoke Spanish and were at home with Mexican food, customs, and music—pluses, in my view. Laura, whom I dated, was the daughter of Mr. Sierra, who kept the books of the Cardenali Brewery in Tijuana. Every morning, in suit and tie, he rode off in his Model A coupe, crossed the border into Mexico, and returned late in the afternoon. When he learned that I had an interest in Mexican history, he gave me a book justifying Lázaro Cárdenas's expropriation of the oil companies. Laura, said the young men who knew her, had the "best legs" in town. She was a wonderful young lady but beyond marriage had no plans for the future. She was, however, a good companion, and her parents, who thought me a suitable suitor, treated me royally. I also remember pert and talkative Alicia Padilla, especially because my Ford stopped running just as we crossed the border at two in the morning.

Roberto, as he tells it, had to come for us just as he was "getting into bed."

Once in a while I talked about my classes at State, and some of the girls appeared to listen but, I am afraid, more out of courtesy than genuine interest because they were not ones to talk to about history, literature, or philosophy. They may have been intelligent but aspired to work in a department store or, if lucky, in an office. After my initial bout of puppy love for Berta, which nearly wrecked my life, I took none of them seriously. I attended their parties and took them to the movies or dancing at Pacific Square, San Diego's ballroom, where the big bands of the era played. About the future, I had other matters on my mind.

One was a part-time job at the Neighborhood House as an assistant to Frank Galindo, who oversaw the playground and coached the baseball teams. I worked from three to seven in the afternoons, with boys from eleven to thirteen, all of whom spoke Spanish, under my care. I remember those days fondly because I enjoyed them and because I did something useful. I came to like many of the boys. They were from poor families, were probably poor students in school, but were friendly and eager to follow me around. There was Camacho, shy and gentle, and the brother of one of the prettiest girls in the neighborhood; the Campo boy, tall and a bit arrogant, whose parents ran the nearby grocery store; and Tortilla, as he was known. Short of stature, a bit on the heavy side, with a round face and a big mouth, Tortilla was gregarious as well as mischievous. I never saw him with shoes on his feet, no matter how cold the day, but a Cheshire cat smile never left his face. On Saturdays, I would bring three or four of them to work at the nursery; Papá, who took a fatherly interest in them, paid each a dollar, a good bit for boys at that time, and our mother gave them lunch in the kitchen. After the first such Saturday, which they enjoyed immensely, there were always boys who wanted to be taken to Pacific Beach. One week I borrowed one of the nursery trucks and took a group of them to a camp in the Laguna Mountains. We cooked our food in the open air over wood the boys gathered, hiked during the day, and at night swam in the reservoir by climbing the fence that was meant to keep us out. It was a wonderful time for me and, I suspect, for them, too. Some days I think about those boys I knew and came to care for and wonder whatever happened to them. To my sorrow, I have been told that Tortilla, one of my favorites, either is in prison or has been in and out of jail.

This was the San Diego that became part of my life on Saturday nights and Sundays, where I met girls and dated, where my social life turned normal, all the more because I had one of the few cars in town, a 1936 Ford Phaeton, with a canvas top, white sidewalls, and leather upholstery. On weekends, Roberto and I had six dollars to spend, money we earned working for Papá. That was money enough to put gas in the car and to take a girl to the movies or once in a while to Tijuana. That, by the way, was more money and more car than anyone else had in Logan Heights. As Roberto, who owned a Ford, says, "We were the dandies of the town."

In 1941, girls were also a secondary consideration because of the military draft. These were days of German subs sinking U.S. merchant ships; of the Lend Lease being enacted; and of a Senate turning its back on neutrality acts. Propaganda urging young men to volunteer for military service was rampant. Wear a uniform, serve your country, and be a soldier, sailor, or marine were the messages. In one such appeal to arms, a picture of two pretty girls and a soldier in the *San Diego Union,* one girl says to the other: "Yes, I gave him a date. I don't understand it myself. It was the uniform." After the Japanese bombed Pearl Harbor, I woke up many a night thinking about what I would do when called to arms. This was not just my worry, but that of scores of men at State, many of pacifist leanings, although a few had volunteered to serve as pilots in the Canadian Air Force. The unlucky ones never came back. Frank Verduzco, who joined the Army Air Force to become a pilot and escape the draft, died when he crashed his plane during his days as a cadet.

Unlike these volunteers who could not wait to fight, I was never a superpatriot. "Our country! . . . may she always be in the right; but our country, right or wrong," Stephen Decatur's famous quotation, stands logic on its head. Consciously or not, I was inclined to believe Michel Foucault, the French philosopher, who wrote that what we call truth is at the beck and call of those who hold power. I am a law-abiding citizen of the United States and at the same time *"no he manchado el pabellón"* (have not brought shame on Mexico), to quote my father. I mention Mexico here because, when I was young, our parents, citizens of that republic, registered me with the consulate in San Diego. From that date until I joined the U.S. army, I was a citizen of both nations.

Waging wars, killing human beings, was morally wrong. To have the blood of another on one's hands is devastating. How else to explain the need for asylums to handle posttraumatic disorders for veterans of combat if not because the compact with patriotism made killers of people reared by the Ten Commandments to respect human life? Yes, when I watched war movies, I, like any red-blooded young man, sometimes hankered to join up, to test my metal in combat, but only momentarily. After all, as Joseph Heller's novel *Catch 22* reminds us, "a concern for one's safety in the face of dangers that were real and immediate was the process of a rational mind." That concern included risking life and limb in World War II. As a fledgling student of history, I knew that, occasional exceptions granted, there was rarely an absolute right or wrong in quarrels between nations.

I was not a pacifist, though of pacifist inclinations, and from time to time had even toyed with being a conscientious objector. Wars rarely settled age-old disputes and not infrequently planted the seeds for new ones. The more I studied international conflicts, the more senseless they seemed to me. Unlike wild animals who kill to eat, men would go on fighting wars until there were no more men to fight them. Given the sundry wars waged by the United States, one could hardly call it a pacifist nation. This country had waged wars from early on, one being the rape of Mexico, engineered by American jingoists who hungered for that country's northern territories. James K. Polk, the wartime leader, as Abraham Lincoln charged, was "deeply conscious of being in the wrong" and felt "the blood of this war, like the blood of Abel . . . crying to Heaven against him." True, Mexico was badly governed, but it neither wanted war nor was prepared to fight it. And by 1898, Spain, the master of Cuba, had conceded each of Washington's demands, yet the likes of Theodore Roosevelt were set on conquering Cuba and enjoying "a splendid little war." Less than two decades later, American soldiers were fighting alongside the French and English in a war waged over empires.

As events in Europe unfolded, I marched in step with what jingoists of that day branded isolationism, but what in fact was a strongly held sentiment in a wide range of American society, particularly among college students and their teachers. Among the isolationists were a number of historians, including Charles Beard, a stalwart of the trade. Merle Curti, Merrill Jensen, and William Hesseltine, important Americanists, also voiced deep reservations. At Stanford University, 60 percent of the faculty disagreed with colleagues who urged a "dynamic defense" in support of FDR's foreign policy. Contrary to what pashas of intervention would have us believe, the United States was not called upon to lead the world; this was simply a chauvinistic assertion of U.S. power—arrogance, according to William Fulbright. True, a rich and powerful country inevitably would engage in world affairs, but it should not attempt to dominate them. The cornerstone of U.S. diplomacy should not be to remake the world into its own image, as Woodrow Wilson, a high priest of American political morality, had done by intervening in Mexican domestic affairs.

World War II, "the Good War," was unique, so it is asserted. "The greatest generation," television news anchor Tom Brokaw claims in his book of that name, did not dispute the righteousness of the Allied cause. That rings false: by the late 1930s, the people's representatives in Congress had passed five neutrality acts with overwhelming support. By 1937, nearly three out of every four Americans favored a constitutional amendment to require a national referendum for any declaration of war; a bare majority in Congress stopped its approval. Brokaw is simply mistaken when he asserts that young American men marched "forward in unison to answer the trumpet's call." Even after the Japanese bombed Pearl Harbor, factory workers got themselves draft deferments, and forty-two thousand draft-age men declared themselves conscientious objectors. Largely to evade the draft, 40 percent of men twenty-one years of age took wives because marriage exempted them from military service. Americans of every stripe, asserts historian David Kennedy, looked upon Europeans as a contentious bunch. Many remembered the horrors of World War I trench warfare and had no wish to subject their sons to a similar fate. It should come as no surprise, therefore, that millions were isolationists. As Franklin Roosevelt, a ferocious interventionist, conceded: "the wind everywhere blows against us."

That Hitler wanted to impose Germany's hegemony over Europe, that he was a militarist who trampled over the sovereignty of nations, and that he had scant regard for human life were indisputable. True, too, that Nazis persecuted Jews, yet in 1938, despite news of the crimes against the Jews, fewer than 5 percent of Americans were willing to accept more refugees into their country. The "greatest generation," if truth be told, was a bigoted one. News of the Holocaust was virtually absent from radio and newspapers; most of us knew little or nothing about concentration camps, nor was the war waged to rescue Jews. That the United States "deliberately embarked on a crusade to . . . stop the Holocaust [is] . . . mythology," asserts Benjamin Schwarz, an editor of the *Atlantic Monthly*. Ending "the mass murder of Jews," he adds, "didn't figure in any way in either American war aims or conduct." In 1940, the full extent of the terror the Germans would visit on Jews, Poles, and Russians was by no means obvious. Had it been so, the isolationist sentiments that I have described might have been muted, but that is the clarity of hindsight. At the time, the travails of Europe were still remote in the minds of a majority of Americans.

The second European conflict, even bloodier than the first, arose out of complex causes. One was the imperialistic ambitions of the Western powers. The Treaty of Versailles, which ended the first war and exacted a heavy toll on a defeated Germany, was a tragic blunder, sewing the seeds for the rise of Hitler's Germany. France and England, authors of the treaty, were determined to keep Germany under their thumb, rule Europe, and enjoy their colonial empires in Africa, India, and Asia while Washington walked hand in glove with them. Ever since the open-door policy, the United States and its European allies had run affairs in China, to the anger of the Japanese, who were no less eager to carry out their version of the Greater East Asia Co-Prosperity Sphere. When U.S. policymakers obstructed Japanese ambitions, they made war inevitable. As *Inside the Oval Office,* a book by William Doyle based on White House tapes, reveals, Roosevelt knew that his ultimatum to Japan of November 26, 1941, would bring retaliation, although not where exactly. But because U.S. intelligence one year earlier had deciphered many of the Japanese naval codes, officials had at least several days warning that the target might be Pearl Harbor.

There I was, caught between the proverbial rock and hard place: a male citizen of a country at war. Equally agonizing, our parents, Papá emphatically, had no stomach for the war. "It is none of our business," he would say. Neither one wished to see their two sons in uniform. That dim view of the military had old roots. Mamá, who disliked peacetime soldiers, believed they were hardly models of ambition. As for Papá, his distaste, which bordered on repulsion, probably dated from his father's experience as a buck private in the Mexican army and from his own experience in the Mexican navy. I recall vividly that parental rebuke of the military when Richard Boronda, one of my teachers in junior high school, had become scoutmaster of the local troop and had urged me to join. My parents said no, seeing the scout's uniform as a first step into the U.S. army.

As the danger of military service loomed closer, Papá began to ask why I would want to risk my life in a "senseless war"? Why not go to Mexico and study at the Universidad Nacional Autónoma de México (UNAM)? He and my mother, who went along with the idea, would support me until I was on my own. I would become a Mexican and live my life in that country. The more Papá urged, the more convinced I was that he was right. However, Roberto, who also faced military service, chose to stay home, so I dropped out of State and set out for Mexico City by way of Nogales, Arizona. When I left, everyone cried, my mother most of all, for I was the first of the family to leave home.

Leaving was a heart-wrenching experience. Until then, home was my nest, where every day I rose in the morning, went to bed at night, and saw my parents, my brother, and my sisters. Except for the brief fling with Berta, I had never thought of leaving home. Yet there I was, on a train—a *mixto,* half cargo and half passenger—and not a *bolillo* in sight, on my way to Mexico City, two thousand miles away, traveling as a Mexican, with papers from the consulate in San Diego. In Nogales, Sonora, across the border from its U.S. namesake, I bought a ticket for a Pullman berth, but the train had no dining car, which meant that passengers had to find food at every whistle-stop. I ate chicken burritos made of flour tortillas in Hermosillo, the first stop; corn tortillas and beef at the next; and freshly cooked fish in Mazatlán; and so it went until we reached Guadalajara. The stopover in Mazatlán, reached at dawn, was memorable, just the way Papá had predicted. Despite the early hour, the train station was awash with people hurrying to and fro, vendors hawking their wares, and the whistles of locomotives. That was how he had said it would be, and, lo and behold, it was true.

When I left home, the political climate of Mexico had turned conservative. Lázaro Cárdenas, the man who revived the revolutionary pledge of 1917, was no longer president, his place taken by Manuel Avila Camacho, a fat army general reputedly of moderate bent. Not terribly bright but amiable, he surprised everyone upon taking office by declaring himself a Catholic believer and turning his back on revolutionary rhetoric. When a German submarine sunk a Mexican freighter, Avila Camacho declared war on the Axis powers.

At that time, Mexico City had just more than one million inhabitants, among them my older cousin Eva, her husband Amador, and their son Carlos, just fourteen. They lived on the southern edge of the city, on Calle Coahuila, blocks from Insurgentes, part of the road to Acapulco. Their house, located in the Colonia Roma, was newly constructed and would be my home until I found permanent quarters. Eva and Amador were in their late forties; she was a Catholic fanatic, hated Lázaro Cárdenas, and belittled Americans. My mistake was not finding a boarding house for students from the provinces, where I would have been among men my age and might have adapted more quickly to life in Mexico City, which I came to dislike at that time. It was not the people or the food, which I had eaten since childhood, or the manners and customs of Mexicans that bothered me; it was urban life, the noise of honking horns and the crowds on the streets at all hours.

I never really got started at the university, although, joined by Eva, I met with an admissions dean and submitted the application for entrance. The heart of the university stood on San Cosme, across town from Eva's home. I rode a crowded bus there, stood all of the way, and returned in the same manner. The university had no central campus; one class might be given in one part of the city, another somewhere else. Mexicans studied history in the *primaria* and *secundaria,* the lower schools, but seldom at the university. Majoring in history, moreover, was hardly an alternative; it was neither prestigious nor lucrative, and a doctorate in the subject was virtually unknown.

Had Eva been more kind and loving, I would have stayed in Mexico. She was rather cold, however; she had lost three of her children by sickness, yet I never saw her weep or lament her cruel fate or talk about the tragedies in her life. She never let me forget that Mexico City was the cultural soul of the republic, that Mexicans might learn from France but not from the United States. She tended to look down on campesinos, country folk, and prized whiteness of skin. She was especially hard on Mexican Americans, especially if they spoke Spanish poorly. I suspect that Eva gave a sigh of relief when her cousin, who spoke highly of Lázaro Cárdenas, left for home.

We make choices for odd motives. What prompted my spur-of-the-moment departure from Mexico was, of all things, a ballad composed in 1912 by a Mexican from Huajuapan de León, a small town in Oaxaca; I knew the chorus by heart. Antonio López Alavés, a young student in Mexico City, was homesick for his native land, so he wrote "Canción Mixteca," a nostalgic remembrance of the *patria chica* (native region) sung today wherever Mexicans congregate. The words of the song, tender and sad, recall that *patria chica:*

How far I am from the land where I was born.
Intense nostalgia captures my thoughts,
And to see myself alone and forlorn as a leaf in the wind,
I want to cry and die of a broken heart.
Oh, land of the sun, I crave to see you.

I was alone in a bedroom in Eva's house when I heard the refrains of "Canción Mixteca" on the radio. As I listened to the words, it was all that I could do to keep from sobbing.

5

The Dogs of War

More than 400,000 men of Mexican ancestry, in bonds of brotherhood, helped fight the "Good War," as today's pundits refer to it. On one short street in Silvis, Illinois, sixty-five young men, the sons of twenty-two Mexican families, heeded the call to arms. So eager were some Mexicans to bear arms, recalls Raul Morín in *Among the Valiant,* a book about them in World War II and Korea, that a *palomilla* (gang) of them gathered outside his barracks to celebrate joining the army.

On the battlefields of Europe, Africa, and the Pacific, on land and the high seas, Mexican soldiers, marines, and sailors fought gallantly and died. Their heroics began early. On the Bataan Death March, one out of every four soldiers was a Mexican. Ernie Pyle, in his wartime book *Brave Men,* writes about Spanish-speaking dogfaces with the Forty-Fifth Infantry Division in Sicily. Mexican paratroopers participated in every one of the major airborne campaigns, the most dangerous of the war. Beatrice Griffith, author of *American Me,* a book about barrio youths, tells of reports in Los Angeles newspapers in which "about one-fifth of the names on the casualty lists and about the same proportion on the lists of awards were names of men of Mexican ancestry." The first draftee in the Pacific theater of war to be given an award for bravery in battle was a Mexican. All told, Mexicans earned more Medals of Honor than any other ethnic group—although most were given posthumously.

As for wartime heroics in the Ruiz family, that fell to Roberto, my brother. After receiving his wings as a second lieutenant at a multiengine base in Douglas, Arizona, Roberto went overseas as a copilot on a B-24 bomber. After several missions, he was given command of his own aircraft and promoted to lieutenant; he flew thirty-two deadly missions over Germany before being sent home. On one, after he had dropped bombs on the target, flack crippled his B-24, and it began to lose altitude, exposing it to even heavier fire. Roberto had to leave the formation and try, as best he could, to return alone to England, a flight made perilous because German fighters swooped down on the B-24. He barely made it over the English Channel and, unable to get back to his base, had to make an emergency landing at an English fighter field. For this feat, Roberto received the Distinguished Flying Cross. He had luck on his side. Strange as it may seem, that is not the episode Roberto most remembers. Once after a harrowing mission, as he tells it, he went to the officers' club to calm his nerves with whiskey—fortunately, as it turned out, because he was not in his quarters when a call came for him to check out a crew just arrived from the United States, so another pilot took his place. The aircraft blew up on take-off.

Yet while battles overseas raged, rednecks still did not welcome Mexicans in uniform. Roberto tells how he was barred from entering a dance hall in Kansas City; when he asked why, the reply was that "we don't allow Mexicans." Hungry Mexicans in uniform traveling in the Southwest encountered roadside café signs that read, "We don't serve dogs or Mexicans." In Richmond, a town in California, bigots chased Sergeant Macario García, a recipient of the Medal of Honor, out of a dingy lunchroom. All he wanted was to buy a cup of coffee. In Three Rivers, a Texas town, a funeral chapel refused to bury the body of Felix Longoria, a soldier killed in the Philippines, because, his widow was told, "the whites won't like it." Heroics on the battlefield, acknowledges Ralph Guzmán, a scholar of the Mexican American experience, did not end anti-Mexican prejudice. The returning Mexican soldier knew that wartime heroics are quickly forgotten.

The home front was hardly better. In San Diego, Consolidated Aircraft, which built B-24s and PBYs, a navy seaplane, the cost borne by taxpayers, at first did not hire persons of Mexican ancestry. The Selective Service Act of 1940 granted workers in defense industries, such as Consolidated, occupational deferments because they were vital to the war effort. Anglos who worked at these plants escaped the draft—at least temporarily. Only belatedly did the Roosevelt administration order Consolidated and other war plants to hire minorities, when it was increasingly difficult because they were in the army. Meanwhile, Mexican Americans in agriculture, an industry every bit as vital to the war effort, enjoyed no deferments; nearly all were drafted into the army. Washington then had to replace them with braceros or workers brought in from Mexico. Even after Roosevelt's order, the employment picture changed little. In 1944 Los Angeles, home to a large population of Mexicans, at Vultee Aircraft, less than 300 Mexicans were employed out of a labor force of 7,500; Consolidated Steel had only 50 out of 4,000; and at California Ship Building, with 43,000 employees, no more than 1,200 were Mexicans.

That said, I turn to my years as a soldier. Home from Mexico, I went back to San Diego State, with the draft hanging over my head like the sword of Damocles. "If I must fight," I told myself, "it will not be as an enlisted man"; I had nothing against privates, but that was not the issue. As one who had known racial insults and who was now a college student, I would not eat humble pie. Having lived near the ocean and heard our father tell of his adventures at sea, I decided to join the merchant marine as an officer, which required two years of college and a passing score on the exam. On the day of the test, I drove up to Los Angeles and took it but never heard if I had passed or not. When I looked up the navy v6 and v12 programs that offered college students the opportunity to stay in school until called to active duty, I was told that they accepted only whites. One day, however, Frank Galindo, the former football jock, said that one of his old teammates was in town recruiting officer candidates for the Marine Corps. Would I be interested? Frank offered to put in a good word for me. Fourteen of us from State went down to the Marine Corps base in San Diego; thirteen were accepted. I was the sole applicant turned down.

The worst was yet to come. I was not a mechanical man; the hard sciences, math, and physics never caught my fancy. If I had to fight, I preferred to be around human beings. Yet the options were drying up, and time was running short. Two alternatives were left to explore, one in the Navy Air Corps; I believed naively that the racial bent of the navy might not apply to its air wing. Still, let me make one thing clear: I never hankered to fly an airplane. The Navy Air Corps asked for two years of college and a physical exam for a commission. I met the requirements; all I had to do was drive to Los Angeles and take the physical, which I passed with flying colors, until I got to the eye phase, where a navy corpsman told me that my eyesight was poor. Dejected, I went home and told our parents, who wisely urged me to consult an eye specialist. "Your eyes are 20/20," he told me, "good enough to fly for any navy." But, he added, "just to make sure that you pass on the next try, if your parents will pay for eye exercises, I recommend that you take them." So I did and returned to Los Angeles. Upon completion of the physical, another corpsman told me that a commander wanted to talk to me. "Son," he said, "there is no place in the naval officer ranks for Mexicans. Try the Army Air Force; they will take you." I drove home caught between despair and stifled rage at the unfairness of it all. "Why didn't you stay in Mexico?" Papá asked. That was how I became an army pilot. Lest you judge the Army Air Force a racial heaven, let me tell you that as a cadet I met only one other Mexican. When in *Bombs Away* John Steinbeck wrote that there was "nothing typical in . . . racial stock" about cadets, he was way off target.

In June 1943, I left for military service. Roberto, also a student at State and faced by the same bigotry, had opted for the Army Air Force as well and had departed two months earlier. Our parents and sisters sobbed when he left, as they did when I boarded the train for Los Angeles. The one consolation was that others from State were also on the train: Harold Summers, a baseball player, and Thomas Rothwell, a La Jolla native. This was also the first time that I would eat just American food, sleep in the same quarters with Anglos, and rarely see another Mexican or hear a word of Spanish.

The Dogs of War / 95

Los Angeles was a stopover, where we were told to find something to eat on our own. But this was June 1943, just days after rampaging mobs of sailors, soldiers, and rednecks, shouting "Let's get the chili-eating bastards," had beaten up young Mexican *pachucos* and torn their clothes off, leaving them naked on the streets, bleeding and bruised. Street cars were stopped, and bigots pulled Mexicans as well as some Filipinos and African Americans out of their seats, hauled them into the streets, and beat them. As Anglo spectators watched and even cheered, the police, instead of arresting the assailants, whisked their victims to jail. Los Angeles newspapers, laying the blame for the disturbances on the Mexicans, dubbed them the "zoot suit riots," which made possible the most-damaging canards, giving aid and comfort to anti-Mexican bigotry. So blatant were the trumped-up charges of disturbing the peace that the judge presiding over the trial against the victims had to dismiss them; yet, unbelievably, he warned them that they better change their attitudes or they would end up in greater trouble. When I went off to find Clifton's Cafeteria in downtown Los Angeles, a landmark according to Summers and Rothwell, I kept looking over my shoulder for bigots in uniform.

At Los Angeles, we joined others and a sergeant who told us that we were bound for basic training in Kearns, Utah, a town on the outskirts of Salt Lake City. It was cold when we reached Kearns in the dead of the night. After an hour or two standing in the cold, our sergeant got an army truck to come for us. Tired and sleepy, we arrived at midnight at the base, which was surrounded by an ugly, barbed-wire fence. The fence, tall and angular, set me to wondering if I were not entering a prison. Needing to call for a truck to pick us up was hardly a hearty welcome and a frightening introduction to army life. After another wait, we were given mattresses, blankets, and sheets and assigned a barracks—two-story, nondescript wooden buildings with rows of toilets bereft of stalls. Not until two days later did we have uniforms. We slept in our underwear in bunk beds, one soldier above the other and both near others. When it was time to get up, either the soldier above, below, or to the left or right, or all of them together would reach for a cigarette, light up and puff away, polluting the air. Farting and snoring went on all night.

We supposedly were future officers in the Army Air Force, but Kearns was basic training done the army way. We were buck privates. Barbers cut off our hair, and for six weeks we marched, did close-order drill, changed barracks on command in the middle of the night, and did KP in the kitchen. The midnight transfers from one barracks to another puzzled me, until I realized that they were done to strip away personal dignity, to break down our will. We were being taught to obey, no matter how stupid the order might seem to us. Two or more times a week we did something special called "policing," which meant walking back and forth over a parade ground to pick up cigarette butts. We stood in line for hours at a time. Hurry and wait, that was the army game: the chow line at the mess hall for breakfast, lunch, and dinner; another to fill out countless forms and to receive blankets and sheets from supply. Medics told us to bend over, spread our cheeks, and peered up our assholes, cynics alleged, to learn the state of our health. Others pushed needles into our arms to vaccinate us against typhus, tetanus, and other maladies; if we were not sick previously, we were now. Gripes were the order of the day: bad food, petty regulations, shoes that did not fit, pants either too small or too big, and corporals who ranted and raved. That was the army's way, which to us civilians felt like some clown had poured a bucket of ice water down our sweaty backs.

The six weeks of basic training over, the army shipped us north on a dirty, coal-burning train to Missoula, where we attended the University of Montana for three months. We arrived looking like tramps because soot from the engine flew in when we opened the windows to ventilate the railroad car and covered us with a blanket of coal dust. To my delight, I caught up with Roberto, who had just completed his stay and was on his way to Santa Ana, California. I saw him briefly, but only after I had to beg a jerk of a lieutenant for permission. A day after our arrival, we were given a test; my companions and I, maybe a hundred or so of us, were then placed in squads ranked by test results. Summers, Rothwell, and I, who scored high, were placed in the top squad and assigned to the same room in a college dorm.

At Missoula, we could leave the campus every weekend. That nonetheless depended on the gigs we got. Six gigs, or penalties, meant a walking tour on a parade ground under the watchful eyes of a corporal, more walks if we received more gigs. These tours were done in dress uniform, rain or shine. Gigs were dealt out for unpolished shoes, dull brass belt buckles, blankets not pulled tight on beds, a bit of facial beard, a speck of dirt on a floor, or a washbasin not entirely wiped clean. The spit-and-polish "shavetails," second lieutenants fresh out of Officer Candidate School, dealt out the gigs and literally stood watch over our daily lives. We learned early to refer to these demands as "chicken shit." When we walked to downtown Missoula, we found a bar, and we drank, hoping that a gorgeous girl would show up. They rarely did, at least not for me. At the end of the three months, each graduation class had a dance, when we were allowed to invite girls from the community. I attended with Rothwell, who somehow managed to find two girls, as he told me, by telling mine that I came from a wealthy "Spanish family of dons."

Santa Ana Army Air Base, on the outskirts of Los Angeles, was the next stop. We were back to barracks life. It was a huge preflight camp where tests determined whether we would be pilots, navigators, or bombardiers. Most of us dreamed of flying a plane, but many did not get their wish; I did, though that hardly ranked high on my overall wish list. We spent two months at Santa Ana, where we became full-fledged Army Air Force cadets, marching and marching, not infrequently at five in the morning. Reveille came to the sound of "Oh what a beautiful morning," a melody from the musical *Oklahoma,* and we went to bed to the sound of taps, both played on loudspeakers.

We also marched to class by squads to the cadence of "one two, one two, hut" so that everyone marched in step; I was one of the squad leaders. To keep up morale, so it was claimed, we were told to sing as we marched; any song would do, one being the air force hymn "Off We Go into the Wild Blue Yonder," which we learned by heart. Because most of us could not carry a tune, there was more discordant noise than music. Again there were inspections, this time in the wee hours of the morning; sergeants or corporals would line us up, and then shavetails with flashlights came by to see if we were spic-and-span. To fail these surprise inspections meant gigs; if we got too many gigs, we slept on the base.

At Santa Ana, we had to listen to snot-nosed corporals who had not gone beyond high school tell us of the evils of "Krauts," "Japs," and "Wops," the devils we were told to kill. The superpatriots who concocted propaganda to dehumanize and demonize the foe had entrusted the job to men who, given their anti-Japanese slurs, had the odor of racial bigots. When not being brainwashed, we studied physics and chemistry, spent hours on meteorology, learning to distinguish between fog and treacherous cumulus clouds and how to dispatch messages by Morse code on the telegraph and to communicate, à la the navy, by flag signals. I also remember having the wits scared out of us by a physician who in graphic language described syphilitic chancres, the pus of gonorrhea, crabs, and sundry venereal ills. His sermon? "Don't fuck just any girl, but if you do, wear a rubber."

At Santa Ana, I lost a good part of a shaky faith in Catholicism. As I explained earlier, I had no wish to kill human beings. It had never occurred to me to be a gun-toting macho just to prove that I was as loyal as the next guy. And had not one of the Ten Commandments said that "you shalt not kill"? I may not have been much of a Catholic, but a bit of the faith still lingered. "Why not say that you do not want to wear a uniform and declare yourself a conscientious objector?" I asked myself. I had discussed these doubts with Rothwell: "Why not speak to the Catholic chaplain on the base?" he suggested. Though dubious, I nevertheless decided to seek counsel from the chaplain, who, a major in the army, turned out to be a homiletic priest and a superpatriot. I explained what was troubling me, telling him of my moral dilemma. When I finished, this man of God could ask only if "I wanted others to think me a coward." I left the encounter angry at myself for having thought that I might find solace in a priest.

We learned to fly at Oxnard, a small, civilian field on the shores of the Pacific Ocean. Class and drill instructors were army, but flight instructors civilians. Had there been no war, Oxnard might have been a vacation spot: not a barracks was in sight, and everything was spotless. Four cadets were assigned to one room. Rothwell, Summers, and I roomed together, along with a young man from New York, and flew Stearman biplanes; the pilot wore a helmet and goggles and sat in an open cockpit behind two wings. This was flying at its best, our flight instructors told us. At Oxnard, I flew solo for the first time, alone at the controls of an aircraft, with hands gently pulling back the stick to get elevation and with feet steering the rudder. As the instructor watched from the ground, I took off at fifty miles an hour, flew around the base, and landed the aircraft. After three months, I could do stalls, power on and power off, spins, barrel rolls, and inside loops, just as the barnstormers had done in their biplanes in the fledgling years of flight. At Oxnard, I decided not to answer to the name Ray, but only to Ramón.

There, too, I made one last attempt to settle my moral quandary. The more I thought about it, the less convinced I became that I should soldier on. "Why not drop out of flight training?" I told myself. When we arrived from Santa Ana, we were, as usual, assigned to quarters, this time four cadets to a room. Summers and I were put in the same room, but not Rothwell. The lieutenant who had made the assignments seemed friendly, so on my own I asked him if he would put Rothwell with us, a move made possible because a cadet assigned to our quarters wanted to be with his friends. The good-natured lieutenant proved flexible, never an army characteristic, and made the transfer. From that time on, I saw him as someone I could talk to.

About three weeks into the stay at Oxnard, I decided to speak to the lieutenant. He not only listened sympathetically but offered good advice. "Look," he said, "you must be practical. If you claim the status of a conscientious objector, you will have to document it on religious grounds; that is difficult. The chances are that you will end up a private and be sent off to a battle front in Europe or the Pacific." On the other hand, he went on, "the cadet program will last another seven months; then more months will be required to prepare you to fly a combat aircraft." By then, he pointed out, "the war might be over." That made sense, so I remained a cadet. I saw him once again after Japan had surrendered, when we flew a B-29 bomber into Florida Blanca, an airfield across the bay from Manila in the Philippines. When we landed, he was standing on the edge of the strip.

I remember something else about Oxnard: I had one date as a cadet, a totally unexpected one. At the dining hall, where we ate breakfast, lunch, and dinner, one of the waitresses was a very pretty, fair-skinned young woman who caught everyone's eyes. Although many tried to flirt, she paid no attention. Gradually, however, it dawned on me that she would smile at me, which did not go unnoticed by Summers and Rothwell, who encouraged me to ask for a date. At first, I brushed aside their counsel, thinking that they were pulling my leg. How silly would I look if I asked and she said no? However, one day, after much prodding, I took the bull by the horns and asked her out; she readily accepted and invited me to see her the coming Saturday evening. It turned out that she was a Mexican American. That Saturday I walked to her home to discover that she was the daughter of an extremely religious family, not Catholics but Protestant converts, who looked upon dating, drinking alcohol, and dancing as Lucifer's deeds.

We left Oxnard for Minter Field, just north of Bakersfield. Minter meant going back to life in a barracks; it was summer and very hot. At Minter, I learned to fly a BT-13, a heavy, sluggish, single-wing aircraft with a wide landing gear. After the Stearman, it was a dull plane to fly. However, I came to like the instructor, a cocky, loud-talking lieutenant. When I was set to take off for the solo flight, he climbed on the wing to tell me, "If you kill yourself, I will piss on your grave." Later, I nearly did when my plane fell into a spin and I failed to hold down the stick that controls the elevators and to kick in place the rudder pedals. I panicked but luckily only momentarily. When I pulled out of the spin, my head was groggy from the many turns of the aircraft, each turn tighter than the previous one.

I had one more close call at Williams Air Base in Chandler, Arizona, the next stop and an advanced flying center, where I flew AT-6s, a 600-horsepower single-engine aircraft with a retractable landing gear, which could climb six thousand feet per minute. In September, near the end of our training, I had gone up with an instructor and another cadet to practice a simulated dogfight. The instructor, an uptight jerk, had taken off first, I went next, and the other cadet brought up the rear. We were flying fast and furious at six or seven thousand feet, trying to keep up with the hotshot ahead, doing barrel rolls, loops, half-loops, and steep climbs when the cadet behind me, eager to earn brownie points, tried to pass. As he did, he collided with my aircraft. Luckily the planes merely touched fuselages. Had they collided with force, we either would have been killed or at least would have had to bail out.

Like Summers, I wanted to fly heavy bombers, either a B-24 or a B-17, but an encounter with a civilian flight instructor at Minter, I suspect, ended that hope. Near the end of our training, we had to practice instrument flying, going up with an instructor, then pulling a canopy over our head to fly blind. We were supposed to shut down the gyro compass and use only the magnetic one, with a needle that turned freely on a pivot when you made a turn. Clearly, it was more difficult to fly by this compass. There was a knob on the dash of the cockpit that had to be locked in place to keep you from relying on the gyro compass. When the instructor, who sat in the seat ahead, told me to pull the canopy over my head and lock the gyro, I could not get the darn knob to stay in place, so I maneuvered the plane as best I could. When we landed, I tried to explain what had happened, but the instructor doubted me. I believe that he put a negative report in my file. I could not be trusted with the safety of a bomber crew, he must have concluded. As a result, I ended up in single engines at Williams and completed flight training as a flight officer, the equivalent of a warrant officer. A few months later superiors at another base where I was stationed thought otherwise and gave me the eagle of a second lieutenant for my cap. When I went off to Williams, Summers, a friend since Kearns, was dispatched to Marfa, Texas, a multiengine, advance-training base, and Rothwell, never a fan of heavy bombers, wanted to pilot two-engine attack bombers. Williams ended my career as a cadet; it was September 1944.

Months later, at Marfa, where I was briefly assigned, I caught up with Summers for the last time; he was now a flight instructor, teaching cadets to fly the "bamboo bomber," a two-engine advance trainer made out of wood. You never had to worry about the landing for no matter from what height you dropped it, it fluttered to the ground. After Williams, I had been ordered to Marfa from Kirtland Field in Albuquerque, where I made a short stopover to fly the AT-11, a two-engine aircraft. From what I could tell, the only recommendation one could make for Marfa, a field 150 miles east of El Paso on the two-lane road that followed the Mexican border, was that it was close to Sul Ross College for women. The airfield, however, was not in Marfa, but between that tiny hamlet and the slightly bigger one of Alpine, twenty-six miles away. Both towns were in a land of perpetual droughts, where two hundred acres fed only one steer and the wind blew and blew.

However, my life took a radical turn at this point. I married. Natalia Marrujo had been born in Hatch, New Mexico, a small town that lies north of Deming and forty miles from El Paso. Its inhabitants boast that it is the "chile capital" of this country. Natalia was the daughter of *hispanos,* descendants of colonial New Mexicans. She now lived in San Diego. Both of her parents spoke Spanish and for all intents and purposes behaved as Mexicans. Before leaving for the army, I had known Natalia for two years or so, dating her on just three occasions. Each time she came accompanied by an older sister. She was two years younger than I, gentle by nature and a woman of exceptional grace and beauty—and, from my point of view, a Mexican, the kind of woman I had sworn to marry, one, to quote Mamá, "I can talk to." She spoke fluent Spanish, was at ease with Mexican ways, enjoyed eating Mexican food, and knew Mexican music, the rumbas and *paso dobles.* She got along well with our mother and sisters and was a good companion. She came from an old-fashioned family, a matriarchy where her rotund mother ran the household and held a tight rein on her daughters, in particular Natalia, the youngest. Until Natalia was twenty-one years old, she was not permitted to go out with a boy unless accompanied by a chaperon. The father, tall and slim, seldom spoke and, from what I could tell, never contradicted his wife.

When I left for the army, I had Natalia on my mind from time to time, once, as I recall, when I was lying on the grass at night at Williams Field waiting for my turn to fly. I saw her again when I went home on a six-day leave from Williams in the fall of 1944, when I had just completed flight training. My parents had received an invitation to a ball in San Diego from the Mexican consulate. I went in their place, and to my delight there was Natalia, who, lo and behold, had come alone. We danced all night to the sounds of a Mexican orchestra, and then I drove her home. On the last day of my leave, I asked her to marry me. She said yes, but her mother said no—emphatically. "Don't worry," Mamá said when I told her what had occurred, "I will get the lady to change her mind," but this time she was badly mistaken. She and Papá put on their Sunday best and went to visit the lady. *"No se puede con esa señora"* (the lady won't budge), Mamá confessed on her return from the visit.

I went back to Albuquerque, this time by car, a Ford coupe I was to drive on two-lane roads in the Southwest. Soon thereafter, on another leave, I returned to San Diego, and this time Natalia and I were married in Nuestra Señora de Guadalupe, the Catholic church Natalia attended. On this occasion, Natalia, for whatever reason, had decided that she would marry whether her mother liked it or not. I suspect that her mother did not approve of the marriage because she thought the Ruizes uppity, especially father and son. She worshiped at the altar of humility, *ser humilde*, and also wanted her daughter to stay home. We had only a few days to plan the wedding but, thanks to Mamá, even had a reception. Natalia had a friend as the maid of honor, but I had no one to turn to; the men I knew at State were in the military. By a stroke of luck, Charlie Carvajal, whose brothers I had known before the war, said he would do it but warned that he was a wayward Catholic who had not gone to church for years. He went as a favor to us, but his sins were so varied and many, as he told it, that the priest had to impose penance on the installment plan. On the day of the wedding, Natalia's father came, but not her mother, though she demanded that we return after mass to receive their blessing. That conferred, she told me to "return Natalia when I had tired of her."

At Marfa, we looked everywhere for an apartment but had to settle for a room in an old, two-story house across from Sul Ross College in Alpine; Natalia washed dishes in a bathroom we shared with others, all military personnel, and cooked on a hot plate. As for our honeymoon, we went dancing at the city hall. As I recall, Natalia and I were the only Mexicans in a sea of Anglos, both soldiers and civilians; whether because of my officer's uniform or our youth, everyone treated us royally, though both Alpine and Marfa, for all intents and purposes, were segregated. Anglos lived on one side of the tracks, and Mexicans on the other.

In Marfa, my career as a pilot virtually ended. I was told that there were no openings for a pilot instructor (why I was sent to Marfa I will never understand) and that I would be shipped off as a copilot on a bomber bound for Europe. This was bad news because I had no stomach for that enterprise and I had just married. To leave Natalia behind after just weeks of marriage seemed terribly cruel, although I knew that soldiers sent overseas did it all the time. Then, to my surprise, the army gave me a temporary way out. I could retrain as a flight engineer for the B-29 bombers just then making their appearance; I would no longer be a pilot. It would be months before I was sent to the Pacific, where the B-29s were bombing Japan. As a result, Natalia and I spent my army career in this country moving from B-29 base to B-29 base.

Until this point, I had been around mostly single-engine aircraft, although I had flown AT-11s at Albuquerque and multiengine trainers at Marfa. That experience, however, had not prepared me for my first glimpse of the B-29. On our way to Amarillo, our destination after Marfa and the place where I would begin to learn how to operate a B-29, we passed through a small town in the scorched Texas Panhandle. As we approached it, we came across a B-29 base, where I saw dozens of them, their big, radial engines and four-blade propellers staring at us. They were the biggest airplanes I had ever seen, tall as a two-story building and with an enormous wingspan.

Then it was on to Amarillo, where I began to learn about the B-29, the initial phase of my training as a flight engineer, the person responsible for the engines on takeoff and in flight. I was one of some fifty pilots, many of whom had been flight instructors, now asked to retrain because of the need for flight engineers. For two months, we took classes taught by specialists, oftentimes former aircraft mechanics, who spent hours explaining how the B-29 was built and how it ran. For me, whose knowledge of mechanics was limited to changing a fuel pump on a Ford, it was a novel experience.

In Amarillo, according to local lore, the winter winds had blown down the barbed-wire fence that once stood between it and the North Pole. It was winter, and the wind blew from dawn to dusk and during the entire night, and it was cold, bitter cold. Amarillo was an army town, its streets at all hours of the day full of men in drab uniforms. When we arrived, we could not find an apartment to rent; everything had been taken by married couples at the air base. By sheer chance, we stumbled upon a run-down auto court with a vacant bedroom and a bath, but we had to share the kitchen with the couple next door. By coincidence, the husband, a lieutenant by the name of Gunther Haig, had been with me at Oxnard and Minter Field and was now also in the B-29 program. The arrangement turned out well because Natalia and Gunther's wife got along famously. That is how our married life began.

At Amarillo, I began to understand more fully the implications of racial bigotry. At San Diego State, I had taken a course that indirectly touched on issues of prejudice. A book we read had a map of the Southwest covered with red dots where Mexicans encountered rednecks. One of the biggest dots was over Amarillo. Not wanting to alarm Natalia, I said nothing to her about the red dot as we drove there from Marfa, but in the back of my head I kept wondering what our reception would be. As it turned out, the only bit of racial bigotry we encountered was on the way there, when Border

Patrol agents stopped us and asked for identification even though I was an army officer in uniform, the kind of harassment Mexicans along the Texas border had long endured and not entirely unfamiliar to me. Before the war, when Roy Snyder and I tried to enter San Luis Río Colorado, just across from Yuma, Arizona, a Border Patrol bigot told Roy that he could cross into Mexico, but if I went, he would not let me back into the United States. However, the people of Amarillo, perhaps because of the uniform, treated us decently.

Being in the army nonetheless gave me other unwelcome looks at racial intolerance and not simply the textbook variety. Yes, I had known bigots at La Jolla and later at San Diego State, but not midcentury American apartheid, what blacks had to endure. At Marfa, I overheard two stupid lieutenants bitch because they had to stand in line behind a black army chaplain who outranked them; at Montgomery, Alabama, I watched blacks get off sidewalks to allow whites to pass; in Kansas, I boarded a Jim Crow railroad car divided in half by a wire screen, with blacks sitting behind it, their faces peering at me; at Biggs Field in El Paso, I saw more German prisoners of war than black soldiers; and on Guam, I stumbled accidentally upon a segregated army camp for blacks. Obviously, in the United States, the so-called land of freedom, there were first- and second-class citizens, depending on skin color.

Anglo antipathy toward Mexicans had logical repercussions. One was group solidarity among the victims. When I arrived for breakfast at the officers' club at Kirtland Field in Albuquerque, the cooks and kitchen help, all Mexican women, rushed out to greet me. They would prepare hot chile sauces and special dishes for me. I was something special because I was a "Mexican" officer in an Anglo army. In Tijuana, when I went dancing with a friend at the Tivoli, a nightclub on Calle Revolución, a Mexican at a table behind us got up, turned to some U.S. naval officers sitting nearby, and proudly said to them, *"Es mexicano"* (he is a Mexican), "and he is an officer." At Amarillo, to celebrate our finding lodging, Natalia and I walked over to a dingy night club. A big band was playing, and, as usual for the era, the place was packed with soldiers. One of the musicians, a saxophone player, was a Mexican, obvious to us but also unexpected because dance bands rarely, if ever, employed Mexicans. The saxophone player must have seen us enter because at the intermission he came over to say how delighted he was to see a *mexicano* army officer. When I was stationed in El Paso and walked downtown, young Mexican women clerks rushed out of stores to gawk at me. It was the novelty that explained this rather flattering behavior.

Yet this behavior was not always typical. On one occasion when Natalia and I were walking in downtown El Paso, I saw a soldier of Mexican ancestry approaching us on the sidewalk. He was a bit portly, not too tall, and a buck private. In those days, soldiers were required to salute officers, even lowly second lieutenants. I never cared much for this army regulation but obeyed orders—that is, I saluted when meeting soldiers. As we approached the man, who had clearly seen me, I noticed that he began to hesitate, not knowing, I suspect, whether to salute. He didn't. He solved his dilemma by turning to look at the plate-glass window of the store he was passing.

After Amarillo, it was Lowry Field in Denver and more schooling, then Biggs Field in El Paso, Texas, the last stop before I went overseas. That was good duty because it was on Mexico's doorstep, across from Ciudad Juárez, where Tía Chayo, one of Mamá's sisters, had her home. Inez, her married daughter who lived nearby, had once stayed with us in Pacific Beach. She was a frequent visitor in our tiny apartment, if you can call a small bedroom and a tiny kitchen in the rear of an old house on Kansas Street an apartment, which we rented from two Mexican sisters, one of whom joined Natalia once a week on the trolley ride to the *mercados* (markets) in Ciudad Juárez, from where they returned with chickens that had to be plucked and delicacies we had not enjoyed since leaving home. No matter how hot the night, we slept on a narrow bed made for one person and got up at three o'clock in the morning so that we might breakfast together.

At Biggs, I met the crew of my assigned B-29. Pilot, copilot, and crew, with one exception, were from the South or from the border states. Only dimly do I remember the pilot. Mac, as he was called, was a tall, decent man who spoke slowly with a southern drawl, as did the copilot. Neither one had been to college. I recall the copilot vividly. Just nineteen years old, big, overweight, and not terribly bright, he had opinions on everything, including Mexicans, whom he called "Spics." On the flight line one time, I overheard him telling the enlisted men on the crew that he did not care for Mexicans, but, upon seeing me, he quipped that he liked me because I was "different."

One man I remember was Damon Hart, the bombardier, at age twenty-seven the oldest of us. He had been a second lieutenant for nearly two years, an instructor of bombardiers. He was intelligent and witty, the only college graduate among us. Some days when I think of Hart, as I do occasionally, I remember that he loved bourbon whisky. Helen, his wife, joined him at El Paso, and the four of us became friends, spending evenings eating, drinking, and jesting about army ways at the officers' club in the Paso del Norte Hotel. Like Summers, I could talk to Hart, who thought army life a "crock of shit." He despised the petty regulations so common to the military and delighted in finding ways to circumvent them. He calls to mind John Yossarian, the mock-Assyrian bombardier in Heller's *Catch-22*, that hilarious roast of Army Air Force life.

I spent two months at Biggs, flying training missions, some lasting twenty hours, getting ready for those long flights over Japan. We flew to Seattle, Jacksonville, Chicago, and far-off burgs in Wyoming and Montana, ever attentive to fuel consumption, my particular responsibility. On the flight to Jacksonville, an engine stopped running on the return, and we had to make an emergency landing in Montgomery, Alabama, to await a B-17 dispatched to pick us up. I remember that flight because over Texas hot-air currents jerked the aircraft this way and that, so much so that I got air sick, vomiting over everyone in the pilot's compartment as we came in for the landing at Biggs.

Saying good-bye to Natalia at El Paso and leaving for the Pacific were among the most difficult things I have done. We had been married for less than a year and were just getting to know each other. It was a heart-wrenching experience that I will never forget. Papá, Emma, and Eva had driven from Pacific Beach to El Paso to say good-bye, get Natalia, and take our car home; at that juncture in our life, Natalia did not know how to drive; my mother would teach her later. I took Papá out to Biggs Field to see the B-29s we were to fly over Japan; I don't know what he thought, for he said nothing. Good-byes done, Hart and I and the rest of the crew rode a train to Herrington, Kansas, a dinky burg where, during World War I, thugs in police uniforms broke into the homes of Mexican families in the middle of the night, roused them out of bed, and told them to move on. From there, it was Hamilton Field, just north of San Francisco, and from there by air to Hawaii.

The memory of that flight aboard an Air Transport Command aircraft would haunt my sleep for years. I recall that we took off and flew over the Golden Gate Bridge, our last sight of the mainland; we watched the bridge disappear from sight, with only the ocean below us and the roar of engines to keep us company. My companions, B-29 crews, were strangely silent, nearly all keeping their thoughts to themselves. Because Japan had not yet surrendered, I am sure that everyone was thinking that we might not come back. After a fueling stop in Hawaii, we made a stop on Johnston Island and then another on an island on the Kwajalein Atoll, both tiny specs of land only slightly higher than the ocean.

After thirty-some hours in the air, we landed on Guam, tired, sleepy, and hungry, expecting to find quarters for all of us; instead we came across what appeared to be a refugee camp. It was an army base in the process of being built. For the first three months, we slept under canvas tents sitting on platforms of plywood nailed to four-by-fours, which we built ourselves from discarded lumber. When it rained, the water dripped through the canvas or ran in torrents underneath the plywood, soaking shoes and clothes. Rats the size of cats were everywhere. It was a scene from John Steinbeck's novel *The Grapes of Wrath*.

On Guam, I joined the Fifteenth Bomb Wing, part of the Twentieth Air Force under the command of General Curtis Lemay, who promised to bomb the Japanese back to the Stone Age. We arrived just after the first atomic bomb had been dropped on Japan, news that every soldier, sailor, and marine welcomed. When the Japanese surrendered after the second bomb, drinking and revelry went on into the early hours of the morning. The clock on hostilities had run out, and I had escaped being an active participant in the killing.

Today, as I look back on the atomic bombs, I can't say for certain what I thought because, like every man and woman in uniform, I yearned to go home. Moreover, after years of statistics on the hundreds or thousands killed in some battle—whether at Stalingrad, where Russians and Germans slaughtered each other, or in Africa and Italy, ravaged from D Day in Europe, or in the Pacific island campaigns against the Japanese—you became numb to numbers of the dead. You came to view them as inevitable, almost normal, and to see years of peace, for which you longed, as a mirage. Nor was I fully aware of the horrendous power of the nuclear bombs, which I later witnessed when we flew over Hiroshima and Nagasaki, their targets. When the first of them exploded, I was at Hamilton Field, only vaguely aware of their awesome force. It was Mac, the pilot, who gleefully read us a newspaper account of the havoc it had created in Hiroshima; Japan was finished, he crowed. Most of us were skeptical—unwilling, I guess, to believe that a bomb, no matter how powerful, would end the war. Now, however, as I think back on the bombs, I wonder how Truman and company could have justified their use, especially the one dropped on Nagasaki, which killed or wounded an estimated 145,000 Japanese, countless innocent children among them. Hiroshima, moreover, was a Christian city, the only one in Asia where the Bible was read widely, where the largest cathedral in Japan stood majestically in praise of the Christian God. Why such a flagrant injustice from men who professed a faith in Christianity?

Just the same, I also saw the havoc wreaked by conventional bombs. It was just after Japan's surrender, a day or two after General Douglas MacArthur had dictated terms. The battleship *Missouri,* where he had held court, had dropped anchor in the harbor alongside its escort of cruisers and destroyers. After a ten-hour flight from Guam, we arrived over Yokohama and Tokyo. What I recall about the port city were the hospitals on its waterfront, where U.S. bombs had ripped gaping holes in the roofs, at times squarely on the giant red crosses painted on them. Of Tokyo, there was little left except for rubble where buildings had stood. Only the emperor's palace was left standing. The devastation was awesome. The giant fire bombing by B-29s killed some 100,000 civilians, men, women, and children, who surely died a grisly death.

After Japan's surrender, we ferried clothing and food for Americans captured in battle and held in Japanese prison camps, once flying to the Philippines for them at the tail end of a typhoon, the worst flight we ever had to endure. We were alerted about it early one morning and told to be ready to take off momentarily, but the hour of departure was postponed again and again. The typhoon stood between us and the Philippines. When we were finally cleared for takeoff, it was eleven at night, and, according to our meteorologists, the worst of the storm had passed. Despite the weather forecast, raging winds tossed the B-29 around as though it were a scrap of paper, while heavy rains pelted us, and in the pitch-black night lightning lit up the aircraft like a Christmas tree. Below us, gigantic waves surely must have ripped open the ocean. That flight still preys on my mind, especially when I read descriptions of powerful hurricanes that carry tornadoes inside of them, with the power to rip things apart as though they are made of paper. When we left the storm behind, a roar of relief went through the aircraft. We spent two weeks on Iwo Jima, each day waiting for orders to leave behind the dust, foul water, stinking food, and heat of the island. I do not envy the Americans who waded ashore and braved enemy gunfire to plant the flag on Mount Suribachi, and I only pity the Japanese soldiers whose decaying bodies were still around when we arrived. At times, too, we flew weather missions over the South Pacific, once over Truck, a Japanese island bombed incessantly by U.S. planes, with the ghostly wrecks of sunken Japanese ships in the harbor visible from the air; it was like peering into open graves in a cemetery.

On Guam, too, I revived briefly my life as a pilot at the controls of a B-24, the four-engine bomber Roberto flew over Germany. Until the coming of the B-29, it was one of the two biggest bombers in the U.S. air arsenal. The aircraft had a tricycle landing gear, which meant that when landing, instead of pulling back on the controls, you pushed the nose down after touching ground. I enjoyed being at the controls of an airplane once more and after two lessons was landing the B-24 easily enough, although on one of them I nearly overshot the runway, coming in too fast and too high. When I finally brought the aircraft to a halt, there was nothing left of the runway.

I spent eight months on Guam. A recent arrival, I lacked the necessary points to be at the top of the list for the return home. The high point of every day was mail call, when some of us, the lucky ones, received a letter from the states. Natalia, who had returned to work at Marston's, never ceased to write, nor did Mamá, with news of Papá, my sisters, and Roberto, now back home and married. My companions and I passed paperbacks back and forth, among them *Gone with the Wind;* when someone had a pornographic book, everyone rushed to read it and then probably spent sleepless nights tossing in bed or having wet dreams. When we could, two or three of us would requisition a Jeep, get a cook to prepare sandwiches, and drive out to a beach, where, we discovered, majors and colonels monopolized the only women on Guam, either nurses or Red Cross workers. On some evenings, even when it rained, we watched movies on a hillside sitting on wooden benches. As the water came down, we hovered together, helmet liners on our heads and rubber ponchos over our shoulders, at times watching Hollywood draft dodgers play war heroes.

At the bottom of the hillside, a few steps above the movie screen, sat a band of Mexicans, privates to the last man, usually four or five of them. They kept together, paying no attention to others around them. It was if they had their own little barrio. Their banter was partly in English and partly in Spanish, and their laughter never failed to catch my attention. "What tickled them?" I asked myself. If they looked up, we would exchange greetings and then go our separate ways, I in the company of Anglo-Americans to the officer's quarters, and they to the soldiers' side of the camp. Outside of the evening movies, I never saw them.

What I recall of those months on Guam was going to sleep in the evening, lying in a narrow bunk next to the table in a one-room, plywood barracks where Hart, Barnes, and others played cards, smoked cigarettes, and drank cans of beer until the early hours. When I got up in the morning, empty cans littered the floor, and ash trays were piled high with cigarette butts. Before going to bed, I walked over to the outdoor latrine set aside for us (which the enlisted men called the "officers' shithouse"), sat there in the dark, and pondered my fate. At the officers' mess, mutton from Australia was served every Thursday; as cooked, it tasted awful and smelled worse.

I returned home unexpectedly. One day while I was sitting on the doorsteps of the plywood barracks I shared with Hart, contemplating nothing more important than the nature of the evening meal and a trip to the shithouse, a soldier came by with an urgent message for a Lt. Ruiz. I was ordered home immediately. Though I asked everywhere, no one could tell why the order had come; I knew the reason must be illness or death. Yet when I said good-bye to Hart, the one man I could talk to, all he could say was: "Do what you can to bring us home." On the flight back to the States, again on an Air Transport Command aircraft delayed for three anxious days by an emergency landing on Johnston Island to repair a faulty engine, I slept poorly, not knowing what I would encounter at home. I landed at Hamilton Field and took a bus to San Francisco, where I boarded a flight to San Diego. Upon arrival, I went for Natalia, who had been staying at her parents' home, a reunion tempered by news that Mamá was in a hospital recuperating from an operation for cancer. Knowing that the operation was life threatening, Natalia and Emma had asked the Red Cross to bring me home. My orders were to return to Guam after a six-day leave. When I reported to Fort MacArthur in San Pedro, California, a captain in charge of reassignments asked if I wanted to stay in the army or get out. If I wanted out, I was to report at eight o'clock the next morning. I was there with bells on.

Unlike other veterans of World War II, I never look back with nostalgia on my army days. Quite the contrary. When first discharged, I had nightmares, especially of that flight from Hamilton Field to Guam. I know that I soldiered, but I have to kick myself to acknowledge it, and musty photographs offer proof. As for getting to know Anglos, I had done that previously, though certainly not as well. Some I liked, and some I did not. With the exception of Summers and Hart, I didn't make any army buddies. Did I learn something from military service? Yes, emphatically so! Soldiering is not for me. I wish to be free, to think for myself, to say what I think, and, within the limits of the possible, to do what I want. Regimentation, the military "Big Brother" way of doing things, I leave to others. In short, I spent three years in the army, time I could have put to better use had human beings sincerely desired to live in peace.

The situation in the world, moreover, has rotated 180 degrees and is no longer the one for which we supposedly fought. Germany and Japan, once hated enemies, are now our allies, whereas the Russians, once mighty warriors for the holy cause, became mortal foes until the collapse of the Soviet Union. Peace, what we supposedly fought for, is as illusory as ever. Since the surrender of Germany and Japan, this country has been continuously at war for sixty years, give or take a few intermissions of peace. U.S. soldiers, at the behest of Washington mandarins, have done battle with North Korea, China, Vietnam, Iraq, Grenada, the Dominican Republic, Yugoslavia, and Afghanistan. Some seventeen trillion dollars have been spent on guns, tanks, planes, and ships of war.

6

The Graduate Student

——

When I saw my mother upon my return from Guam, she was lying on a hospital bed, my sisters, brother, and father sitting beside her. Though she left the hospital, she never recovered. Soon afterward, sick and in pain, she had to bury her sister Aurora, whose liver literally disintegrated from the alcohol she had imbibed over scores of years.

At home, the family business was in terrible shape. Fearful that death might come to Roberto or me, our parents had let the nursery run down; nor had it been possible to hire men to do the labor; they were either in the army or in the defense industry. So instead of returning to college, I set out to restore the nursery. I will never forget the pride our mother took when she saw the renovation taking place. Though again and again I asked her not to return to work, she would come out to sell to her favorite customers, no matter how much I scolded her. She was too active, too full of life, to be simply a housewife.

I was back at San Diego State, this time on the GI Bill, when the cancer flared up again. It was October 1946, when I heard the doctor say that her death was inevitable. I was there alone with her in his office, the first in the family to know the frightening verdict. When she asked if he had said something of importance, I could only lie. I went home and told Natalia and waited until the next day between classes to tell Roberto, also a student at State, and that afternoon we told our father. He was out in the nursery when we came to give him the doctor's verdict. He flew into a rage, wanting to disbelieve what we told him, insisted that we consult another physician, then calmed down and sobbed. Roberto and I told our sisters, who cried as though they would never stop.

Despite visits to the doctor, our mother's pain grew steadily worse, until she had to return to the hospital. She lasted three weeks, half of that time in a coma, drugged with morphine so that she not suffer unduly. It was the Christmas season, when groups of happy men and women strolled through the halls singing carols. For years after her death, I could not bear to listen to "White Christmas." Roberto and I were in the hospital room when our mother gasped her final breath; at that moment, the offshore winds and the trees and flowers she loved so much stood motionless.

On Guam, when told that I was to go home, I feared that someone in the family had taken sick or died. I thought that if it were not our father, at least he could hold the family together because he was the chief breadwinner. How wrong I was; our mother was the family's strength. Her death shattered us. To recall an old truth, "one never knows what one has until one loses it." Words cannot express a loss of this magnitude. My brother and I were married and on our own; however, Berta, Emma, and Eva were young, very much in need of a mother's love. We buried her in the Catholic cemetery of San Diego, where she rests. As though it were yesterday, I recall praying with passion at Mamá's deathbed and believing that my prayer was valid, but it was all in vain. That June I graduated from San Diego State with honors in history.

It has been more than half a century since our mother died, yet I do not remember a time when I did not think of her. She was my best companion for the first twenty years of my life. It was to her I turned when I had a problem or when I wanted something special done. When I fell sick, she nursed me back to health; once, she did so at the cost of her own health and ended up in the hospital with pneumonia. As I began to date girls, she wanted to know who they were. That ended when I married, although in the short time she knew Natalia she tried hard to be her friend, going out of her way to help Natalia escape my ire over something not done.

At times, I wonder if she ever regretted coming to this country and leaving behind parents, sisters, and brothers, most of whom she never saw again. When I think of her, I remember how she would stand and stare out the kitchen window. There wasn't much to see, for it was open countryside. I would ask, *"¿Mamá, que estás viendo?"* (What do you see?) She would smile and say, "Nothing." What was she thinking? Of her first marriage to Victor Mora and of his untimely death? Or perhaps she just looked? How I wish I had asked her to tell of her life in Parral and El Valle de Allende, her parents, and her brothers and sisters.

Just once did she return to the land of her birth. In 1940, she took Berta and Emma to meet their Mexican relatives. In San Diego, the three took the train to El Paso, crossed the border to Ciudad Juárez, and boarded another one for Mexico City, stopping on the way in Parral and El Valle de Allende to visit Carlos Maldonado, a nephew she helped raise, and his family. Then it was on to Mexico City to see Eva and her husband. Eva and Carlos were the offspring of Rosalía, our mother's oldest sister, who died young. That journey ended Mamá's ties to Mexico.

Papá did not take Mamá's death well; he was a solitary man, but he needed his wife. When I came to see him one time, I caught him drinking from a whiskey bottle he had stashed away in the garage. What a shock it was because he usually drank sparingly. In the years I had known him, only on two occasions had I seen him tipsy. During Prohibition, when Americans banned the manufacture and sale of demon rum, which our parents thought puritanical nonsense, they had made red muscatel wine in wooden barrels in an old shed; Papá would have a glass of the wine with his dinner, but if not for Terencio, Tía María's husband, who dropped by to see whether the wine was ready for a "taste," it would have spoiled.

To our utter surprise, life was to change dramatically. Without telling any of us, Papá wed again. A few months after our mother's death, he went off to Mexico and married a woman from Texcoco, a suburb of Mexico City. When he returned, he said nothing to any of us. My sisters, who were still living at home, had no way of knowing that a woman they had never met would be coming to take their mother's place. She arrived a few months afterward and took up residence in the house we called home. She was everything our mother was not, half our father's age, insecure, distrustful, selfish, and eager to rid herself of my sisters. Soon Eva married and left the house, as did Emma, but Berta, the more docile of the three, stayed around until she found a job on the UC Berkeley campus.

All three of my sisters married men of Mexican descent, though they were raised in Pacific Beach, lived their lives among Anglos, and went to La Jolla High. The racial prejudice of those days dictated that Anglo men their age not date them. My sisters were intelligent, academically capable, well mannered, and attractive. Berta and Emma had won the Gold Cup awarded each year to the best female athlete at La Jolla High. Eva married first, a young man who at the age of twenty-one had risen to the rank of chief petty officer in the navy during the war. With dreams of his own, he enrolled in a technical college and enjoyed a successful career in electronics. Berta eventually married the son of a Protestant minister and, as a student at UC Berkeley, known for his proclivities toward parties.

Emma, hardworking and ambitious, had wanted to go to college, but our father, being the macho that he was, thought college inappropriate for women. He held to the old Mexican belief that a high school education was more than enough for a woman, who would marry, have children, and stay home. That was not Emma's view of the future, but though she pleaded, Papá would not bend. Our mother, meanwhile, though she sympathized with her daughter, had problems of her own. The war was going on, her sons were in the military, and she was no longer well, so she acquiesced to our father. Emma, like Berta, had to attend a secretarial school and then get a job as a secretary. Then she married a young man just out of the army who, he assured her, wanted to attend college and build a better life for himself. Well, he did, but not entirely on his own. Emma put him through college, working to supplement the money from the GI Bill, and had a daughter at the same time. Not only did she help her husband get through college, but eventually she enrolled in Pomona College, got her bachelor's degree, and then earned a master's from Scripps College. Later, as she taught high school classes, she made certain that her daughter, even when married, graduated from Scripps College. After Emma divorced, she married an Anglo professor of botany who had taught her first husband in college.

In 1947, for the master's degree, I enrolled in the Claremont Graduate School, one of four sister institutions, the others being Pomona, Scripps, and Clarement McKenna. Lying east of Pasadena, Claremont was a college town that nestled amidst a barren landscape turned green by man at the foot of mountains to the north; orange groves surrounded it on all sides. When temperatures dropped during the winter, growers lit smudge pots, the billowing clouds of smoke keeping the fruit from freezing. East of town lay acres and acres of vineyards, grapes for the making of wine, and even one or two wineries, yet in the town teetotalers ran the show; not a drink was to be had, though some professors had well-stocked wine cellars. If you walked along the railroad tracks, you came across Mexican men laboring among the glossy leaves of orange trees and Mexican women packing the oranges in boxes at the packing plant. You could also see them at night dressed in *folklórico* costumes singing and dancing at Padua Hills, an outdoor theater patronized by the wives of professors and the town's elite. On the eastern edge of Claremont, in a tiny enclave of Mexicans, a grocery store sold tortillas, *chorizo, queso ranchero*, and on Sundays *menudo* (tripe soup).

I chose the Claremont Graduate School in part because it was near home and in part because of Abe Nasatir, who had spoken of a professor there who thought he knew "what was wrong with Latin America." Hubert Herring was not that, but of all the college teachers I had, I best remember him. By the time I left Claremont, he had become both mentor and friend. Hubert did not have a Ph.D., just a master's from the Union Theological Seminary. He had been a minister in the Congregational Church and was the son of a minister. He wrote about contemporary Latin America, not essays meant for other academics, but articles for journals read by intelligent, well-informed readers, such as the *New York Herald Tribune,* and books that dealt with current issues. He spoke disparagingly of academics who spent their time digging up dusty documents in archives to write about sixteenth-century Spanish explorers in the wastelands of the Southwest.

Hubert was a tall, balding man with a big round face on which he perched a pair of glasses. When I saw him for the first time, he was in a white linen suit, the kind you see in Hollywood movies about English colonials in Africa or India. He had a joint appointment as a professor at the Graduate School and at Pomona College, where he taught the history of Latin America. From the start, we got along well. I was the sole student of Mexican descent, which proved advantageous. In Claremont, for a change, being of Mexican extraction, speaking Spanish, and having lived in Mexico gave one special status.

One reason Hubert caught my fancy was that over years of travel in Latin America he came to know a host of politicos, writers, and artists, including Ramón Beteta, then the minister of finance in Mexico. Beteta was someone I knew by reputation, for as a young man he had been a teacher of a relative of mine in the public schools, was later a leftist idealogue of some note, and ultimately became a Cardenista who sadly betrayed his earlier convictions and got rich. Hubert loved to talk about these people—a novelty for me because until then I had never studied with anyone who knew Mexicans. Unlike sundry academics, he also knew how to write; his knowledge of grammar was scanty at best, but he was the master of the crisply written sentence and the pithy paragraph. He and his wife Helen would ask Natalia and me for lunch or dinner, and from time to time Hubert would come by the apartment to invite me for a beer—if I would help him in his garden.

The year 1947 marked the start of the Cold War, when cocky Harry Truman, a clothing salesman turned politico, sat in the White House. His presidency, as John C. Culver and John Hyde argue in *American Dreamer: The Life and Times of Henry A. Wallace,* aborted American liberalism and arguably ushered in the day of the Cold War. Thanks to Truman and his supporters, the New Deal country became a Cold War state and, instead of a modus vivendi with the Soviet Union, gave birth to the Truman Doctrine, federal loyalty boards, and an anticommunist foreign policy. Before long, Americans were in bed with their World War II foes and had made an enemy of their recent ally. I never cared for Truman, though I took comfort in his victory over Thomas Dewey in the election of 1948, mostly because he was a Democrat. But I voted for Henry Wallace, convinced the confrontation with the Soviet Union was a tragic mistake. As events bore out, Truman's Democrats were hardly disciples of FDR, whereas Republicans, under the leadership of men such as Senator Howard Taft, were aching to turn the clock back, as their enactment of the antilabor Taft-Hartley Act testifies.

Hubert would ask my opinion of events in Mexican history or of contemporary developments, believing that I, a man of Mexican ancestry, might have fresh insights. On one occasion, he asked me to speak to the Mexican history class he taught at Pomona College. He wondered why someone had not written a first-rate biography of Benito Juárez, the Indian president of Mexico whom he admired. He acknowledged Mexico's turn to the right after the reforms of the Cárdenas years and the failure of the Revolution of 1910 to improve life for the majority of Mexicans. He never doubted that racial prejudice existed against Mexicans in the United States. That, plus the hand of friendship he offered, was why I came to look forward to seminars with him and to hour upon hour of talking about Mexico. He was the first and only professor of Latin American history who took a personal interest in me, thought me promising, and encouraged me to pursue a doctorate. Hubert understood something close to my heart: that I wanted to interpret Spanish American life and culture to Americans and that because of my cultural background I might have something unique to offer. A few years ago Mary Chapman, Hubert's assistant, asked if he had lived long enough to read my book on the Cuban Revolution, which she praised. I wish that I could have told her yes. Hubert, however, had died before *Cuba: The Making of a Revolution* saw the light of day.

Hubert surely never expected me to write a thesis on Spanish adventurers in the Southwest, yet that is what I did. I was eager to get a Ph.D. and did not want to waste time researching a fresh topic for a master's thesis, so I chose to expand and rewrite my senior thesis on the Santa Fe Trail that I had done for Abe Nasatir. I departed Claremont with a master's in Latin American studies, with history as the major and Spanish American literature as the minor.

I began to study for the doctorate at UC Berkeley in 1948. Berkeley was an urban metropolis with the feel of an Ivy League town. The city spread out on one side of a hill, with streets sloping east to west, across the bay from San Francisco. Telegraph Avenue, its main thoroughfare, was lined with bookstores, shops, and restaurants catering to students, as was Bancroft, on the southwest edge of the campus. All day and into the early evening, the streets teemed with activity, much of it from students and faculty. Berkeley had a plethora of old, two-story homes, some the work of the architect Maybeck, with shingled sides, dormers on their roofs, and big porches. Leafy shade trees had usurped sidewalks of many streets. A three-hundred-foot bell tower on the university campus, known as the Campanile, poked skyward and looked out over the city.

But Berkeley was a housing nightmare. There wasn't an apartment to rent, so we had to settle for housing that UC provided for veterans in Richmond, a dirty industrial town ten miles from the campus, during the war a shipping and petroleum hub. The rent was cheap, but the apartment, characteristic of wartime housing for workers, was one room with a bath and a tiny kitchen on the second floor of an old army-style barracks. Every morning we left at seven in order to find a parking space for our car within walking distance of the university; if we were not in the library by eight, all seats and tables were occupied.

Anglos were the warp and woof of Berkeley. It was hardly a racial paradise, with blacks, the sole minority, relegated to the outskirts. It was a segregated town, as we learned in due time. Anglo bigotry complicated our house hunting. Once, after we read a newspaper ad for a vacant apartment, we drove to the address, where Natalia, who is fair of skin, spoke to the landlord and re-turned to tell me that it was still vacant. When I got out of the car and walked over to his office, however, I was told that the apart-ment was rented. That bigot, clearly, was not renting to swarthy Mexicans. Against stupidity, it is foretold, "the gods themselves struggle in vain." After three months of fruitless searches, we found a studio apartment on the north side of Berkeley—tiny, just two rooms, but a short walk to the campus.

For a short time in Berkeley, I was reunited with my brother Roberto. When he had a job in San Francisco, he, his wife, and his two children lived just south of us. Roberto and I joined the YMCA to play handball on its courts at night, and on Sundays we now and then came together for dinner; his wife was a wonderful cook. In our youth, Roberto and I had joined our father on Sundays to see Westerns at the movie houses of San Diego. I guess that we never forgot those days because when a film starring Randolf Scott, the movie cowboy of the late 1940s, came to town, we were in the au-dience and watched the hero settle scores, always looking bronzed and healthy and speaking in that accented and courtly diction of his. By now, Papá was no longer the father of old, but Roberto and I were still cowboy fans.

Berkeley was a hotbed of graduate students who, I learned quickly, existed in an isolated society where racism and sexism ruled the day—primarily, as a Jewish student observed, to the ben-efit of Anglo Protestants: ethnics, as we know them today, were rarely around. And you could count the number of women on the fingers of one hand; investing time and funds in them, professors believed, was a waste of time and energy, a canard reminiscent of the silly opinions of Edward Clarke, a Harvard professor who ar-gued in the late 1880s that women could not withstand the rigors of a college education, and if they tried, their brains would grow bigger and heavier, and their wombs would shrink. The savants at Berkeley, perhaps less fatuous, merely believed that women would marry, have children, and never become serious scholars.

Until well into my doctorate, I spent all of the days at Berkeley as the solitary Mexican; then near the end of my time there another one appeared suddenly. John Martínez, a shy and likeable navy veteran with a smile on his face and the son of a working-class family, had abandoned the Catholic Church and embraced the Mormons. He was married to an Anglo woman, the mother of his five children, and dreamed of a doctorate in Mexican history. John and I got along well but, I soon realized, had little in common; he talked like an Anglo, knew little about Mexico, and voted Republican.

The late 1940s were a time of transition, when the deprivation of the war years gave way to dreams set aside to soldier. My companions had seen a lot of life before returning to academe. Veterans almost to a man, some had faced combat in Europe, others in the Pacific. They were older, more mature, married, and hard-working, wanting to get on with their careers, aspiring to teach and write history. They lived in modest apartments, paying for them with the GI Bill, stipends from teaching assistantships, and their working wives' salaries. Fraternities, sororities, and student life in general held no interest for them. They hailed from Boston, New York City, and places in Michigan, Kansas, Indiana, Oregon, and Washington. Two or three of them had attended Harvard and Yale and were scions of wealth. A dozen or more aspired to a doctorate in Latin American history. The students I knew best were either in Latin American or U.S. history, two of my fields of study.

My companions were a hard-drinking bunch: when we got together, we gulped down bourbon, straight or on ice, and exchanged gossip about professors and small talk, but with other thoughts going on behind, to paraphrase Noel Coward, that paragon of bourgeois society. As good liberals, we argued over the "Red scare," politics, U.S. imperialism, German responsibility for the war, the Soviet Union, and the Cold War. Democrats all, we voted for Adlai Stevenson in 1952 and grieved when he lost the election to Dwight Eisenhower.

Sadly from my perspective, the more conservative of these students were the future historians of Latin America, who took for granted the triumphs of the Mexican Revolution; believed Juan Domingo Perón, the strong man of Argentina, a fascist; and labeled

Eva, his wife, a whore. What boggled the mind, however, was their response to the overthrow of the Arbenz regime in Guatemala in 1954, a military coup cooked up in Washington and carried out by the Central Intelligence Agency, largely on behalf of United Fruit, a U.S. corporation fighting to derail land reform. To execute this shady enterprise, Washington held trade concessions over the heads of recalcitrant Latin American leaders; suborned local businessmen; cultivated dissidents in the oligarchy, church, and army; and then funded and equipped an exile invasion force from Honduras. The United States justified this blatant intervention in the affairs of a sovereign state by alleging the need to rid Guatemala of communism—a preposterous indictment. Yet, with an exception or two, my colleagues, future scholars of Latin America, swallowed this tale hook, line, and sinker.

These were also paranoic times, when Red baiting was to the current culture as the 1950s were to the 1930s—not the locomotive of change but the caboose. In Washington, Joe McCarthy and the nefarious House UnAmerican Activities Committee went around asking Americans "if they were or had been communists?"—scaring the wits out of faint-hearted liberals. These modern-day vigilantes, including a California version in Sacramento, wanted perversely to destroy people in order to save their souls. Fawning over "pinkos" and communists had led the country down the road to moral perdition. In the race to escape being labeled a "Pinko" or a "Red," friends turned against friends, while in the academic world fellow travelers turned rabid anticommunists, displayed their metamorphosis in books and articles, and won the applause of cowardly back-scratchers. Communism was evil, concluded most Americans, who turned a puerile anticommunism into a mendacious brew of American patriotism.

In the California halls of ivy, chancellors scurried for cover. When right-wing demagogues in the legislature in Sacramento demanded that professors at the state universities sign loyalty oaths, campus leaders acquiesced, as did most professors, more concerned about jobs than principle. "I have nothing to hide," they would say, "so why shouldn't I sign?" One Berkeley professor, it was said, explained that he had not taken a strong stand against the loyalty oath because it would lead to "terrible gastrointestinal ills." Even war veterans had to swear to uphold noncommunist ideals before draft-dodging politicians. A few professors, I acknowledge, refused to buckle under and lost their jobs, tenure notwithstanding.

One explanation for this less than valorous behavior was that most American historians, including Berkeley's, saw themselves as intellectual warriors in the struggle of a "free world" against "totalitarianism," originally in the form of German Nazis and now Russian communists. This assertion, the underpinning of American Cold War ideology, became the lynchpin of so-called scholarly studies of Nazism and communism on campuses across the land. Historians were called upon to rearm Americans spiritually for the coming Armageddon with Russian communism, which was identified with a disdain for "objective historical truth." Scholars who had questioned the wisdom of FDR's interventionist diplomacy, among them Charles Beard, found themselves ostracized. Beard, charged Stanford historian Thomas A. Bailey, had "prostituted history to his own ends" because of his "Marxist-Leninist-Stalinist philosophy." In that political climate, continues Peter Novick in *That Noble Dream,* "Beard's earlier stance made him a pariah," so much so that "he was jeered at meetings of the American Historical Association." Lionel Trilling lamented that perhaps never before in history had intellect so "associated itself with power." Outside of "physics, no other academic discipline participated more wholeheartedly in that association than did history," says Novick. Signaled out for specific attack was Marxism, equated with "economic determinism of the crudest sort." Pacificism, rampant among youth of the 1930s, it was claimed, had left them unprepared for the war they had to wage; it was either fight or live in servitude. With a few exceptions, this intellectual climate prevailed in the Berkeley history department.

Since the days of Herbert E. Bolton, Berkeley had been looked upon as one of the premier universities for the study of Latin America. For this reason, Hubert Herring had urged me to apply there. Berkeley appealed to me because it was close to home and because Hubert had spoken highly of two young historians of Latin America, James F. King and Engel Sluiter, who taught there. What I did not know was that both had studied under Bolton, though neither one was a borderlands specialist. When I met Bolton, then a doddering old man, he boasted that he had picked his two finest students to replace him.

Jim King—of normal height, neither heavy nor slender, and never without his thick glasses—was a pleasant man, well meaning and liked if not respected by his students, but unfortunately not very intellectual. In the years I knew him, we never discussed Spanish American cultural life, let alone *pensadores,* the thinkers and doers. It was difficult, if not impossible, to have any kind of conversation with him, let alone one dealing with philosophical issues. I never understood why he had become a scholar of Latin America, a culture and way of life so foreign to his personality. He was the editor of the *Hispanic American Historical Review* but knew no Latin Americans outside of one or two Venezuelan scholars who studied the institution of slavery at the end of the eighteenth century, the topic of King's dissertation. He had published two articles on the subject; so far as I know, he never published another. King was far from being a born teacher, and his seminars were rarely stimulating. Sometimes he had not looked at the paper that was being read in the seminar and, if tired, was known to nod off. He held one historical conviction: the "black legend" of an evil Spanish Conquest was simply wrong; British and American historians had unjustly maligned the Spaniards.

Sluiter, another Latin Americanist, deeply versed in books but shallow in himself, seemed to walk as though he had something important on his mind; I always suspected that for him belief was harder to shake than knowledge. He was a cold fish; personal warmth was not one of his traits, an opinion most graduate students held. However, he could talk, which I know because I was his teaching assistant, but he inspired no one because he circled his subjects but never seemed to land on them, wasting time on the details of the voyages of every Spanish and Portuguese explorer.

I once had the temerity to suggest that it might be better to combine the voyages of exploration into one lecture, but he paid no
attention. If memory serves me right, I don't believe that I ever
heard him speak highly of Spanish American culture. To the contrary, he once said to me: "we [Americans] can do everything better than you [Mexicans]." When he retired, the sum total of his
scholarship added up to one or two articles on the Dutch in Brazil,
intruders in the seventeenth-century Portuguese colony as sugar
planters and slave masters. During his years at Berkeley, he spent
his time collecting documents on the Dutch in Brazil for what, he
implied, would be his magnum opus.

The department also had a professor who taught Mexican history and was an editor of colonial materials, specifically Spanish
New Mexico. He never wrote anything about Mexico. Neither he
nor King nor Sluiter took me under his wing.

I also recall John D. Hicks, chair of history, with whom I took a
course and a seminar in U.S. history and who drew six hundred
students to his course, the exams graded by five graduate assistants.
A good speaker, he lectured with a microphone attached to his la-
pel. Hicks, however, had his peculiarities. A midwesterner and the
son of a Protestant minister, he was as American as apple pie, a
critic of anything he considered attacks on cherished "American
values" and a Cold War warrior. He rarely faulted anything American; one day an assistant was reading an article in the *Daily Cali-
fornian,* the campus newspaper, on student beliefs. One belief was
that God was an American. When his assistant laughed at that,
Hicks pondered for a moment and then replied, "I'm sure that God
wishes he were an American." Hicks, I realized quickly, knew little
of the peripheral world and was unsympathetic. When it came to
American deeds abroad, he was hardly objective. His hero was
Theodore Roosevelt, to whom he paid tribute for his "progressive"
politics, his role in the Spanish-American War, and the building
of the Panama Canal. That Roosevelt, as president, had robbed the
Republic of Colombia of a slice of its territory, threatened Venezu-
ela with intervention, and betrayed Cuban patriots' aspirations for
independence troubled Hicks not the least. After I objected to a

lecture justifying General Pershing's invasion of Mexico in pursuit of Pancho Villa, Hicks in jest started to call me Pancho Villa.

One of the better scholars at Berkeley was the tall and slender Kenneth Stampp, a native of Wisconsin and an up-and-coming historian of slavery in the United States. On first contact, you had the impression of meeting an austere and cold person, but much of that impression disappeared once you came to know him, and he certainly mellowed over time. He was, however, very Anglo, more dour than open. Yet, as one of his teaching assistants, I looked forward to his lectures, finding them well crafted and provocative.

I came to admire Stampp because of his stance on the issue of race in America. He had no stomach for Ulrich B. Phillips, author of the "Plantation Legend," a racist diatribe, and the southern school of historians who sometimes referred to black slaves as "sambos." Some of them, Stampp wrote to his mentor at Wisconsin, are "damned Negro-hating [historians] . . . who crucify the abolitionists for attacking slavery." If he had lived in the 1850s, he went on, he "would have been a rabid abolitionist." Stampp's book *The Peculiar Institution* is a landmark study of slavery.

Stampp attracted large numbers of graduate students, probably more than any other professor. None of them spoke ill of him; they admired him and were proud to study under him. One was Jack Sproat, a bright and gregarious man who had endured a year on Guadalcanal as a warrant officer in the war. I remember him especially because I have seldom met someone whose politics so closely resemble mine. When Jack was getting ready for his oral exams, Stampp assured him that the queries would be on "familiar stuff"; to Jack's surprise, they dealt largely with constitutional history, which he told me he "knew almost nothing about." Jack went on to be one of Stampp's star pupils. He had a knack for writing, as his book *The Best Men,* about moguls from the late nineteenth century, reveals. But, as he admits, he lacked the inner drive, the desire to spend countless hours shut up in a room bent over a typewriter, what it takes to publish. I came to know Jack quite well; Natalia and I spent hours carousing with him, including an evening party when one of the drunken guests fell out of a bedroom window. Jack went on to become a popular teacher and chairman of the University of South Carolina history department.

One who surpassed Stampp's expectations was Leon Litwack, the son of a gardener in Santa Barbara; younger than the rest of us, he was a campus radical at Berkeley, politics he never abandoned. After military service and a doctorate, Leon went on to teach at the University of Wisconsin and then returned to Berkeley. He writes on blacks before, during, and after the Civil War and always sympathetically. He wields a heavy pen when decrying American racism. *Trouble in Mind,* one of his books, won the Pulitzer Prize. I see Leon from time to time when I go to Berkeley; "our drive to get ahead," he tells me, derived from the fact that we were "not Anglo Americans." Leon is a Jew.

My outside field was Spanish American literature, so when I could, I audited a course on Spanish American literature. Natalia, who also had enrolled at Berkeley, was taking classes taught by Arturo Torres Ríoseco, a noted Chilean scholar. Torres rarely prepared his lectures, relying instead on students to ask questions; his responses would take up the rest of the class hour. His rejoinders never failed to give a Spanish American perspective; he held no brief for U.S. interventions in Latin America. Yet he was not uncritical of his countrymen. Quite the contrary! What sticks in my mind from the class was an assertion Torres made time and again: Hispanoamérica was the home of any municipal, state, or national bureaucrat's *filosofía de que no se puede* (it can't be done). Later I enrolled in one of Torres's seminars; the topic was Rubén Darío and *modernismo,* a school of late-nineteenth-century poetry. At San Diego State, I briefly had studied Spanish American poetry, a subject not close to my heart. Torres was the one and only *hispano* professor I had in all of my years in the United States.

At Berkeley, no longer was I left out of social life. I was sought out by others. One such person was Sam McCall, a native of Bend, Oregon, and a graduate of Reed College who wanted everyone to know that his family had roots in Massachusetts. Tom, an older brother, went on to become governor of Oregon. Sam spoke with a weird Boston accent, dressed as though he were a student at

Harvard, brown tweed sport coat and dark-gray pants, and carried a green book bag over his shoulder. The son of a mother who was a women's "lib-er" before that term was coined, Sam was a witty charmer with superb talents as a raconteur, but he also suffered bouts of acute depression. Sam collected odd friends, one a young woman by the name of Lavinia Joyce of the shoe family dynasty whose saucy language was "refreshing, but only for a while," as a friend put it.

Sam was the social cacique of a band of students who dwelt in a decaying Victorian house on Telegraph Street, blocks from Sather Gate, the entrance to the campus. Everyone referred to the house as Throckmortons, and invitations to its parties, which Sam largely dictated, were highly prized. I met Sam because I played tennis, a sport I took up there at Berkeley. We came to play nearly every afternoon on the university courts, usually just the two us, but sometimes doubles with friends. After a game on Friday afternoon, our wives would join us for drinks and dinner at Sam's place. The residents of Throckmortons had an elegant cocktail party every semester for invited faculty and students. Sam and his close friends, foppishly turned out in tuxedos, presided over these affairs. Sam later asked me to serve as a host, in tuxedo and black tie, for this dignified frivolity. I recall Sam, too, because he was in part responsible for my wish to teach in a New England college. He died while he was teaching in a community college in Bakersfield; he never completed his doctorate.

Sam was hardly an exception at Berkeley, where we met Anglos with few if any racial hangups, at least not in dealing with us. Then, too, the veterans I studied alongside, natives of places far from Mexican communities, did not bring with them prejudices typical of the Southwest. They were generally more sophisticated, though not all of them. One student, whom Natalia and I knew quite well, had married a Mexican American woman; he confided to Natalia that on one occasion he was asked why he had married a "goddamned Mexican."

When I enrolled at UC Berkeley, I had moments of uncertainty. Compared to San Diego State and Claremont, the university, monstrous and alien, appeared foreboding. "How would I fare?" I asked myself, especially when I took the first exam in the huge class on twentieth-century U.S. history. Dozens of the students were graduates seeking a doctorate in the field, and teaching assistants graded the exams. I studied day and night for the first exam, worried because I had never confronted competition of this caliber previously. I made a B plus on it and As after that; from that point on, I knew I could make the grade at Berkeley.

To become a doctoral candidate, a student had to pass written exams in three fields of history, then, if successful, an oral exam in the major and outside fields. In addition, he had to pass exams in two foreign languages, one supposedly in the language of his research interests. I opted for Spanish and Portuguese but to my astonishment was told that I could not take the Spanish exam because I was a native speaker, even though I would be working with Spanish books and documents. I must take German and French. So I enrolled in a special class for students preparing for the German exam; I was the first of fifty or more to pass the test; French I studied on my own and had no trouble with it.

I was also the first of the hopefuls in Latin American history to take the departmental exams; most students waited two and three years. At the beginning of the fall semester, one year after arriving at Berkeley, I took the written exams in modern European, Latin American, and U.S. history and passed all three, and two months later I took the oral exam. I did it by staying home, reading textbooks in each field again and again, and reading monographs about the topics the professors at Berkeley emphasized. All I needed now for the doctorate was to write a thesis, the most difficult part of the program, as I eventually realized.

That challenge, however, proved the most rewarding. With an Opportunity Fellowship for minority students from the John Hay Whitney Foundation and a William Harrison Mills Fellowship from UC Berkeley, I went off to Mexico. Natalia graduated just as I was ready to take off. She majored in Latin American studies, specializing in Spanish and Spanish American literature. For the trip, we bought an old Mercury, had it painted, and set off for Mexico in the summer of 1950. First we drove home to say good-bye to our parents; Papá beamed when he heard that I would spend an entire year in the country of his birth. Our first stop was El Paso, and from there we went by the recently opened Pan American Highway to Mexico City, much larger now than the one I remembered. Miguel Alemán—the son of a revolutionary general and at this time an opportunistic politico in cahoots with bankers, speculators, and businessmen—sat in the National Palace. He set out to industrialize Mexico, but during his days in office graft and corruption enjoyed a heyday.

We set up housekeeping in a small house on the edge of Chapultepec Park, in the Colonia Hipódromo-Condesa, a legacy of the Porfiriato. What a novel experience, especially for Natalia, who knew only Mexican border towns! We were to experience what Mexicans refer to as *sabor a barrio:* the sights, noise, and smells of a neighborhood. We were among *vecinos* who had known each other for generations, some of them born in the homes of grandparents. Our neighbors, men and women we passed on the streets, as well as their children, spoke only Spanish. The ubiquitous cries of ambulant vendors pierced the air, among them *tortilleras,* women selling tortillas, and men on bicycles laden with mops for the kitchen, towels for the bathroom, and baskets for clothes to wash. From down the street wafted the appetizing fragrances of a *panificadora,* a bakery where early in the morning and late in the afternoon freshly baked *bolillos* sat on shelves. Here and there we came across *fondas,* where men and women tempted passers-by with *antojitos:* tamales, tacos, and corn on the cob. Blocks away a *mercado* beckoned; merchants hawked roses, gladiolus, and calla lilies the colors of a rainbow. A cobbler, the old-fashioned type who knew how to make shoes, was a short walk away, while newspapers and magazines were at our doorstep. In the evening, one heard the music of *cilindros,* men turning the handles of box organs. On Saturdays and Sundays, children played in the streets or at the park across the street where aging Mexicans sat on benches, earning themselves the title *banqueros* (bench sitters).

Once settled, we paid Eva, my cousin, a visit and from that time on saw her frequently. She had not necessarily mellowed; she was still the arch conservative and Catholic fanatic, but because I was married and no longer a burden, I suspect, and because she took a liking to Natalia, we got along better. Eva would invite Natalia to accompany her to fashion shows and the two of us, along with Amador, her husband, to play canasta, games she always wanted to win. Amador, an official of the national railroads, was pleasant enough but seldom made known what he thought and stayed away from home as much as possible. On Saturdays, he would come home, change his suit, and leave, not to return until late that night. For those days, Eva had to make certain that the maid had washed and ironed a clean shirt, else Amador was annoyed. "Your cousin," he told me once, "wears iron panties." Eventually I learned that he had a mistress; I remember he gave me this advice: "Don't ever take on two women; you can't satisfy them." Amador died in the arms of his mistress. When he lay sick in his bed, a woman knocked on the door, and Eva answered; she was Amador's mistress. "I am here," she told Eva, "to care for Amador."

Our house in order, I began my work, thinking that I'd write on *indigenismo,* the struggle to lend a hand to the exploited Indians, which dated mainly from the Revolution of 1910. One of its key aspects was rural education, a topic I ultimately chose for my dissertation. The research took me to the Ministry of Education in downtown Mexico City. As best I could, I chased after the men in charge of rural schools, most of whom I found willing to talk to me but were hardly completely candid. They were members of the ruling party, the Partido Revolucionario Institucional (PRI). Moreover, the ministry's archive was limited at best; it did not even have a complete set of its *memorias,* the yearly records of activities. So I had to look for sources in other places, among them the Biblioteca Nacional and the Instituto Indigenista Interamericano, where I met Manuel Gamio.

In the 1920s, Gamio, an anthropologist, had been under the secretary of education but had to flee the country when he denounced graft by department officials. During his exile, he had come to the United States on a Guggenheim grant, which he used to write a study on Mexican migrants. He was a stalwart *indigenista,* an advocate for the downtrodden Indian. Tall and slim, with the face and complexion of an Englishman, and once a student of Franz Boaz, he had overseen the famous study of San Juan de Teotihuacán, an Indian village on the outskirts of Mexico City. He had published essays on the Indian question—*Forjando patria,* a pathbreaking book on the forging of a Mexican nationality—and, of more importance to me, gave life to the concept of an "integral education." Schooling alone would not remedy the plight of the poor. When I met Gamio, he was no longer a young man, but still vigorous enough to head the Instituto Indigenista Interamericano, the office for the study of the Indian people of Spanish America. I spent hours discussing rural education and Mexico in general with Gamio, who greatly admired Lázaro Cárdenas, referring to him as *"lo mejor que ha producido México,"* the best Mexico has produced.

A pet peeve ruffled Gamio's calm: Indian campesinos' resistance to discarding old habits. The object of his angry denunciations were usually the Otomí, who dwelt in the Mezquital of the state of Hidalgo, a region northeast of Mexico City, arid and bereft of fertile lands. Their poverty was a national disgrace. Some lived in caves dug out of the ground and covered with maguey stalks, and they cultivated tiny plots of rocky soil. They were poor and malnourished, in part because of their almost total reliance on corn for food. As Gamio explained, the Otomí diet would improve if they substituted soya beans, rich in protein. He would tell me again and again that tortillas, a basic of the Otomí diet, could easily be made from soya bean flour. But, as he added, the Otomí were *tercos,* stubborn; they preferred to die of malnutrition rather than alter their ways. I will carry to my grave Gamio's parting comments when I came to say good-bye: "Were I still a high government official," he declared, "you would not leave Mexico." No one has ever paid me a greater compliment.

At the Instituto Indigenista, there was also Juan Comas, the undersecretary of education in the last Spanish republic. He had arrived in Mexico when President Cárdenas, a staunch supporter of the republic, had opened Mexico's doors to refugee republicans. A physical anthropologist and a prolific writer, Comas was fifty years old, smoked incessantly, and never sat still. He was married to Camille Destillieres, an American woman from New York City. Camille had edited one of the editions of Madame Calderón de la Barca's *Life in Mexico,* an account of the days of Antonio López de Santa Anna, the fool who ruled the country eleven different times. I remember Comas, too, because he was the editor of *América Indígena,* a journal where my first article appeared. "Hijos olvidados," the forgotten children, was a stingy rebuke of Mexicans for their treatment of their kin across the border, and, thanks to Comas, "El Color: El enigma de los Estados Unidos," my analysis of the role skin color plays in American life, saw the light of day in *Cuadernos Americanos,* one of Mexico's best journals. Comas and Camille became our friends, and in their company we spent many a night drinking red wine and bemoaning the fall of the republic.

Unfortunately, Natalia fell sick, spending weeks as a patient at the British-American Hospital in Mexico City and then having to return to San Diego to recuperate, while I stayed on to finish my research. How I remembered Arturo Torres Ríoseco and his *"filosofía de que no se puede"* when I had to ask for a visa extension from the Ministry of the Interior for Natalia, who, sick in bed, was unable to leave the country. Armed with a written request from her physician, I would appear at a window only to be told by a faceless bureaucrat that I was either at the wrong window or that nothing could be done.

Without the help of Angélica Castro, an anthropologist who headed the Ministry of Public Education office of bilingual programs for Indians, I could not have done my fieldwork. Angélica proved not only a friend but an amazing fountain of information on Indians and their schooling. With her, I attended reunions of Tarascan Indians in Michoacán, visited Internados Indígenas (schools for Indian children), and by rowboat and mule back traveled up the Papaloapan River in Veracruz, where the Miguel Alemán administration was building dams and relocating Indians. I spent a week in an Indian village in the upper reaches of the river with Pedro Carrasco, a Mexican anthropologist who had set up camp, eating with him and sleeping on an army cot in an adobe hut shorn of doors and windows but not of ugly spiders.

Through Angélica, moreover, I met Lázaro Cárdenas. We were in Pátzcuaro, Michoacán, where Angélica ran into a schoolteacher who had just seen Cárdenas in Uruapan, a small city not too far away. Angélica asked if I would like to meet El General? "Of course," I replied, jumping at the chance to talk to the man I so much admired. The next day we drove to Uruapan. Cárdenas then headed the Comisión del Río Balsas, a federal agency in Michoacán. When we arrived, we found ourselves among hundreds of campesinos and politicos from Mexico City waiting to talk to El General. How, I wondered, would I ever get the opportunity to see him? Angélica, however, was not fazed. She made her way through the crowd to the office of a *licenciado* (lawyer) in charge of appointments, as it turned out a close friend of both Cárdenas and Angélica. "Don't worry," he assured us, "I will speak to El General." That done, he went to him and returned to tell us that I had an appointment for that afternoon and that El General had ordered him to take us to lunch. During the conversation at lunch, I recall that I had the temerity to ask the *licenciado* if Cárdenas were *honrado,* honorable and honest. From my perspective, it was a logical question because Mexican generals as well as politicos in those days were notorious for their ill-gotten gains. *"Honrado, honrado, no; honrado, si,"* was his reply.

I shook hands with General Cárdenas and then spent an hour or so asking questions about contemporary Mexico. At that time, Miguel Alemán, the governor of Veracruz in the days when Cárdenas was president, headed the republic. No longer a Cardenista, he had tossed aside the agrarian promises of the revolution and given free reign to businessmen who wanted to industrialize Mexico. In the opinion of the old Cardenistas, Alemán had betrayed them. An astute politico, Cárdenas did not speak ill of Alemán, even insisting that Mexico had to industrialize, but, he emphasized, not in the manner that it was being done. What he lamented, obviously, was that Alemán had left a coterie of cynical and allegedly corrupt politicos and business tycoons free to establish monopolies at the expense of most Mexicans. Cárdenas was right, of course, as the eventual failure of the Mexican-style import-substitution policy confirms. Had the federal government taken the lead to direct and control the effort, making certain that monopolies did not arise, import substitution might have tasted success.

Living in Mexico City, nonetheless, offered more than just meeting people and making friends. It meant watching Palillo on the stage of the Teatro Blanquita, a comic with the guts to voice his outrage at the chicanery of the Alemán regime, for which he was jailed every time he opened his mouth. It also meant exploring a rich past, to be found everywhere: Teotihuacán, site of the legendary pyramids of the sun and moon built by ancient peoples, perhaps the Toltecs; the ruins of Tenochtitlán, where Cuahtémoc, the last Aztec emperor, had presided and what Hernán Cortés and his hordes had burned to the ground; and countless colonial churches and the majestic cathedral that faced the Zócalo, Mexico City's central plaza. There, too, stood the Palacio Nacional, a colonial structure where Mexico's presidents decided policy and where Diego Rivera painted his Marxist interpretation of Mexican history. A block or so away, at the old Colegio de San Ildefonso, Rivera, José Clemente Orozco, and David Siqueiros had covered three stories of patio walls with murals and launched an artistic renaissance not matched anywhere else in the Western Hemisphere. At the agricultural college of Chapingo, "Mother Earth," one more of Rivera's murals, graced the walls of the colonial church. And then there were the Orozco murals at the Supreme Court, at the Palacio Nacional de Bellas Artes, and, best of all, in the Hospicio Cabañas and the Palacio de Gobierno in Guadalajara—done with dexterity, color, and passion, testimony to a great artist's cry for social justice.

When I returned to the United States in 1951, I saw that much had changed at home in San Diego. Our father had dismantled the nursery, sold the property, and purchased a small house not too far from the shores of Mission Bay. The man who was always active, always puttering with something, was no more. When his wife was around, he was a changed man, no longer the father I admired. Alone, his old self surfaced; he wanted to know about Mexico, what I had seen, the people I had met. He did not say it, but I began to suspect that he was itching to return home.

In Berkeley, I completed my dissertation in 1953 and received the Ph.D. a year later; the icing on the cake was a Phi Beta Kappa key. My dissertation topic was Mexican rural education, a study of schools in campesino communities, isolated villages inhabited by poor mestizos and Indians who spoke only their native language. The crusade to educate them sprang from a Mexico that still had faith in the ideals of the Revolution of 1910. Many of these schools, *casas del pueblo,* humble one-room adobe buildings, dated from 1921, when Mexicans began to teach the poor to read and write, as well as to give them rudimentary tools for a better life. There were cultural missions, bands of teachers, carpenters, masons, and nurses who went from village to village preparing young men and women to teach; campaigns against drunkenness, a bane of country life; and doctors who cured the sick and taught campesinos to purify their drinking water. These were exciting times, and that is why I picked the topic of rural schooling for my dissertation. The next step was finding a job in a college or university at a time when jobs were scarce, especially for Latin Americanists, but candidates, among them my companions at Berkeley, were plentiful.

7

The Holy Grail

———

Well, there I was, Ph.D. in hand at a time when jobs were as difficult to find as the holy grail avidly sought by medieval knights. We were living in the postwar era, the 1950s, but colleges and universities were stuck in the 1930s, when hard times stunted growth. Higher education was not a priority for federal largess, which, with the advent of the Cold War, was bequeathed on weapons, soldiers, and highways. Hardly anyone at Berkeley or anywhere else in the country was getting a teaching job.

This was especially so in Latin American history, a peripheral field, where appointments were few and far between. Schools in the Southwest were more likely to teach the subject than those in the East, where, at best, a professor taught it in conjunction with others. What departments taught marched in step with Washington's foreign-policy preoccupation, which in the 1950s was the Soviet Union, the Cold War enemy. When China embraced communism in 1949, courses on China began to appear on the pages of university catalogs.

Yet it was with a high heart that I set out to look for a job. Naively I believed that I had an advantage over other candidates. I was bilingual; I spoke Spanish fluently and could write it. Of Mexican ancestry, I knew the culture of Mexico and had lived and traveled in the country and even published articles in Mexican journals. Why, as I saw it, would a university or college not want someone of this background on their faculty to interpret Latin American history and culture? Well, I was mistaken; they did not.

It was a lesson I would learn again and again. When it came to finding a job in the academy, someone of Mexican ancestry, no matter how well he might know Spanish American life and culture, had few allies. That was not so for others. Anglos could always count on the "old boys' network." They took care of each other. When I began the job search, Anglo men filled nearly every position. Amazingly, they even excluded their own women: mothers, sisters, daughters, and wives. Jews were just starting to enter the history profession; they gradually became numerically and intellectually important. As they did, they began to imitate Anglo behavior, recruiting their own.

In the 1960s, a handful of African Americans began to infiltrate academic ranks, usually teaching African American history. They were never numerous but, compared to Mexicans, enjoyed a tremendous advantage. Since 1619, when the first slaves were introduced to the English colonies, blacks had been an integral part of U.S. history; when teaching U.S. history, you could ignore race relations, as was usually done, but not slavery or the Civil War, supposedly fought to put an end to it. Over and above that, Anglo-Americans never forgot completely their responsibility for the horrible crime. I suggest that some of them felt shame for how their forefathers had exploited blacks. In the liberal 1960s and 1970s, this meant atonement—up to a point: paying homage to African American scholars, hiring an African American person to teach African American history, or establishing an African American studies department.

Nothing of the sort existed for those of Mexican ancestry. Despite the despicable treatment accorded Mexicans, which included murder, feelings of guilt seldom troubled Anglos. Nor was the history of Mexican Americans an integral part of the national experience, at least in the minds of most history scholars. Worse still, I was in Latin American history and the sole applicant of Mexican descent. Not until the 1970s did I start to come across scholars of similar ancestry, nearly always teaching Chicano (Mexican American) history. At most, there was one in a department, with few outside of the Southwest. Why, after all, teach Chicano history in

New England or in the South? When I attended the annual meetings of the American Historical Association, I saw no one who
looked like me.

I also began the quest for the holy grail when professors of Latin
American history were the stepchildren of the guild. Yet hopeful
that a liberal arts college might be interested in what I fancied were
my unique qualifications, I wrote scores of letters but, aside from a
reply from Bowdin's president, received a batch of printed rejections. Why my interest in a small college? Well, it dated from Berkeley and to conversations with Sam McCall, who had gone to
Reed, as had a coterie of his friends. When they came together,
there was talk of Reed, where students knew each other, professors
called each other and the students by name, and academic standards were high. This was not always so at big, state institutions.
At Berkeley, too, I had heard of colleges from "Pete," an advertis-
ing executive who had two things on his mind: booze and Williams College, his alma mater. He was a neighbor of ours when we
had a cottage in the Berkeley hills. When his physician told him
to stop drinking, Pete gave up whiskey but on weekends drank a
gallon of wine and, when tipsy, spoke nostalgically of Williams.
Even before Sam and Pete, I was aware of the hallmarks of the liberal arts college while at Claremont; Pomona College was one of
the best of them. As well as being Hubert's first wife, Helen Herring had been a student at Smith, and Hubert had written a book
titled *Neilson of Smith,* about one of its hallowed presidents.

Yet there I was, a jobless hopeful. On top of that, Natalia and I
were virtually paupers. We had gone through our savings, the
money from the GI Bill had run out, and I was no longer a teaching assistant, a job that paid peon's wages anyway. We were in deep
trouble; nonetheless, we were not ready to fold our tent because
until then we had always managed somehow to survive. Free of
the army, I had gone back to San Diego State with more than three
thousand dollars saved while I was on Guam, a not inconsiderable
sum for those days, and funds from the GI Bill, especially helpful
because Natalia had enrolled in college. On weekends, I worked
alongside Papá and for the next five years of graduate study kept

our heads above water by teaching part time at a private school in Claremont, by selling men's clothes at Capwells (a tony Oakland department store), by earning extra income as a salesman on Saturdays and Sundays for an Oakland nursery, and by delivering Christmas packages for the post office in Berkeley. After Natalia graduated, she found a job in the manuscript division of the Bancroft Library, the Western and Mexican collection at Berkeley, where she helped Robert Burke, its head, catalog the José María Vallejo, Thomas Mooney, and Oliver Larkin papers. But even with Natalia's income, we had barely enough to keep our heads above water.

Just when things looked bleak, by a stroke of luck I replaced Burke's wife, one of John Hicks's graduate students, in the U.S. history course she taught in the School of Pharmacy at UC San Francisco; the next semester I taught Latin American history as a night course in the extension division of the university. That meant driving into San Francisco at night and coming home tired and weary. The rule for pay in extension was simple: the more students, the more pay; and conversely, the fewer, the less pay. Neither of the two groups of students dedicated much time to the study of history.

Any port in a storm, I told myself, so I wrote Sacramento for an emergency teaching credential, hoping that I might teach as a substitute in the Oakland and Berkeley schools. No matter how many degrees you had or how well prepared you were, you needed a credential to teach public school. For one year, I was "on call," as the school chiefs put it. Early in the morning, when a substitute was needed, I was told by phone to go to such and such a school to teach such and such subject. In the course of one year, I taught sixth grade in an elementary school where racial diversity but also disunity reigned supreme among students; the eighth grade in an upper-class, all-white junior high, whose students thought so well of me that they wrote a petition asking the principal to keep me on; and shop, music, and biology in high school. If the absent teacher had left assignments for the students, I fared passably well; if not, I was in trouble, especially in the sciences and math, where my knowledge was sketchy at best. As a "music teacher," I devoted an entire day to playing records and keeping order; when I struggled to get a record on the turntable, one student, a boisterous female, quipped that teacher "cannot find the hole," to the laughter of the class.

I taught in minority schools in Oakland, mostly all black; in one, keeping order came before teaching. If I turned my back, erasers and chalk flew through the air. The morale of its teachers, mostly Anglos, could not have been worse. I once was transferred at midday from one high school to another with disciplinary problems because a substitute teacher could not control the students. I had been there previously, so I knew the students, one in particular, a Mexican American kid who thought he could get away with murder. I took him into the coat room and told him that if he did not behave, I would spank him.

Eventually we began to hear news of job openings. They were not, however, what I had hoped for. That may sound strange because, as the old saying goes, "beggars can't be choosers." One job was in Tennessee, at a school no one at Berkeley had heard of; when King, my doctoral mentor, suggested that I apply, I had to find reasons to say no. After all, if I were to get the job, King, supposedly responsible for placing his students, would surely forget me once I was "placed" and leave me stuck in an institution where no one seeking a Latin Americanist would think to look. So I told him that a Mexican would be out of place in that part of the country. King was not entirely pleased with my response, but he asked another of his students to apply, and that person got the job.

When my prospects looked bleak, a lucky break occurred. Robert Burke, Natalia's boss, was a friend of Earl Pomeroy, a well-known historian of Western history at the University of Oregon. The department was searching for someone who could teach the U.S. history survey course and a Latin American history course. Burke, who liked Natalia and knew that I wanted a job, asked if I were interested. If I got the job, I would replace William Appleman Williams, the diplomatic historian, for one year. I thought Oregon was a good place to launch a university career. With Burke's help, I applied but fretted that I might not get the job. I did get it, but not before Pomeroy, who did not care for the iconoclastic Williams, asked Burke if rumors were true that I was a radical. What Pomeroy did not want was another Williams in his department; one radical was enough.

The temporary post at the University of Oregon started my career as a professor of history, what I had aspired to be since that first day as a freshman at San Diego State. Being a professor up to this point had been merely a dream; now I would live it. Eugene, home of the university, was a hard day's drive from Berkeley and a long, long way from Mexico, by character and miles. Across from Eugene was Springfield, a lumber town, where big rigs loaded with logs traveled up and down the main street. Eugene was a college town of twenty-eight thousand Anglos; in the two years I taught there, I saw only one other Mexican. I was alone. It was Natalia who kept me in touch with my heritage by cooking Mexican dishes, making tortillas, and sharing the delights of Mexican music. She also helped make ends meet; the city library hired her to run the reference desk. One thing I will never forget about Eugene: it rained, it rained, day and night from October to May. It rained so much that the ground rotted, or so it appeared. It was not a heavy rain, more like a drizzle, but it never stopped. This was raincoat weather. In the spring and summer, Eugene was lovely, the color of lush green, rhododendrums and azaleas in full bloom under towering fir and pine trees.

Central Avenue, the main thoroughfare, split the campus in two; the history department, housed in one of the brick buildings, faced it. History was a good department. Its luminaries were Gordon Wright, a historian of modern France, Earl Pomeroy, and the up-and-coming William Appleman Williams. A graduate of Whitman College, Gordon, a shy, tall man, was known for his up-side-down smile; instead of twisting up, the ends of his mouth dropped when he smiled. He was a native of Oregon, a man happy to be teaching there, a fine scholar, and an excellent teacher esteemed by one and all. He was one reason why people on campus spoke highly of the department. One of the grand, if infrequently observed, ceremonies of academicians is the Mt. Rushmore question: What chairman's picture would you add to the stone monument in South Dakota? At Eugene, the answer was always Gordon. He was that rarity: a chairman who could make tough decisions without unduly angering his colleagues. The department was basically a happy one. I got along well with Gordon, though I found it difficult to talk to him; he always seemed busy.

Earl and Gordon were a kind of Mutt and Jeff duo; one was tall and the other short, but equally shy. However, when Earl felt at home, he liked to talk—if he was not writing a letter. His office was a jungle because he kept copies of all of his correspondence. Earl wrote on the American West and, like Gordon, enjoyed national recognition for his scholarship. It seemed as though he was constantly writing a book. Also like Gordon, he enjoyed entertaining colleagues at home; both had wives who endeavored to make newcomers feel welcome. Natalia became especially fond of Mary, Earl's wife. She was earthy, a kind of flower child, though a mother of four. On one occasion, when she took her children to the public library, a woman there, upon seeing them poorly dressed and without shoes, urged Mary to see the local welfare agency for help. To Earl's dismay, Mary enjoyed telling this story.

Bill Williams, the diplomatic historian, was different. Blond and blue-eyed, neither tall nor short, he was not known for his sense of humor. He took everything seriously, in particular politics and U.S. foreign policy, his specialty. He was one of the best teachers on campus; students flocked to his classes. A graduate of the Naval Academy and a veteran of World War II, he had been wounded in combat. Predictably, most graduates of military schools—whether Annapolis, West Point, or the Air Force Academy—are conservative in their politics and are glorified patriots. Bill, however, was building his scholarly reputation as a radical in politics and as a critic of U.S. foreign policy. His first book placed the responsibility for the Cold War on the shoulders of Washington. Later, in the 1960s, when fear of risking life and limb in the unpopular Vietnam War briefly turned American college students, usually gung ho patriots, into radicals, Bill's books and articles were read widely.

Bill could be blunt, as I learned when I first met him at a dinner where he was explaining why he had voted for General Eisenhower, a Republican, and not Adlai Stevenson, an idol for most of us. If U.S. political behavior were to improve, he insisted, things had to get worse. At that time, I was sure he was mistaken, and I told him so; I am not so certain anymore, now that I realize that there was not a dime's worth of difference between the two candidates. Some in the department did not care for Bill, though he and Gordon got along fine. Over the years, I came to know Bill much better and once even shared a room with him in Denver, Colorado. When Bill left Oregon for the University of Wisconsin, some were glad to see him go, but it was a huge loss because he went on to transform the field of diplomatic history from a discipline in which scholars simply studied embassy dispatches to one in which they sought to explain the whys and wherefores of foreign-policy decisions by looking at domestic issues.

More important for me, I was not the only newcomer. There were three others, among them John Selby, a Harvard graduate with a doctorate from Brown University. All three were in their late twenties and easterners who in their souls believed Oregon to be in the sticks. From the day they arrived in Eugene, they dreamed of the day when they would have a job in an eastern school. Their wives, also from the East and equally homesick, shared a similar opinion, and the tone of conversation at our dinner gatherings was often nostalgic. I confess that I missed Berkeley and so had something in common with them. John and I became good friends and proud parents almost simultaneously in our second year in Eugene. Our firstborn saw the light of day at the Sacred Heart Hospital in Eugene; I will never forget that hospital because the holy sisters demanded that I pay the bill before I took Natalia and our child home. We named our daughter Olivia Teresa, her middle name my maternal grandmother's; when we left Eugene, Olivia had started to crawl on her hands and knees. When I came home in the evenings, I had to open the front door of our house slowly lest I hurt Olivia, who waited on the other side, her face turned up to see me.

The job at Eugene was for one year; I was hired to teach a course on Latin American history and two identical sections in U.S. history. Oregon was my baptism as a university professor; I was on my own, free to do what I wished with the courses assigned to me. I had never taught such courses previously, so I had to decide what to emphasize and, more important, how to teach history. Before arriving at Eugene, I had come slowly to the conclusion that good teaching was an art rather than a science. Great teachers, moreover, were born not made! Yes, you could improve your teaching, but the knack is God given. However, never having dreamed of becoming a rich man, I knew that it was more fun to know something than to own something.

The goal of the history teacher was to alert the young to the significance of the past for an understanding of the present and to encourage them to open their minds to fresh ideas. Unlike John Dewey, I did not see myself as the caretaker of a "social order." As T. S. Eliot wrote, a function of education was to "help us to escape, not from our time—for we are bound by that—but from the intellectual and emotional limitations of our time." Students must be taught to question, to make the word *why* an integral part of their vocabulary. Why did certain events occur in history, and what was the role of men and women in shaping those events? Were the forces of history, as Tolstoy argued, more powerful that the actions of any individual? Was there such a thing as a "great man" in determining historical events? Or as Marx argued, were economic and social forces and the inevitable conflict between classes the keys to history? I had begun to ask these questions of myself as a student, but it was as a professor at Oregon that I had to grapple with them as a teacher. I did not find final answers because teaching is a lifelong learning process; to quote an old Latin proverb, "by learning you will teach, by teaching you will learn." No matter how many hours the good teacher spends reading what the sages have said or working with students, he or she is always learning, acquiring knowledge as well as new perspectives and ways to impart them. History, after all, is much more than a catalog of inert facts, dates, and names. The job at Oregon set me on the path to becoming a teacher.

Teaching large classes of students meant preparing lectures, a first for me, which meant rushing over to the library to find out what specialists had written. Teaching Latin American history was not terribly difficult, especially Mexican history because it was close to my heart and because I more or less knew the material, though finding books on the subject proved frustrating. The history department at Oregon had never attached much importance to Latin American history, and the meager holdings in the library testified to that.

The course in U.S. history was a different kettle of fish. I was a neophyte. However, I could count on help from Selby, a scholar of the colonial era who also was teaching a section of the U.S. course. I would ask him what he was teaching in class, why he picked certain topics, and what books he assigned students to read. We would spend hours discussing what was important and why. At Berkeley, moreover, I had taken a doctoral exam in U.S. history and had been a teaching assistant for Kenneth Stampp and another professor in the field, so I was not completely out of my depth. To avoid having to prepare three lectures a week, I stumbled upon an approach that has served me well ever since. Instead of lecturing on Friday, the third class hour, I held discussions on current events. By this method, I was able to probe contemporary topics I thought important, among them race relations. The idea was a huge success; the students liked it so much that when the second semester began, enrollments nearly doubled. At Eugene, too, I started on the long road that in the profession leads to scholarly recognition. I began to revise my doctoral thesis for publication, coming to my office at night to work on it. The first article I published in English began to take shape during those nights in Eugene.

Although Natalia and I missed our Berkeley friends, we made others in Eugene. One was Charles Johnson, the dean of the business school, whom I met on the squash courts, a sport I took up because rain made playing tennis impossible. After we came to know Chuck and his wife, we spent weekends sharing a cabin and conversation around a warm fireplace at Coos Bay, a small town on the Pacific Ocean where giant waves broke on the rocky cliffs below.

Tall and slender, his hair cut short, the always amiable Chuck was not the typical academic bureaucrat and certainly not what one expected from a business school. In the two years I knew him, I don't recall one conversation about business, his faculty, or campus politics. He was more apt to talk history than to talk shop, as we referred to campus affairs. After we left Eugene, we saw Chuck twice again—in Boston, where he was spending a year at Harvard on a fellowship, and in Northampton, Massachusetts, when I was teaching at Smith College; he and his family stayed with us. There is a tragic ending to this story; Chuck became president of the University of Oregon in the 1960s, but, unable to quell the student turmoil of those days, he was fired. Unable to accept defeat, he committed suicide.

The University of Oregon at that time had a reputation as a party school, which it was trying to live down. It drew students from California who wanted social activity more than an education. To be invited to join a fraternity or sorority was to be accepted; there was a "Sammy House," a Jewish fraternity because Jews were seldom, if ever, asked to join an Anglo-American house. Every month or so, the frats put on big parties and invited girls from a sorority. One of the students, now my friend, was Roger Martin, who hailed from Portland, where his father had a business. Of the hundreds and perhaps thousands of men students I have taught, he was the only one to bring his father to meet me. Roger was a BMC, a big man on campus, and a loyal fraternity brother. That is how I came to know life in fraternities and sororities: over time, Roger invited Natalia and me to his frat parties, where, to our initial surprise and then delight, a bottle of whisky awaited us. Roger went into politics, headed the Republican majority in the state legislature in Salem, and was a candidate for governor in a Republican primary, but lost out to a man who in the general election became governor.

Oregon's football team, known as the Ducks, was an integral part of campus life and played in the Pacific Coast Conference but seldom came out on top. The coach was Len Casanova, formerly of Santa Clara, a Catholic college with big-time football aspirations.

Some of his football players were students in my classes, so Casanova would drop by to ask how they were doing and, I suspect, to encourage me to be kind to them. But Casanova, whom I came to like, was also a staunch Catholic who thought me a wayward one who needed redemption. His visits to the office were made in part to discuss football and in part to save my soul from hell. I have a different memory of another coach at the school, however. On a lecture tour I was making of alumni clubs, a woman approached me to say how much she had enjoyed the talk. Afterward I overheard this coach tell another that the woman, whom he found attractive but who had failed to notice him, "liked her meat well done."

Probably because of my teaching success, Gordon and his colleagues saw fit to keep me on for another year and, to my delight, to promote me from instructor to assistant professor. When I returned for the second year, I hoped for a third and perhaps even for a permanent appointment. Quirinus Breen, the medievalist, a gentle and kindly man, had asked if I would like to stay on at Oregon. Of course I said yes. I enjoyed my classes, colleagues, and students. Unfortunately, my hopes quickly evaporated. There would be no third year and no permanent appointment, so I began to explore possibilities for another job, writing letters to other departments, and soon realized that the picture looked bleak. I even flew back at my own expense to Storrs, where a professor at the University of Connecticut had indicated an interest. James F. King, my mentor at Berkeley, could not help; he knew of no job openings. I was desperate: my final year was drawing to a close, our limited funds were exhausted, and I had no prospects of a job. To exacerbate matters, for the first time in my life I began to get chest pains, the first of them while drinking beer on a Saturday evening at the Selbys.

Not knowing what to do about a job, I wrote Arturo Torres Ríoseco, the Chilean professor at Berkeley, and almost begged for help. Why he listened, I don't know, but he recommended me for an opening to teach Spanish American literature and Spanish at Southern Methodist University (SMU) in Dallas, Texas, and to teach

Spanish and the Spanish Golden Age at Hamilton College in New York State. I had taken courses in the literature of the Golden Age at San Diego State, but nothing since then and had merely a passing interest in Spain, so I applied for the SMU job, which was closer to my interests, and got it. In June, Natalia, Olivia, and I left Eugene in a station wagon, Olivia in a crib in back. The trip south was hardly a joyous one, for though I was grateful to Torres, I wanted to teach and write history. Teaching verb conjugations (especially those nasty irregular ones), the subjunctive, pronouns, and Spanish pronunciation were hardly my priorities.

Between Eugene and Dallas, we spent the summer in Mexico City. If I were to turn the thesis into a book, I had to do more research in Mexico. Unlike in our earlier visits, this time there were three of us. We had to find an apartment big enough that we could afford, no easy task in Mexico City. We entered Mexico at Ciudad Juárez and, but for Olivia, might not have gotten into Mexico without paying a *mordida* (bribe) to a customs agent. Just when things looked bleak for us, Olivia, who had been asleep in the back seat, awoke and stuck her head out the window. Upon seeing her, the agent, a *cabrón* until then, changed completely. *"Que chula"* (What a lovely child), he uttered, patted Olivia on the head, and told us to move on.

Our stay in Mexico, though brief, gave us time to renew friendships. We saw my cousin Eva, Amador, and Heriberto Maldonado— Eva's half brother, a distant relative of mine and, more important, a friend whom I had known since my yearlong stay in 1950–51. He was ten years my senior, a man of pleasant disposition and the father of three. He and Juanita, his wife, were from Villa López, a small town not too far from Parral, Chihuahua, where my mother and her sisters were raised. He was old enough to remember uncles and aunts of mine. He had come to Mexico City to become a physician but for some reason had dropped out of the university. When I met him, he had an office job with the National Railways of Mexico, which, in the manner of all lowly bureaucratic posts, paid poorly.

Heriberto was a gentle soul and never assertive; he was the

proverbial hen-pecked husband, a fact that troubled Eva. When Natalia and I visited the Maldonados, we never knew if they were on good terms with Eva, who often found ways to criticize Juanita, who was hardly meek and mild. The bitter feelings between the two women could go on for months; Heriberto, however, always found time to see his sister without telling Juanita. Natalia and I were on good terms with both families, so either Eva or Juanita often wanted us to hear her version of the story. Neither was very objective. On a number of occasions, we even managed to repair hurt feelings on both sides.

When the summer ended, we returned once again to the States. Dallas in 1957 was a segregated, southern city. African Americans were off by themselves; Mexicans were rarely seen on the streets; and whites, as Anglo-Americans called themselves, had the run of the city. Bigotry was all around us. When we went to see the football team play, we found that the stadium had two sets of fountains and restrooms, one for "colored" and the other for whites. At first, I did not know whether to enter the "colored" restroom or the other. Yet we had no trouble finding a place to rent. By chance, when we began to look, we found one across the street from the university. It was one-half of a duplex, and the neighbor on the other side was a young woman who took a liking to Natalia. One day when Natalia and the woman were together, Natalia chanced to see an African American walk by the alley of the duplex. The woman's immediate reaction was to ask Natalia if that bothered her. If so, she volunteered to call the police. Oddly, the only prejudice I encountered was in the classroom, when a dumb football player made some comment about me, a Mexican, teaching the Spanish language. Dallas was also dry; you had to belong to a private club to drink liquor in public: you bought a bottle of whiskey, wrapped it in paper, and carried it to a private club, where you purchased setups—glasses and ice. Anyone could join a club; at the door, you simply paid a token fee. It was hypocrisy gone wild. Buying a bottle of booze, however, was not always easy because entire parts of the city were completely dry.

I never felt entirely comfortable in segregated Dallas, though we made friends on and off campus. However, there were also Mexicans in Dallas, but one had to look hard to find them. We could buy Mexican groceries, and on Sundays Natalia would give me a soup kettle and help strap Olivia in the car seat, and off Olivia and I would go to buy *menudo* at a local Mexican grocery. We also could buy tortillas, what Mexicans eat with every meal; Natalia did not have to make them.

In 1996, I went back to SMU to give a faculty seminar and to talk about a book I was just beginning to write. I was much impressed. Compared to Berkeley, UC Los Angeles, and even UC San Diego, it was a small campus, but intellectually lively. William Taylor, one of the best colonial scholars of New Spain, taught there. It was a changed place from the days when I was there. When I arrived on campus in 1957, it was a very white school, attended by very white students, the sons and daughters of wealthy Dallasites, members of frats and sororities housed in gaudy buildings. Football was the sport, and football players were campus heroes. Its president was a former SMU football star, big and overweight, who left intellectual matters to others. Its academic standards were low, and, with important exceptions, it had a mediocre faculty. Some of those exceptions were in the history department, where Herbert Gambrel, its chair, and Paul Bohler and Dick Powers, two able younger members, welcomed me. Testimony to the department's vitality, its medievalist, a strange man, left SMU for a job at Princeton—proof, I assume, of scholarly credentials. Gambrel, an older man, was a widely acclaimed scholar of Texas history. Had I stayed at SMU, Dick and Paul told me, Gambrel would have asked me to join the history department. With his help, I published an article in the *Harvard Educational Review;* then, on my own, I published another in *Social Research,* a much-read journal out of New York City, no mean accomplishment for a young professor teaching at SMU. Dick and Paul, meanwhile, helped preserve my sanity.

Sanity is the perfect term. John Cook, the chair or, in reality, the head of the Department of Spanish, ran it like a personal fiefdom. Not only was he an SMU alumnus, a Ph.D. from the University of Texas, but in some sixty years of life had never lived outside of Texas, his native state, and had never taught anywhere else. I don't think that the department at SMU had ever had another chair. Dr. Cook, as he wanted to be addressed, *was* the Spanish department. He was wealthy and conservative and the owner of a telephone company; as he told me when I met him, his teaching salary was pocket money. He had published his doctoral thesis long ago and nothing ever since. He spoke Spanish poorly, with a Texas drawl, and came to campus only during the hours he taught. You had the feeling that he was not thinking: one side of his brain was merely fondling the other.

You may surmise that I came to dislike him, and you would be entirely correct. That dislike began on the day of the first department meeting. Besides Dr. Cook, there were four of us: a woman in her fifties, the only one with a doctorate; a woman who taught to supplement her husband's salary; and a young man who had yet to complete his doctoral thesis. He spoke Spanish well, knew a good bit about Spanish American culture, and possessed a social conscience, but unfortunately dedicated most of his time to his duties as a Greek Orthodox priest. When he was not teaching, he was at his church. We got along splendidly, but I rarely saw him in the afternoons. No one in the department did any scholarship, a theme rarely if ever a topic of conversation. The Spanish department was the weakest on campus; I had been hired, I learned from the dean of the graduate school—a man I came to like—to strengthen it.

My three colleagues, Dr. Cook, and I met a day before classes began. I had been brought to SMU to teach a course on Spanish American literature and lower-division Spanish-language courses to freshmen and sophomores. I felt no qualms about the literature course; not only was it one of my doctoral fields, but the novels of Spanish America, especially those of the Mexican Revolution, had always fascinated me. But Spanish grammar was unplowed ground for me. True, I had studied it in high school and at San Diego State, but that was years ago, and I had never cared for it. Yes, I spoke Spanish, but Mexicans and other Spanish Americans do not learn to write Spanish by memorizing rules; grammar is rarely stressed in Mexican schools. So there I was, having to learn grammar so that I could teach freshmen and sophomores. I thankfully could rely on Natalia, who relishes knowing the intricacies of the language, to help me teach it to beginners.

On that astonishing day when the Spanish department faculty first met, Dr. Cook informed us that on the next day he would tell us what classes we would teach and give out the schedules. When I told my friends in the history department, they thought I was joking. On the following day, we trekked into Dr. Cook's office to hear the news. In all the years of teaching, I have never heard of a comparable episode at any college or university. Dr. Cook dictated what we would teach, the hours when we would teach, and the days when we would teach. To my surprise, his colleagues, like children, meekly accepted their fates.

A month or so of Dr. Cook and I was ready either for another job or for the insane asylum. I wrote everyone for help. It was the right time to do so, for university expansion had taken off. The end of the war had finally produced a flood of university students; to accommodate them, new campuses sprang up, for which additional faculty had to be recruited. The drought in teaching jobs was over. By November, I had expectations for jobs at three state universities in California, the University of Wisconsin, and Smith College. Unbelievably, all offered me a job. Smith and the state universities were offering a history position, and Wisconsin was asking me to join its Spanish and Portuguese department. As though it were yesterday, I remember that when I traveled to New England for the interview at Smith, I almost came to wish that I were still a Catholic so that I might ask the Almighty for help, so much did I want that job. When the offer came by way of a telephone call, I accepted eagerly. My dreams had finally taken shape.

8

Marvelous Journey

———

Before joining Smith College, I set forth on a journey that I won't ever forget. It began in Mexico City, then went through Central America to Peru and Bolivia, and came to an end in Buenos Aires, Argentina. Traveling mostly by land, I climbed over the Andes, the longest and highest mountain chain in the world and, in so doing, traversed South America from the Pacific to the Atlantic.

I embarked on this adventure after spending part of the summer of 1958 working on what became my first book. I was at the Huntington Library editing the diaries of William Marshall Anderson, a Confederate sympathizer from Ohio who had spent time in Mexico. I knew nothing about Anderson but held contempt for the slaveocracy, the idyllic picture of cotton plantations and benevolent masters of Margaret Mitchell's *Gone with the Wind* notwithstanding.

Jim Holliday, tall, lanky, with a booming voice and once a classmate at Berkeley, had come across the diaries in a dusty attic in an old house in Circleville, Ohio, while looking for letters of the men and women who rode wagon trains to California during the Gold Rush. The diaries, seven shopworn notebooks on tattered paper, made little sense in part because Anderson, not knowing any Spanish, misspelled names of persons and towns along with virtually everything he came across in Mexico. They told of his adventures surveying land in the province of Coahuila for a cockeyed colonization dream of Maximilian, the Austrian prince Napoleon attempted to foist on Mexico during the days of President Benito Juárez.

At Oregon, I had told Roger Martin, as he remembers it, that I wanted to travel through South America before "I was too old to do it," a comment he judged odd because at the time I was in my early thirties. The trip, he recalls, was to start the next summer. He says that he "jumped at the chance" to join me. Unbeknownst to me, he invited three of his fraternity brothers to join us. One reason I wanted to make that trip was that though I would be teaching the history of the southern republics at Smith, I had never been to any of them. How, I asked myself, could I talk about a people I had known only by way of books? What I had in mind was travel in the manner of *New Worlds to Conquer,* a book by Richard Halliburton, a renowned writer of adventure tales I had read in my youth.

While in Dallas, I had forgotten the trip to South America, but Roger hadn't. After two months at the Huntington, I had completed everything on the Anderson project but the introduction and was looking forward to finishing it when, unexpectedly, a telephone call came from Roger, saying that he and three companions would be arriving the following day to plan for the trip. Sure enough, when I got home the next day, there were Roger and his fraternity brothers camped out in the patio of the house Natalia and I had rented.

The "four gringos," as Roger says, and I met again later in Mexico City; they had been there for a week, having earlier stopped off at Mazatlán and Guadalajara. None spoke Spanish, and none had been to Mexico previously. It was their first visit to a Spanish-speaking country. To escape the carping I anticipated from my gringo companions upon visiting our poor neighbors, I reminded them of the parable of the bred-in-the-house Boston lady who, when asked why she never traveled, said, "Why should I? I'm already there." A foreign country is not designed to make you comfortable. It is there for the comfort of its own people.

The first leg of the journey from Mexico City was by train to Ciudad Oaxaca, a day's travel to the south. The city lies in a state heavily populated by Indians and the site of the pre-Columbian cities of Mitla and Monte Albán, religious monuments carved out of stone and testimony to the prowess of their Zapotec builders. The city of Oaxaca was a virtual museum of colonial artifacts and churches, one dedicated to La Virgen de la Soledad, Mamá's patron saint. Reminders of three centuries of Spanish colonial rule were everywhere, starting with the baroque cathedral in the heart of the city. There were homes of the colonial elite, sumptuous, two-story stone mansions with thick walls built around a patio. The cuisine, too, was unique, starting with the traditional *mole*, a rich and thick chocolatey sauce poured over turkey, chicken, or pork. Even a cup of chocolate, a provincial delicacy, had its own taste and aroma. In Ciudad Oaxaca we ran up against our initial barrier: lodging for five persons was not always easy to find, especially because we were unprepared to pay for quarters in luxury hotels. By a stroke of luck, we found rooms at one of the inns on the plaza, where the ringing of church bells every half hour kept me awake most of the night.

On the way out of the city, we encountered another problem: tickets for five persons on first-class busses were difficult to come by. If we wished to get on with the trip, it would have to be by third-class bus. We were in for a novel adventure. The bus, earlier a school bus in the United States, was on its last legs, windows either broken or missing, and cushions on seats barely visible. It rattled and swayed as we drove along bumpy country roads, stopping here and there to pick up or drop off villagers, men and women who pushed us aside as they entered or got off. Some carried boxes of chickens or small pigs; when the animals did not fit on top of the bus, they were brought inside. We saw a slice of Mexico closed to tourists: the beauty of the countryside, villages standing still in time, the life of campesinos, as well as the toll that neglect and poverty exact on human beings.

The rail route through Chiapas, the next province, took us, as natives claim, by way of a *selva siempre verde,* a tropical rain forest always green. This region of the Soconusco, lying just north of Guatemala, was overgrown with plants of sundry varieties, from the giant ceiba, the sacred tree of the ancients, to mangos, bananas, and cacao bushes. For me, someone who thought he knew Mexico, it was a learning experience. It was, to quote a Mexican truth, *"el México desconocido,"* unknown Mexico. That night we slept in a place called Arriaga. At midnight, we arrived at a forlorn train station, where we were to board a train the next morning, but far from the center of town. We were dead tired and eager to go to bed. By chance, a man loitering nearby told us of a cheap hotel that had seen better days and stood across the tracks. From what we could make out of the facade of the building, the paint had long ago disappeared from its walls, a victim of heavy rains and hot weather; merely the drab color of aging timbers remained. It was two stories tall, with a veranda that swept around the second floor, above a porch on the first. We paid our fees to a woman who took us upstairs, where, she informed us, it was less hot, and gave us cots to sleep on. But it was too hot inside, so we moved ourselves out to the veranda. No sooner had we gone to bed than scantily clad women kept walking by the beds. At times, too, we heard the squeaks of bedsprings under the weight of human bodies. We were in a whorehouse.

The next morning, bright and early, we showered outside with cold water, ate a breakfast of mangos and bananas, and boarded the train, listening to the train's pulse, the click-cluck, click-cluck that resounded below our windows, from which we saw campesinos tilling land with oxen and wooden plows. Thinking that we could eat on the train's diner, we took no food with us, but there was no diner, so we spent the rest of the day saying no to food vendors who crowded each train window to sell tortillas, dishes of meat, and God knows what else, preferring to scrounge for something to eat at every train stop, always worried that we might end up with Moctezuma's revenge. It was hot and late again when we arrived at Ciudad Hidalgo, a small city on the southern rim of Chiapas. So we decided not to look for lodgings, preferring to sleep on the concrete slab in front of the customs house and get an early start the next day. When I asked the customs agents if we could, *"Claro,"* came the reply, *"Los cuidaremos"* (Of course, we will watch over you). So we did, though I enjoyed not a wink of sleep. The customs agents probably thought we had lost our minds because malarial mosquitos infested the region. The next morning we said good-bye to our guardians and walked over the Río Suchiate on a wooden bridge to Tecún Umán—to Guatemala.

Travel by a narrow-gauge train began our trek to Guatemala City. From there, Chevrolet vans and Mercedes busses carried us, stopping at every village where passengers boarded or got off, as they had in Mexico. They were so few that we got to know each other, though I had to serve as the go-between, translating from Spanish to English and back again. We got off to stretch our legs on the outskirts of one tiny hamlet where a man in a corral was catching pigs and cutting their throats with a knife for market. One of my companions, in typical gringo fashion, condemned the Guatemalteco for killings pigs in a cruel manner. But, then, is there a humane way to kill an animal?

We stayed less than a week in Guatemala City, a place high in the mountains, seldom hot and mostly chilly, bathing in cold water in a cheap hostel. We saw the cathedral, a colonial legacy, as well as the Universidad de San Carlos, the topic of a heralded book by John Tate Lanning when I was a graduate student. In the city, Roger saw for the first time "the ugly American face of some U.S. citizens," among them "the reprobate preying on young native girls." From there, we rode to San Salvador, capital of El Salvador, and went swimming in the Pacific Ocean at La Libertad, a beach known for its black sand. On the road to San Salvador, we shared a bus ride with a whorehouse madam on her way to visit parents; she was talkative, well dressed, and known to one and all. No one on the small bus looked down on her because of her profession. Then it was on to Tegucigalpa, capital of Honduras, the poorest of the Central American republics.

On these bus rides, my companions were a curiosity. Passengers wanted to know what they were doing riding busses. Why were they not on an airplane? My friends would explain that they were college students traveling on limited funds, that I was a professor, and that we were bound for Buenos Aires. Roger, with whom I have discussed the trip, says that in these conversations he and his companions "prided themselves on showing the better side of

America." At each stop, we looked for inexpensive hotels and more than once stayed in boarding houses for university students. Some were eager to talk to us, to compare notes, as were my companions. To save our funds so that we might reach Buenos Aires, we washed our own clothes, ate at *fondas*, rode buses, and walked and walked. Walking is a superb way to meet people.

One lesson I learned on our trip through Central America: rampant nationalism is not a prerogative of the powerful. At each border stop, immigration agents wanted passports, dozens of photos, health certificates, and proof that we had no intention of staying in their countries. Unless you had tickets for plane or bus rides to get you out of the country, you were in trouble. We had none, so we found ourselves constantly in hot water. Again and again we had to explain that we were bound for Buenos Aires and that we would return to the United States once we got there.

Originally we had planned to ride through all of Central America, from Tegucigalpa to San José, then to Panama City, and from there to Colombia. However, time and money were running short, so at Tegucigalpa we chose to skip these countries and fly to Lima, Peru, the "City of the Kings," as Pizarro, its conqueror, had baptized it. The city lies on the coast, but behind it tower the Andes, a rocky mountain chain whose peaks seem to touch the heavens. Not once during our stay did we see the sun; it was always overcast, yet its hinterland, we were assured, had eternal sunshine. Under colonial rule, Peru and Mexico, where rich deposits of precious metals were discovered, were the kingpins of Spain's empire in the Americas, a gaudy society introduced to Americans by Thornton Wilder, who made actress Micaela Villegas—called La Perricholi and mistress of a Spanish viceroy of the eighteenth century—a central character in *The Bridge of San Luis Rey*. The Inca Empire had rivaled the Aztec's in power and glory, and so, as with present-day Mexicans, Indian blood runs in the veins of most Peruvians. Without the Indian people, there would be no Peru, a truth easily acknowledged as one looks out at the mass of humanity, a conglomerate of varying hues, shadings of Indian red, brown, and Mongolian yellow. We arrived in Lima just as Peruvians were celebrating their independence and watched Indian soldiers march under the command of European types. Nowhere had I seen such a marked racial disparity between officers and men.

Lima—a colonial city in the Spanish mold, replete with parks and plazas, wide boulevards, and elegant houses built around patios in the rich Miraflores *colonia*—had much to remind one of Mexico City. At its core was the Plaza San Martín, and on one of its sides stood the Gran Hotel Bolívar built of white stone in modified Renaissance style. The Universidad de San Marcos was a contemporary of its kin in Mexico City, both the first universities in the Western Hemisphere. There was the cathedral with foundations laid in the sixteenth century, one of the oldest in Spanish America, and the abode of the Santo Negro, the black saint. We visited Callao, Lima's port, where Chinese restaurants had taken over, and watched a soccer match between Peruvian teams.

Where to go from Lima was the next question. We had two options: we could ride a bus to Cuzco, high in the Andes, and visit the fabulous pre-Columbian city Machu Picchu, heart of the Inca Empire, or drive south to Arequipa and get on with our journey. Again, we counted our money and the days left in the summer; time was of special importance to me because I had to finish the Anderson manuscript and report to Smith College in the fall. We chose to skip Cuzco; looking back on it, that was probably a mistake. Cuzco and Machu Picchu are the most remarkable sites in Peru and perhaps in all of South America.

Getting to Arequipa, a city atop the mountains of southern Peru, was not easy. We could buy tickets for a bus ride, which no one we spoke to urged us to do. So we hired a man and his car to drive us to Arequipa. The trip—over flat plains, deserts, and sand dunes, where scrawny fingers of the Andes touched the sea—took the better part of a day and a night that turned bitterly cold. What I remember best of the trip, besides the desolate geography, was the *ceviche*, a raw fish and onion dish, we ate on the way; I had eaten *ceviche* in countless Mexican restaurants, but never as tasty as this one. Another novelty was our driver, who spent hours on end telling me about the woman he bedded in Arequipa. Again we arrived late at night, and although our driver knew the city, we had a terrible time finding a place to stay. It seemed that we drove around for hours before going to bed in a flophouse patronized by our driver, who, it turned out, had no mistress in Arequipa. The beds sagged, and it was cold, bitter cold. On that journey, I came down with a fever and a cold.

After a day in Arequipa, we got on a narrow-gauge train bound for Puno, a town perched on the peaks of the Andes mountains and home to Quechua speakers, one of the two ancient languages of the pre-Columbian people. In Quechua, Arequipa means "Here we rest," a most appropriate name given the city's location at the foot of a long, upward trek into the Andes. Arequipa sits at 7,500 feet above sea level, in a fertile valley nestled by three majestic volcanoes, named by the ancient dwellers El Misti, Chachani, and Pichu-Pichu. Homes were constructed of petrified volcanic lava.

The train we boarded creaked into motion as we pulled out at dawn, again to the click-cluck, click-cluck of iron wheels on iron rails, and got to Puno in the evening. The train ride took us into the heart of the Andes. It was a rail line that wound its way upward and upward, on hairpin curves—switchbacks where from the windows we could see our locomotive coming toward us as the train entered a curve, giving us a view of the cars behind us. We rode on the edge of deep precipices and wide ravines as well as through tunnel after tunnel, long and short, cut through solid rock. It was an unforgettable ride, but it had its down side. The higher we climbed, the more people got sick—nearly everyone, my companions and natives alike, with heads hanging out of train windows, vomiting what they had eaten that morning. We reached Puno just as the sun was setting. With its winding and narrow cobblestone streets that appeared always to climb and dingy adobe houses facing each other, Puno had more the appearance of a forlorn hamlet than a city. "How did you use your time?" I once asked a colleague who had spent an entire year as a graduate student in Puno. He replied that he had "smoked marijuana and learned to speak Quechua."

That night we boarded a steamer that would carry us overnight to Bolivia on a voyage across Lake Titicaca, 12,500 feet above sea level and half the size of Lake Ontario. The ship, an ocean-going vessel, had been hauled up to Lake Titicaca by English investors who had built the railroad, a spectacular feat of engineering. We ate supper with arrogant and boisterous German tourists and had to listen to middle-aged American school teachers gripe about traveling conditions, but, thankfully for my cold, we slept well in cabins of our own. On the Bolivian shore, another train carried us over the altiplano, the monotony of its bleak landscape broken by an occasional village of adobe huts and the never absent llama. Like Peru, this was the land of the potato, which the poor ate in sundry dishes, and a country where women, none five feet tall, wore black derby hats and four or five skirts. La Paz, the site of a silver bonanza in colonial days, perched in a valley 12,000 feet above sea level but, unbelievably, surrounded by snow-capped Andean peaks that towered above it. We had to descend in order to reach the city. Compared to Mexico City or Lima, La Paz did not offer much to see. The Spaniards left behind few testimonial wonders to their centuries of activity. We lingered days in La Paz, fighting the altitude and the biting cold and lying in heatless hotel rooms while trying to buy tickets for the train ride to Villasol, our last stop in Bolivia.

We were warned not to leave without Pullman accommodations, but in the haste to move on we ignored the advice, to our ultimate regret. It is said that train travel is the great leveler because it induces the heady spirit of comradeship. Well, yes and no. On second class, at every train stop—and it seemed as though there were countless of them—passengers could not leave their seats because Indian women, every one of them carrying huge bags on their shoulders, crawled through the open train windows and took those seats, as my companions quickly learned when they stepped outside for fresh air. On one such occasion, as Roger and his friends waited to get back on, an Indian woman was boosted through the window and her pile of parcels were passed through to her. She stacked them on three of the seats Roger and the others were occupying and ignored them. As they stood in the aisle, a young

Bolivian soccer player (with anti–United States bias, according to Roger) predicted in a loud voice that they would make a "typical Norteamericano scene." Instead, they waited by the aisle until the woman, a hardy country type, asked if they would help rearrange her parcels. By the end of the trip, Roger believes, she had become their "friend," and "the soccer player was noticeably disappointed." For my part, as night approached, I had dreaded visions of a sleepless night guarding my seat. Luckily, at one of the stops, thanks to a good-hearted conductor, I was able to buy a Pullman berth. Until then, not one had been available, no matter how much we cajoled agents and porters. Selfishly I abandoned Roger and his friends to their fate. In Villasol, which turned out to be a hamlet, we slept in a room and were awakened by the grunts of pigs outside the door.

On the next morning, we crossed by foot to La Quiaca; we had entered Argentina. Everything began to change, especially because we all acquired Pullman berths, except that it took Roger and company a day to figure out that to get a bed they had to bribe the conductor. The trains ran on time and were much better, newer and cleaner. The food, mostly beef, was tasty, and red wine plentiful. Tucumán, the Argentine province where we started our journey, was one of the poorest in Argentina but, even so, far richer than the Bolivia we left behind. As the train moved south, the countryside began to change, no longer hilly or mountainous but flat and green. We were traveling through the outer pampa and soon through the pampa itself, a 250,000-square-mile fertile plain where Argentines raised fine beef and farmed wheat for export. It was a land shorn of trees. It is said that Charles Darwin once quipped that "trees do not love the pampas." No longer were there Indians in bowlers; the closer we got to Buenos Aires, the more European the inhabitants appeared. From the windows of our train, we started to see gauchos on horseback, the legendary Argentine cowboy: baggy trousers, their ends pushed into boots worn just below the knee, and flat-brimmed hats. When beef was king, the gaucho was Argentina. As we traveled through the pampa, I began to recall stanzas from "Martín Fierro," a poem by José

Hernández, and to remember reading "Santos Vega," another of the gaucho poems, which spoke of manly deeds, fights to the death, and a cowboy's life on the pampa. This pampa scene, I thought, must have been how the American Middle West appeared at the end of the nineteenth century.

Buenos Aires, our destination, was a cosmopolitan city of majestic parks, wide avenues—especially Avenida 9 de Julio, which runs through the city center—and urban plazas in the French style, such as the Plaza de San Martín, named after the father of Argentine independence and designed in 1909 by the chief of public works in Paris. The city incorporated a grid overlaid with diagonal avenues running inland from the river front in the form of a fan. We walked among towering buildings and elegantly dressed men and women who wore their Spanish and Italian ancestry on their faces. An Argentine, so goes one story, is "an Italian who speaks Spanish, dresses like a Frenchman, and thinks he's English." In the heart of Buenos Aires stood the Casa Rosada, where Argentine presidents preside; its cupola encapsulated the nineteenth-century architecture of the city. The Colonia La Boca, now the abode of artists and a place for artisans' shops, was just starting to attract visitors. In the context of food, Argentina meant beef, beef, and more beef. The pampa, a place of cattle ranches, kept Buenos Aires steak houses *(parrillas)* stocked with an endless supply of beef, leaner and tougher but more flavorful than the U.S. variety. Roger recalls that at La Cabaña, a famous steak house with a stuffed Hereford on the sidewalk, we ate thick, juicy, and tender "Chateaubriand King Edward XVI steaks, salad, dessert, and good red wine for the paltry sum of U.S.$1.39." Our desert was *arroz con leche,* rice with milk, sugar, and cinnamon, a dish Mamá had prepared from time to time.

Aside from the beef, what I most remember about eating in the city was the good and cheap wines, the reds in particular. They were heavy and, to the American critic, unbalanced but—like Portuguese reds, which I came to know much later—tasty with food. At Oregon, I had taught a history course that included Argentina, so I was not unaware of its long wine history, which dated from the sixteenth century, when Spanish missionaries planted vines from Peru and Chile in the province of Mendoza. Yet it was essentially an artisan trade until the arrival of thousands of Italian immigrants, many of them amateur wine makers, in the late nineteenth century. When they settled in Mendoza, they made the province the heart of the wine industry. Wineries could also be found in Salta and Jujuy, provinces we traversed by train on our way to Buenos Aires. For a variety of reasons, few outside of Argentina knew anything about its wines, so we were delighted to discover them.

Buenos Aires was the home of the tango, the sensuous Argentine dance that got its start in the latter part of the nineteenth century; music for it was provided by a *bandoneón* (bandonion), a type of accordion; working its bellows, as some argue, is "in itself, an act of nostalgia, . . . like riding a steamer or kneading dough." One characteristic of the instrument is its difficulty with volume control; it always sounds louder than it actually is. The bandoneón, which sits on the knees of the *bandeonista* is, like the accordion, an instrument of suddenness: it can never be suitably introduced because "it asserts itself as a kind of non sequitur." Yet, as the Argentines play it, dolorous and joyous, it is capable of unadulterated sentimentality, as the melancholy sounds of the tango testify. When introduced, the tango, the rage of the *arrabales* or slums, was thought too racy for women to perform in public, so male couples, some dressed in butcher's uniforms, danced together, according to photographs of the era. Try as I might, I have never mastered—according to my wife—its intricate steps. *"Adios muchachos compañeros de mi vida,"* an old and famous tango, was one of my father's favorites: the lament of a gaucho who must say good-bye to lifetime companions. A singer by the name of Carlos Gardel, who died a tragic death in a plane crash and whom I knew from his records, made it famous from one end of Hispanic America to the other. The 1950s, when we were in Buenos Aires, were part of the tango's "golden age."

Buenos Aires was also where my American travelers learned about Argentine sensibilities. At a travel agency, Roger and his friends, instead of waiting for the attractive young woman behind the desk to attend to them, simply grabbed the flight schedule. When she saw this, she said to me, *"Para usted haré todo lo posible* [I will help you], but I won't turn a finger for them." Tellingly, Roger does not remember this incident.

I wanted to stay longer but had to return home to see my wife and daughter and to complete work on the Anderson diaries. A week, more or less, was what I spent in Buenos Aires, a city so unlike others in Latin America, both French and English. There I boarded a plane for home, flew through a pass in the Andes between Aconcagua, the tallest of its peaks, and lesser ones, all capped in white snow and ice, stopping briefly in Santiago, Chile, then on to Lima, where I took a Peruvian airliner bound for Panama City, which had to make an unexpected stop for repairs in Guayaquil, the port city of the Republic of Ecuador. Repairs accomplished, I landed in Panama just minutes before a Mexican airliner took off for Mexico City; my bags were transferred from one plane to the other on the landing strip. Three days later, after visiting my cousin Heriberto and his family, I landed in Tijuana, where Natalia and Olivia were waiting for me. I had been away long enough for Olivia, just a year old, not to recognize her father.

For Roger and his friends, as it turned out, the trip was a memorable one. Later, one of them went on to the Thunderbird School in Arizona and became an international banker, spending a number of years in South America, a good part of them in Buenos Aires. Our trip, he says, was a key factor in the career choice. For Roger, it "ranks as one of the top experiences" in his life and led to a lifelong interest in international travel; he has been almost everywhere, except Australia and Antarctica. Like Mark Twain, Roger insists that "travel is fatal to prejudice, bigotry and narrow-mindedness." Because of the experience on the journey south, he does not make reservations in major cities, except for a few extended stays. He shops for bed-and-breakfasts or small hotels even in the most rural areas so that he can meet the natives. This habit, he writes, stems directly from the South American trip, when by choice and financial indigence we stayed in out-of-the-way places. Roger still remembers how I arranged our stay in a small hotel in

Buenos Aires. "You told the four of us to keep out of sight while you went into the lobby and explained that you were a teacher of modest means traveling with four poor students, and struck a very good deal." Roger's iron-clad rule is never to stay in American-style or American-owned hotels. "I cannot tell you how many fascinating experiences and new friends I have made in this manner," he says. "By comparison, can anyone remember someone of interest they met at a Hilton Hotel?"

And what did I learn from the journey to Buenos Aires? Well, much that should have been obvious from the start: Spanish America is hardly homogeneous. The term *diverse* fits better. Mountains dictated life in some countries—Bolivia, for example— whereas flat plains dominated others, in particular Argentina. Some were heavily Indian, Peru and Bolivia to name two, whereas others were European, Argentina specifically. A few were neither European nor Indian; perhaps Chile best fitted this category. Much of Central America was tropical, a lush, green landscape, hot and humid, yet the highlands of Guatemala were cold. In South America, snowcaps adorn the Andes, an imposing range of huge and jagged rocks, the year round. Yes, the countries shared certain characteristics—namely, the Spanish language, Catholicism, and Roman law, as well as the omnipotent city, a Spanish bequest.

I also came to understand that Mexico, the land of my ancestors, was only partly Spanish America. What most Mexicans' neighbors shared with them was—again—language, Catholicism, and Roman law, but also an infatuation with Mexican popular music, the boleros of Agustín Lara and the mariachi, but the commercial variant and not the traditional version shorn of horns. Then there was literature, modern novels especially, those of Carlos Fuentes and Juan Rulfo in particular. Guatemala, once a Mexican province, was the last stop for *cerveza a la mexicana,* where one feasted on corn tortillas and never wanted for chile sauces. True, as far south as Honduras one could eat tortillas, but its tamales were poor cousins of the Mexican variety. From then on, it was another culinary world; though Peruvians liked to boast that they, too, ate chile, nowhere there did one enjoy *salsas de chile,* a Mexican delicacy.

So I came to conclude that talk of a Spanish American culture distorts the truth. Distant cousins, yes, but hardly brothers and sisters.

9

Smith

—

Smith College offered the kind of teaching job I had wanted since I was at Berkeley: at a tony liberal arts school where learning took precedence over vocational goals. National politics, nonetheless, tempered that joy. We had a Cold War, when Ike, a soldier-hero, sat in the White House alongside Richard Nixon, a notorious Red baiter, and heeded the advice of men ready to assert Washington's hegemony over the "Free World," while most Americans, who worshiped Ike, blotted out memories of war and the Great Depression and hated communists.

New England denoted a one and only experience. Nature and man's hands had sculpted a topography very unlike California's—a bizarre landscape of hills, streams, and fir and pine trees nourished by heavy rains and winter snows. Old colonial houses; simple, wooden churches; and cemeteries of men and women long dead were commonplace. These relics of yesteryear called up memories of the majestic cathedrals and rolling aqueducts of colonial Mexico. Unlike my native California, New England had a past. Driving there and watching the scenery turn green was an adventure, especially once we crossed the long bridge over the Mississippi River and left behind St. Louis, a city built of aging, red bricks, so unlike western hubs. No matter how the years go by, I still recall the sight of Northampton, the home I had chosen for my family, as we approached it by car.

A place of abandoned mills and home to Smith, Northampton bordered the banks of the Connecticut River and was seven miles from Amherst College, a men's institution, and the sprawling campus of the University of Massachusetts. Just beyond was South Hadley, site of Mount Holyoke College, also for women. Townspeople looked upon professors, whom they mistakenly judged well paid, as pillars of a world for the wealthy; merchants welcomed them with open arms, whether they were shopping on Main Street or visiting the boutiques on Green Street, which had a coffee shop and a bookstore, the only one in town.

Between classes, professors, mostly the men, congregated at the coffee shop, one being Al Fisher of the English department, who, when younger, had married and divorced three Smithies. After one of them left him, she wrote a book under the title *How to Cook a Wolf*. Smoking a cigarette and holding a cup of coffee in his hand, Al usually could be found at one of the tables, eager to listen to campus gossip, especially if it involved professors who played around with Smithies. When I arrived at Smith, Al was no longer married, just an aging charmer who had enjoyed better days.

Our house, a three-story Victorian that was the property of the college, sat on a bluff above Paradise Pond and just steps from the biggest dormitories. Day in and day out, we were among Smithies, a novel experience; both Natalia and I were graduates of public institutions, whose students were mainly commuters. At Smith, they rode bicycles to class, during the winter in raccoon coats, with scarfs wrapped around their necks and woolen hats pulled down over their ears. On weekends, they deserted the campus, bound for Dartmouth, Yale, or some other men's campus. Saturday mornings the hallways of the classroom buildings were stacked with the luggage of students leaving for the weekend. To us, this pageantry was a novelty, especially in the winter when a blanket of snow covered streets, houses, and trees.

Our house had been the residence of a professor spending her last sabbatical in France; her husband had recently run off with a Smithie. Eventually the college said it was ours to keep, largely as an inducement to remain at Smith because I had received an offer from Dartmouth College. What I most remember about the three-story house was the noise from the furnace in the basement, which during the winter months ran constantly, eating up fuel oil to heat up the water for the metal heaters that stood in the upstairs rooms giving off weird sounds at night. The college sent someone to fix anything that went awry, to put up storm windows, and to clear the driveway of snow. The path from the house to my office in the library wandered by the president's house, where during the summer Nelly Mendenhall, his wife, from the kitchen window might invite me for a drink as I passed by on the home in the evening.

We spent our first New England Christmas in Northampton. Early in December, the snow began to fall, turning trees and lawns a milky white. Natalia and I had seen snow in Denver during the war and later in Eugene, but not like this. This was heavy snow, just as Christmas cards pictured it. Student carolers came to serenade us; all that was missing was a horse and a sleigh. That excitement, however, did not last forever. After a year or two of the dreary cold, we began to dream of March, when spring arrived; as the crocuses broke ground and then the daffodils, so did our hopes that spring was on its way, only to have them frozen when more snow descended on us.

Six years later we purchased a house just outside Williamsburg, ten miles north of the campus. Built in 1792, the house perched on nine acres of land on a knoll above a village that dated from the seventeenth century. Of brick and mortar under a slate roof, the house, which resembled an English country cottage, was painted white, with windows and shutters of wood in black. Two chimneys bracketed the house like a pair of matching bookends. Attached barns in faded red paint ran out from its rear, their roofs of corrugated tin. From the kitchen and dining-room windows, we could see the countryside; in the fall, when the leaves changed color, we had a kaleidoscope of colors around us. Across the road was a cemetery with grave stones that harked back centuries; we could not have asked for quieter neighbors. Old houses, however, have problems; ours needed fixing. Before we were through with the repairs, we had remodeled it—to the horror, I am sure, of purists, a fixture in New England. In one barn, we kept the cars, and in the other a horse for Olivia. The two of us built a stable for Tiburcio, the name we gave the gelding, and on the lawn above the house put up jumps for Olivia to take on the horse. In the winter when it was cold, sometimes below zero, Olivia and I got up at the crack of dawn to feed Tiburcio, clean out the stable, shovel the manure onto a wheelbarrow, and dump it outside.

While at Smith, too, we filled out our family. Maura, our younger daughter, was born six years after we arrived, at the Cooley Dickenson Hospital. Natalia and I will always remember the hospital, not only because of Maura's birth but also because it was where Olivia, our firstborn, had an operation to repair a small hernia—our initial brush with health problems for our children. We took her to the hospital, where they sedated her and, while we watched, wheeled her by us to the operating room. She was just two years old and looked small and frail on that big bed with wheels. We kept a vigil until they brought her, still sedated, out of surgery. We went home and slept badly, and bright and early the next morning we were back at the hospital, where we found Olivia laughing and jumping up and down on her bed in the children's ward. For a time, Natalia stayed home to care for Olivia and then for Maura, but when the college offered her a temporary post, she accepted and taught Spanish for three years, moving from there to Holyoke Community College and then to the Northampton School for Girls.

Northampton and Smith were miles apart from Eugene and Dallas, not merely distancewise, but timewise, too. Not only was Smith an old school, but Northampton, a town dating back to the seventeenth century, was an integral part of colonial history, where Jonathan Edwards, a stalwart of the "Great Awakening," the famous religious crusade, was born. His father, also a minister, had his church in the town.

Originally a red-brick school founded in the 1880s, Smith was a women's college. We addressed the students as "Miss," and they in turn addressed us as "Mr.," "Mrs.," or "Miss." Most of the students were serious; only once in long while did I encounter a bad apple. We did not hesitate to assign ten books a semester; not until I left Smith did I learn that students at other schools thought ten books an "awful lot of reading." Smithies could also write; they knew their grammar, spelling, and sentence construction.

What troubled me was that these students tended to think alike. Once in a while I ran into a hard-core conservative but seldom a radical. Even the tiny handful of African Americans, though bitter on the subject of race, rarely dissented, though occasionally a bright Jewish student from New York City might surprise me. These were the passive 1950s, when Republicans managed affairs in Washington and spineless Democrats ran to keep up with them. Rarely did a student want to be labeled a conservative, even though thinking like one and voting for Ike and Dick. They claimed to be "liberal Republicans" and read avidly David Riesman's *The Lonely Crowd,* a critique of the American tendency to conform, which claimed that when a society became "other directed," people sought peer approval by accepting group dictates. Smithies worshiped the book, unable to see that Riesman, perhaps unintentionally, had careers in business—which many of their parents had—in his gunsight.

Whatever else Smith may have been, it was an elite school. Its students, a majority from eastern states, were chosen with care. They were daughters of college-educated parents who read newspapers and books and enrolled their children in private schools, such as Emma Willard, Dana Hall, and the Chapin School. Though the campus was tinged with a bit of a social conscience, money ran it; members of the board of trustees were usually well off. Minority students were almost absent, except for an occasional Jew or African American, usually the daughter of a Republican. The only daughter of a working-class family was the student from Northampton or nearby Hadley who attended Smith on a fellowship because her father or mother was a gardener or cook on campus.

Not infrequently I taught the daughters of millionaires; one of them, an American businessman in Brazil, flew a horse to Northampton because his daughter complained about the one she rode. Smith had an indoor riding ring and horse shows. In our classes, we had the daughters of ambassadors, Central Intelligence

Agency chiefs, chairmen of the *New York Times,* and heads of the New York Stock Exchange. These students, the beneficiaries of small classes and dedicated teachers, received an excellent education.

Tradition and pageantry were highly prized. As graduation day dawned, alumnae from all over the country filled the campus. They arrived to celebrate class reunions, occasions for old grads to talk about their days on campus. One event was a very special one: there was a parade; the oldest grads, all dressed in white and some walking with the help of canes, led it, behind a college band playing martial airs. Professors, their wives, and children watched from the sidelines. On the reviewing stand in front of the library, Thomas Corwin Mendenhall, the college president, surveyed the scene with benevolent eyes.

Tom, as we knew him, was popular with old grads and students alike. Tall, a bit portly, and a flamboyant dresser, he looked very much the part of a college president. Before donning his robes, he had been master of a house at Yale and coach of its rowing team. He was also a professor of naval history and for a year or two lectured in one of my courses. In the fall, just as the semester was under way, the Mendenhalls hosted black-tie balls for the faculty. By the mid-1960s, faculty radicals, the beards, and sloppy clothes put an end to these affairs. Fancy balls were no longer in style.

Most of us who taught at Smith thought well of Tom, who tried to keep us happy. Soon after we arrived, Natalia fell ill and required an operation, and we had neither money nor a health plan to fall back on, but a check arrived by mail with a note from Tom: he wanted us to know that Smith had not forgotten us. At another time, I went to see Tom in his College Hall office to complain on behalf of four of us who played tennis that the men's dowdy shower room on one side of the women's gym had no hooks on which to hang coats and pants; the next day, when we arrived to change into our tennis clothes, there were hooks on the walls. Tom personally had put them there.

Unlike trustees and students, the faculty at Smith came from less well-heeled backgrounds. True, there were graduates of

Harvard, Yale, and Columbia, but also and increasingly so from New York's City College and Brooklyn College. By and large, western universities were poorly represented and usually held in low esteem, with the exceptions of Berkeley and Stanford. A large majority of professors were Anglo-Americans, though Jews had begun to join their ranks. I was the only professor of Mexican ancestry, but a woman from Spain and a man from Argentina taught in the Spanish department.

There was something remarkable about Smith: its faculty believed in what the college stood for. This was especially so among old-timers who had been teaching for years. As Jean Wilson, former chair of the history department, told me, "Mr. Ruiz, we don't need outsiders telling us who to keep." She was referring to the common practice in universities of asking for outside opinions whenever a promotion was contemplated for a colleague. At most institutions, whether in academe or business, there exist rivalries and petty politics. At Smith, common sense usually prevailed when appointments and promotions came up for a vote; we got along no matter how big our disagreements. Some colleagues did not care for others, but we all spoke to each other and even shared a drink or two at the faculty club.

Women in large numbers taught at Smith. They made up nearly half the faculty, were heavily recruited, and carried real weight in departments or on campus. When they spoke, men listened. One I came to appreciate was Vera Lee Brown Holmes, the Latin Americanist I replaced. A tall, gangling, and dour Canadian, she was a scholar, the author of the massive two-volume *History of the Americas,* which, unlike Herbert E. Bolton's version, wrestled with the question of why some countries move ahead and others stay behind. She was instrumental in my coming to Smith. She wanted her course "The History of the Americas" taught by someone familiar with the concept. Thanks to Abe Nasatir, I had taken the Bolton version at San Diego State.

By car, Smith was just three hours away from New York City, or we could ride the train, at first from Northampton and then from Springfield, Massachusetts. The city had theaters, film houses, museums, and of course restaurants galore. Nearly every major publishing house had offices in the city, and sessions with editors were arranged easily. There were meetings of the American Historical Association, as well as those of its special committees. I began to review books on Mexico for the *New York Times,* a special honor for those of us in Latin American history, a subject never considered a high priority for the nation's newspapers. Why I was asked remains a mystery. It began simply enough: one day, to my utter surprise, a letter arrived at Smith from the *Times* asking if I would review a book on Mexico.

The proximity to New York City also meant that I saw celebrities occasionally, the first of them on my way to interview for the job at Smith. I had boarded a DC-3, the twin-engine World War II workhorse, at La Guardia airport for the trip to Bradley Field, an airport serving Northampton. The other passengers and I, except for one seat, had filled the plane but were kept waiting on the ground for some unexplained reason, until suddenly a woman got on the plane and walked by me on her way up the isle; it was Eleanor Roosevelt. She was the first of the celebrities I met, but not the last—among them Dorothy Day, the Catholic crusader; Dean Acheson, architect of Washington's Cold War diplomacy, with whom I had dinner; and Helen Gahagan Douglas, the actress, for whom Natalia and I hosted a cocktail party. She spoke eloquently and cheerfully about nearly everyone in Washington, until Richard Nixon's name cropped up; she never forgave him for the Red baiting he employed against her during the campaign for a senate seat in the election in California of 1950. Thanks to a lecture I gave at the Chapin School in New York City, I also came to know Herbert Matthews, an editorial writer for the *New York Times* who was celebrated for being the first American reporter to interview Fidel Castro in the Sierra Maestra and who went on to write two widely read books on revolutionary Cuba. With Matthews, I spent an evening with the head of the Cuban Interest Section of that government.

In Northampton, apart from cocktails and dinners at colleague's homes, not too much occurred, so when time and money permitted, we were off to spend a weekend in New York City. For someone raised in tiny Pacific Beach, Park Avenue and the jostling crowds on Times Square, previously known to us only from watching Movietone News, made memorable visits to the city. I met scholars of Latin America teaching at Columbia University and at the City Colleges. We saw Broadway theater, once catching Jason Robards, that premier interpreter of Eugene O'Neill's plays, in the role of a troubled leftist intellectual in the shameful days of the witch hunts.

When I arrived at Smith in the fall of 1958, I was an assistant professor; I left as a full professor. In those twelve years, I like to think that I brought to the campus a fresh perspective on Latin American history. The principal course that I inherited had fallen on hard times, and the survey was struggling to survive. As Vera Lee Brown Holmes got older, she had been unable to keep up enrollments. I worked hard to revive them; when I left Smith, I had as many as eighty students learning about Mexico, Argentina, and Brazil, the countries I emphasized, and the senior seminar had more applicants than I could accept—large classes by Smith standards. Some of the students were women from Mount Holyoke College and men from Amherst College. That increased enrollment plus two books—*Mexico: The Challenge of Poverty and Illiteracy* and a small volume of essays titled *The Mexican War: Was It Manifest Destiny?*—earned me tenure and eventually the full professorship.

For a while, I thought that we were set for life in New England. Given our ties to Mexico, that belief may have rung hollow, but from our perspective it made a lot of sense. Smith attracted some of the best students in the country. This was the age of segregated schools, when Ivy League colleges shut their doors to women. The brightest among them, particularly on the East Coast, attended one of the Seven Sisters, the women's institutions. Smith was the largest of them, with strong departments, especially the art department, where Russell Hitchcock and Phyllis Lehmann, historians of note, and Leonard Baskin, the artist, reigned supreme, and the English department, where Newton Arvin and Daniel Aaron, distinguished literary critics, stood out.

At a small college, you get to know colleagues, not just because they teach alongside you, but because you socialize with them. These were both departmental and campuswide relationships. One of my oldest friendships dates from my first day at Smith. Frank Ellis, a scholar of eighteenth-century English literature, a specialist on Daniel Defoe and Jonathan Swift, joined the faculty when I did. He was a rather tall man, with auburn hair combed to one side but thinning at the top, a sign of approaching middle age. Blessed with a hearty laugh and a boyish grin, he never failed to shake hands, whether welcoming you to his home or entering yours. He was a veteran of World War II, hailed from Kansas, and thought of himself as an easterner—through his wife having some claim to it. Connie was from New York, had gone to Vassar, and during its transition from a woman's college to a coed one had chaired its board of trustees. Frank got along splendidly with the older women professors who dominated conversation at the afternoon tea parties in the library; he never missed one, and I never attended one.

I remember fondly Ely Chinoy, a graduate of Brooklyn college, a sociologist of note, and the author of a reputable book on auto workers. Suspicious of pretentious Anglo colleagues, he, unlike Frank, came from a poor family and took pride in being a Jew. He could never fathom why Frank, whom he hardly knew, and I were friends. He was one of the liberals on campus, though hardly a firebrand. Richard Young, a professor in the English department, had lost a leg in World War II when his jeep ran over a land mine and, after a whiskey or two, became testy. Richard Judson seldom spoke of his Jewish father, but waxed on about his sailing prowess, and wrote on seventeenth-century Dutch art. With his wife Kelly, a graduate of Smith, he joined the Ellises and Ruizes and sometimes the Youngs at tailgate parties at football games between Amherst and Williams Colleges.

I will never forget those affairs: the "Potted Ivy League" at its traditional best, when old grads, nearly all red-blooded Anglos, came together, ostensibly to watch a football game—rain, sleet, or snow—between two rivals. The games, whether at Williamstown or Amherst, took place before no more than two or three thousand fans, the men in coats and ties and their wives in fur coats, as well as students and their dates, everyone sitting on temporary bleachers. The grads came largely to see companions of yesteryear, drink martinis, eat a hearty meal, and yell their heads off. None of us were old grads but nonetheless joined in the merrymaking, not caring which team won. Our wives cooked pork sausages on a charcoal burner, and Frank, who enjoyed bar tending, served martinis, the more the merrier. At these events, I realized then, as I do now, that I was a long, long way from Pacific Beach.

At Smith, I was free to interpret Spanish American life and culture to my heart's content. True, I aspired to be a scholar of national repute. Universities that specialized in Latin American studies, such as Texas and Berkeley, would have appeared ideal, but they did not come calling. When they brought people in, they wanted scholars to walk in step with the dictates of current fads in the profession, which meant writing for the *Hispanic American Historical Review,* publishing books with university presses, and reading papers before audiences of peers. Departments hired to fill specific slots—nineteenth-century Peru, colonial Mexico, or modern Argentina, for example. They seldom went out of their way to hire a person of superior teaching skills. In the candidate's baggage, that skill might be a plus, but departments always discovered ways to circumvent the commitment to good teaching—although usually touted on the printed page of university catalogs.

At these universities, a Mexican background was hardly an asset. Their professors rarely prized ethnic or cultural diversity; they wanted scholars in their mold, no matter how little Spanish they spoke or how oblivious they were to Spanish American life. It mattered not a whit to most of them whether I, given my background, might bring a Latin American perspective to students on campus and perhaps fresh insights to research. That is why in 1957, when an opening at the University of Texas occurred, I never bothered to apply, though I taught at SMU just down the road. Later events tended to confirm my wariness because the man picked for the job at Texas—a New Englander and Harvard graduate denied tenure at his alma mater—retired as a full professor best known for the monographs he failed to write.

I wrote my doctoral thesis on Mexican rural education, the schooling of campesinos. Since then, one or two others have explored the subject, but the education of campesinos or of urban workers, equally important, rarely draws the attention of history scholars of Latin America. However, the Spanish version of my dissertation, *México, 1920–1958: El reto de la pobreza y del analfabetismo,* which the Fondo de Cultura Económica published, was for years used by professors who taught at the Escuela Normal Superior in Mexico City, the most prestigious of the pedagogical institutes.

Smith, on the other hand, prized cultural variety, as the number of European professors, some in history, testified. To my colleagues, especially the older ones, I was a Latin American, and students often saw me that way, too. I aspired to teach, and Smith demanded that its professors teach and teach well. Bad teaching meant denial of tenure or skimpy salary raises and slow promotions. Initially I was delighted but with the passing of time came to dislike having to teach outside of my research interests.

One other factor explains my eagerness to live in New England. An advantage of living in the Southwest was that I was usually among Mexicans and in some cases close to Mexico. That, nonetheless, was also a burden because prejudice against Mexicans, a standard fare in those days, grew the more Mexicans there were. By the 1950s, I had had my share of the bigotry, whether subtle or not, and did not wish for Olivia, our daughter, to have to put up with this nonsense. As Arturo Arnaiz y Freg, a scholar in Mexico, once told me, "If you wish to escape this bigotry, go east." That was good advice. Easterners were just as bigoted, but not necessarily against Mexicans, whom they rarely saw. The bigots hated Jews, Italians, and the Irish, to name just three. In New England, so far as I can tell, I personally never encountered racial hostility.

In Northampton, I met just one other Mexican, a graduate student in philosophy from Mexico City. Margarita Valdez—a bright, articulate, very tall, and thin woman—was terribly upset, and rightly so, over soldiers' murder of Mexican students at the Plaza de Tlaltelolco in 1968. This bloody butchery cost the despotic rulers of Mexico dearly, marking the start of the decline of the myth of the caring president. It was plain that Gustavo Díaz Ordaz, who ordered the massacre, was anything but a benevolent ruler. The fall from grace of the PRI began at Tlaltelolco. Margarita had something else on her mind: Luis Villoro, the distinguished Mexican philosopher whom she swore she would marry. It was through her that we came to know Luis, a friend since those days. Margarita would later become a professor of philosophy at UNAM in Mexico City.

Yes, Natalia and I missed things Mexican. We compensated by spending summers in Mexico, where we saw old friends and renewed ties with relatives. We attended the theater, where we watched a performance of Bertolt Brecht's *The Maids* and heard *My Fair Lady* and *Cat on a Hot Tin Roof* sung in Spanish. A highlight of one of our visits was hearing the composer and singer Agustín Lara, *el músico poeta,* at the Teatro Lírico; he personified the bolero, a rhythm of Cuban ancestry he made "Mexican" by adopting the distinctively French tradition of songs that combine poetic lyrics with catchy melodies.

In Northampton, Natalia also cooked Mexican dishes, not just once in a while but daily. We drove to stores in Hartford and New York City to buy special ingredients, returning with chile peppers; red *mole* to make *pollo en mole poblano,* a Puebla delicacy; and bags of *masa harina,* corn flour to make tortillas. Natalia and I spoke Spanish to each other and with Olivia and Maura. Unless you speak the language, you cannot keep alive the culture, and we did not want to toss into the wastebasket years spent with parents and relatives from another world.

On a Fulbright in 1965, we spent a year in Monterrey, the industrial bastion of northern Mexico, a city two hundred miles from Laredo, Texas. These were the years of the Milagro Mexicano (Mexican Miracle), a recipe for industrialization under the tutelage of a rich and powerful conservative mafia blind to the plight of workers and campesinos. Monterrey was undergoing a metamorphosis from a provincial capital to a sophisticated metropolis and was now home to one million people. A cultural center had been built, where actors from Mexico City performed the latest plays. Studio artists were finding customers for their works, and boutiques and cafés were making their appearance, catering to young people eager to ape their cousins in Mexico City.

I was in Monterrey to teach at the Facultad de Economía of the Universidad Autónoma de Nuevo León, the state university. What a year it was; reflecting on it, I don't think I ever enjoyed a group of students more. One stood out above the rest: Ignacio Olivares, the student body president even though a junior. Nacho, as he was known, never missed a class. He was not brilliant but conscientious, usually completing his homework on time, a must in the class on Mexican economic history taught on the discussion method, which challenged students to think for themselves and not just regurgitate what they read. Neither very conservative nor liberal, Nacho was a pragmatist and seldom ventured opinions on Mexican politics, though, if pushed to take a stand, he conceded the absence of social justice. He was a PRIista who voted the ruling-party line. Liked by all and respected by his mentors, Nacho was the last person I thought who would rock the PRI's political boat, yet that is exactly what he did later, during the student protests of 1968, when the regime had soldiers shoot students in Mexico City and relied elsewhere on goons of diverse sorts. When this occurred, Nacho, whose loyalty to fellow students knew no bounds, joined the ranks of the protestors and for doing so was tortured and beaten to death in Guadalajara—by thugs, it is claimed, hired by the wealthy of Monterrey.

On the brighter side of life, students, Nacho among them, asked me to be their faculty sponsor on a visit to the Universidad de Guadalajara, and Natalia and I attended university dances, where two bands played: one that played rock 'n' roll for students and one that played rumbas and *danzones* for faculty. We sat at the main table, guests of Eduardo Suárez, the dean, and his wife, Alicia. The two could not have been more different; he was introverted, and she, if not gregarious, was certainly outgoing. He was swarthy, anything but handsome, and she fair of skin, almost pretty and popular. We had been in Monterrey only a week or so when they invited us to dinner. At the end of the year, when I was about to leave, the third-year class, my special responsibility, hosted a farewell dinner for us at a private home. By that time, we had made a host of friends, among them a psychiatrist whose parties lasted until three or four in the morning. Natalia took classes, and we joined the Club Hípico de Monterrey, the riding club, and bought a horse so that Olivia and I might ride.

At night, I caught up with the recent fiction by Mexican authors, thanks to Salomón González Almazán, a colleague with literary interests at the Facultad de Economía, who always came up with something new to read. Not since Berkeley, when I was boning up on Spanish American literature, had I kept abreast of the latest fiction by Mexicans. At Salomón's urging, I read *Aura,* a stream-of-consciousness piece, a style I dislike; *Las buenas conciencias;* novels by Carlos Fuentes, author of *La muerte de Artemio Cruz,* a master work; and Juan Rulfo's *Pedro Páramo,* set in the days of the revolution, a novel that ranked him among the giants of Spanish America. I had to read it again and again before I could grasp completely its meaning. The *Tres cuentos* of Agustín Yáñez, author of *Al filo del agua,* a ponderous novel, was a joy to read. Juan José Arreola's *La feria* and Gustavo Sainz's *Gazapo*, a novel about urban youth, were others I remember reading.

Had I not wanted to return to Smith, I would have stayed on another year. That might have been a mistake. Suárez, the dean of the Facultad de Economía, had asked that I teach one more year, offering to match the Fulbright stipend. I nearly accepted, tempted in part because we could have kept Olivia and Maura in Mexican schools; Maura, as a matter of fact, learned to speak first in Spanish, then, back home, in English, which she mastered easily. Fortunately, as it turned out, I chose to return to Smith. I say "fortunately" because near the end of the semester Suárez had to resign because of sexual harassment charges against him.

Since those days, Lucas de la Garza, son of the governor of Nuevo León in the early 1940s, has been a friend of mine. We taught together at the Facultad de Economía, and when classes were over for the day, Lucas would sometimes invite me to his house, where his mother, with the help of a servant, would serve us dinner in the kitchen. She was everything but pretentious. She once joked that her son was so enamored of revolutionary change that, had she not opposed it, "he would have expropriated the family ranch and given the lands to campesinos." Lucas is a *cuate* (buddy), as he puts it, of Cuauhtémoc Cárdenas—son of the late president, a former governor of Michoacán, until recently mayor of the Federal District, and three times presidential candidate of the Partido de la Revolución Democrática (PRD). When Cárdenas ran for the first time, Lucas, then a stalwart of the PRI, resigned his post as *secretario de gobernación* of Nuevo León, second in ranking only to the governor, to join his *cuate* on the campaign trail. Had Lucas not resigned, he might have become governor of his state. On Cárdenas's third try for the presidency, Lucas was his campaign manager.

What I most recall about Lucas are the *tertulias* (soirees) we had at the home of Ario Garza Mercado, son of a former congressman. Mari, his wife, was a friend of Natalia; the two took classes together from Jaime and Pablo Flores, up-and-coming artists. On weekend evenings, we would come together for food, drink, and talk, joined by Salomón and perhaps others, all politically left of center. These *tertulias* could last until the wee hours of the morning. The topic was always Mexico and invariably the so-called Mexican Miracle, which spurred the gross national product but betrayed the promises of the revolution and relegated concern for the underdog to the trash barrel. Lucas and I were usually the most outspokenly critical, particularly of the conservative and corrupt PRI bosses and their wealthy business allies.

On the way back to Northampton, we stopped off in Austin, Texas, so that I could teach a summer session there. For the first time in my career, I met professors of my own background. One was George I. Sánchez, whose book *Forgotten People* I had read at San Diego State and who, like me, had written a book on Mexican education. This encounter with Sánchez, I confess, left me disappointed because he turned out to be a critic of the Cuban Revolution and, if not conservative, a Texan in his politics. Much younger, Américo Paredes was starting his career as a scholar of Mexican American folklore, a career crowned by his book *"With a Pistol in His Hand,"* which relates the struggles of a Texas Mexican against the persecution of Anglos. I also had Mexican American students in class, specifically one from Crystal City, the birthplace of the Raza Unida Party, a militant civil rights band. I don't remember much about him, except that he was jovial and wanted to teach school, yet he became a stalwart of the party.

Of lasting impact, I met Arturo Azuela, eventually a prolific novelist, but then studying for a master's in mathematics. He had heard about me from Romeo Flores Caballero, a native of Monterrey and a student of mine. Arturo started attending my lectures, and after class we would discuss Mexican history. Azuela, of course, was a famous name in Mexico: Arturo's grandfather was Mariano Azuela, author of *Los de abajo,* the first of the novels about the Mexican Revolution. The world is a strange place, however. Arturo gave up his mathematical ambitions to write novels and to teach at UNAM, whereas Romeo, who earned a doctorate in history at Austin, abandoned his early aspirations to enter politics and became a *diputado federal* (congressman) for the PRI. As a student at Austin, Romeo delighted in poking fun at the hypocrisy of Mexican bureaucrats and politicos of the PRI. He did it very well, for he was a born comedian. Today, he is a PRIista, wealthy and no longer fun.

The 1960s, so unlike Ike's era, were years of unrest. The turmoil began in 1959, when Fidel Castro and his band of young rebels toppled the corrupt regime of Fulgencio Batista, along with his wealthy allies a puppet of Washington and of U.S. sugar interests. The U.S. quota for sugar served as the underpinning of the Cuban economy and likewise was the reason for its ups and downs. Seasonal unemployment was rampant, poverty always there, and racism never out of sight. More than one-fourth of the Cubans were either black or mulatto; they were not only poor, but also were excluded from beaches and hotels reserved for the rich and wealthy tourists. Gambling mafias from Las Vegas ran the casinos for the pleasure of Americans and rich Cubans. When the Fidelistas started to introduce social justice, American investors balked, but the Cubans began to nationalize their properties anyway, to the anguish of Washington. Wealthy Cubans and their middle-class allies, mostly white, began to flee to Miami, as Nixon talked of a communist plot. When Washington canceled the sugar quota, the Fidelistas turned to the Soviet Union for help, and the U.S. embargo followed.

Until then, Cuban affairs had never been high on my priority list. At Berkeley, no one had offered a course on Cuba, and no question on Cuba had ever been asked on our doctoral exams. In 1927, Charles E. Chapman, a professor at Berkeley, had published *A History of the Cuban Republic,* a racist diatribe not taken seriously by anyone today. On my own, however, I had done some reading on Cuba, especially because of the Platt Amendment, which converted Cuba into a virtual colony of the United States. I was familiar with the Cuban struggle for independence, their efforts to throw off the American yoke, and sympathized with them. Cubans had every right to be free of the United States and to manage their own affairs.

Initially Cuba had sympathizers. Fidel was seen as a romantic revolutionary, young and idealistic. Then, when he jeopardized U.S. holdings on the island, sympathizers turned critics. I recall a debate with Donald Sheehan, a historian and future president of Whitman College, in which he labeled Cuban communism "immoral." In those days, I also began to write editorials on Latin America for the *New Republic,* then a supposedly leftist journal; the day I sent the editors an article that upheld Cuba's right to confiscate foreign property and they refused to publish it was the day that concluded my brief flirtation with the magazine. Convinced of the justice of the Cuban struggle, I joined the Fair Play for Cuba Committee. When John F. Kennedy went along with Nixon's scheme to employ disgruntled Cuban refugees to invade the island and it failed, I jumped with joy. At last, a Latin American nation had withstood the arrogance of U.S. leaders and survived.

During these years, lamentably, no scholar of Latin American history left his reputation imbedded in stone. Like politicos, pundits of television, newspapers, and magazines, scholars almost unanimously judged events in the Southern Hemisphere by whether or not leaders, dictators included, hued to Washington's anticommunist paranoia. Historians fawned on the Mexican Revolution of 1910; never mind that prominent Mexicans, among them Mariano Azuela, a medical doctor with Francisco Villa, had painted a divergent picture in *Los de abajo*, a gripping novel. Howard Cline became dean of Mexican history with his book *Mexico: Revolution to Evolution, 1940–1960*, which eulogized the shameful doings of Miguel Alemán and his cronies, who in truth shot down agrarian reform, crushed strikes, replaced labor spokesmen with *charros* (lackeys), and stuffed their pockets with loot from graft and corruption. John J. Johnson garnered rave reviews with his books *Military and Society in Latin America* and *Political Change in Latin America: The Emergence of the Middle Sectors*, depicting army officers and the middle class as pillars of stability and democracy. In *Arms and Politics in Latin America*, Edwin Lieuwen, a former classmate at Berkeley, put forth a panacea to end the turmoil once and for all: train soldiers to behave like professionals and stop the *cuartelazo*, the military coup. A few years later, *cuartelazos* by professional armies in Brazil, Argentina, and Chile laid to rest that notion.

No surprise, therefore, that Americans were soon reading anti-Fidelista diatribes, usually by authors who spoke Spanish poorly or not at all and had never studied Cuban history. Theodore Draper popularized the "betrayal thesis," the view that middle-class Cubans had fought the revolution for bourgeois ideals—elections and capitalism. By veering left, Fidel had turned his back on them; he had "betrayed the revolution." This was nonsense, as any reading of the Fidelista platform amply demonstrated. So I decided to write my own interpretation, underlining that Cuban aspirations could not be separated from U.S. imperialism. However, publishers kept rejecting the manuscript, so I would look for more material and rewrite. All told, ten rejections arrived by mail, punctuated by unanswered calls from editors and embarrassing replies from colleagues responding to queries. In desperation, I gave the manuscript to Howard Quint, a professor at the University of Massachusetts; he recommended it to the editor of its press. *Cuba: The Making of a Revolution,* published in 1968, was an instant hit; all reviews, with the exception of one by a Cuban refugee, praised it. A few days after a laudatory review appeared in *Book World,* W. W. Norton bought the rights to its publication. In December 1968, *Book World* listed it as one of the twelve best history books for the year.

The book won me entrance into a fraternity of iconoclastic scholars who, unlike their predecessors, no longer simply hued to the anti-Marxist line. During the late 1960s, younger historians had started to question the so-called empirical truths characteristic of the earlier Cold War era. As historian Howard Zinn explains it, we can approach objectivity only by noting the subjectivities faithfully. Issues of race and class were not simply relegated to the dust bin; they took center stage. For the new scholars of the antebellum South, for example, the opinions of African slaves were just as important as those of their white masters. Until then, only Kenneth Stampp and a handful of sympathizers had questioned the veracity of the dominant slavery scholarship of white historians, many of them from the southern states. Others took the class issue by the horns to show that there was more truth in the views of the poor than in those of the pampered rich. A few leftist historians even found jobs in prestigious universities. I could, on occasion, speak my mind. One opportunity came with the invitation to participate with prominent leftist scholars at a meeting in Estes Park, Colorado. Arnold Toynbee, who was there, wrote the introduction to *Struggle Against History*, a book of essays developed from the conference, mine among them.

How many times I spoke on Cuba, I don't remember, generally before college audiences. How many times did I not fly in single-engine planes to give a talk on Cuba at some isolated college campus? One I remember vividly: a week at Beloit College in Wisconsin, along with Saul Landau, the filmmaker; Lee Lockwood, the photographer; and Maurice Zeitlan, a sociologist. The school's custom was to cancel classes so that students could attend these lectures. I gave the evening talk in the chapel; halfway through it, the doors in the back of the chapel opened, and five students in various modes of dress began to walk down the central isle, carrying aloft protest banners against the war in Vietnam. As they approached, I debated with myself whether to continue the talk or cede the podium. Because I sympathized with them, I sat down and waited for them to speak. A black female explained why they were there, asked for faculty support, thanked me, and they left the hall by the way they had entered. The applause from the audience for the protesting students and for my willingness to allow them to speak was deafening.

At first, few at Smith paid much attention to the war in Vietnam, where the people were fighting to shake off French colonialism. With victory, the communists in the north wanted to unify their nation, but their brethren in the south, prodded by Washington, resisted. John Kennedy and then Lyndon Johnson, encouraged by hawkish advisors, saw a communist plot to overrun Southeast Asia orchestrated by China and the Soviet Union. If Vietnam fell, so would all of Southeast Asia. For pundits in Washington, communism, not nationalism, was the culprit. Kennedy first and then Johnson started to dispatch troops and war supplies to buttress the South Vietnamese regime. With Kennedy dead, Johnson, a militant anticommunist, made the war a U.S. one.

Wars are fought by soldiers, and the South Vietnamese were doing a poor job of it. To justify to Americans the need to dispatch more troops, Johnson and his circle of allies concocted the tale of a North Vietnamese attack on U.S. ships in the Gulf of Tonkin. The senate bought the flimsy story; incredibly, only two senators objected, one being Ernest Gruening, author of a book on Mexico. To recruit young men to risk their lives in far-off Asia, American leaders, at first with public support, called on the military draft. Washington had to draft more men as the war went badly and the Viet Cong and ultimately the North Vietnamese army killed more and more of them. When that occurred, the war became unpopular, particularly on college campuses, where students took to the streets, burned flags, and defied their leaders. "Hell no, we won't go" was their cry. But in Washington, first Johnson and then Nixon, elected president in 1968, refused to pull out of Vietnam.

According to the "quagmire" thesis, a popular explanation for the tragic U.S. blunder, well-meaning American leaders stumbled into the war. Arthur Schlesinger Jr., the historian and Kennedy aide, wrote that "the Vietnam adventure was marked much more by ignorance, misjudgment, and muddle than by foresight, awareness, and calculation." No American leader "knowingly defied prescient warnings in order to lurch ahead into what they foresaw as inevitable disaster."

A book by A. J. Langguth, *Our Vietnam: The War, 1954–1975,* disputes this claim, but the author is not the first to do so, merely the latest. His account is a welcomed antidote to the fairytale version of those who carried out the blunder—among them Robert McNamara, who portrays them as intelligent servants of their country. These ultrapatriots, however, were disciples of the Cold War mentality; they saw everything in black and white. Communism generally and the Soviet Union specifically were evil. None of these intellectual warriors displayed Third World sympathies or knew anything about Vietnam, nor had they known, either in their writings or in person, of a U.S. debacle on the battlefield. Once U.S. troops were in Vietnam, moreover, neither Johnson and his Democrats in 1964 nor Nixon and his Republicans in 1968 dared pull them out for fear of an election debacle, for Johnson in 1964 and for Nixon in 1968. No one claims that Kennedy, Johnson, or Nixon made decisions on the war in Vietnam solely on perceived political fortunes, but, as Langguth argues, they were influenced greatly by this consideration. When the war dragged on, the public grew restless, especially after the Tet Offensive of 1968, which saw U.S. marines fighting to defend the U.S. embassy in Saigon.

African Americans, at the same time, had launched a civil rights crusade, demanding the overthrow of Jim Crow in the South, asking for an end to segregated white universities and relying on the law to gain admission. They participated in marches and countermarches, sit-ins, angry rallies; Anglo-American students gradually began to join them. As time went by, Martin Luther King Jr.

joined his struggle to the anti-Vietnam War protest. At Smith, colleagues and students were hardly in the forefront of the antiwar movement but rarely disputed the justice of African Americans' demands. Soon the bravest among them headed south to take a stand against racial bigotry.

From the start, I never supported the war, believing it racist and immoral. By what right did the United States, the richest and most powerful nation in the world, invade a small, impoverished country thousands of miles away? My sympathies were with the Vietnamese. To help the antiwar protest, I did what I could, speaking at teach-ins at the University of Massachusetts, at Amherst College, and at Smith, where most colleagues watched from afar. When I charged that it was a racist war, even liberal friends dissented. *Gooks,* the denigrating moniker applied to the Vietnamese, recalled memories of the use of *Japs* in World War II. As for African Americans' demands for social justice, why would I, a Mexican, the skin the color of the earth, not think them just?

Smith College, however, was not at the helm of antiwar movement; that position was left to Berkeley and to kindred public universities where men, after graduation, faced the military draft. Although many women took leading roles in the protests of the 1960s, Smithies were less willing to rock the boat, being the offspring of a bourgeois culture. Their parents, by the same token, were inseparable from a U.S. regency supportive of the war and for centuries acquiescent in the cruel exploitation of African Americans.

10

Exile's Return

How true the old adage is that you can never go home again, which I learned by heart when I went back to the old haunts. Why return? Certainly not nostalgia; I was not unhappy in New England, where I had a host of friends and a good job. Once in a while, I admit, I felt a bit of nostalgia for bygone days, of parental memories in a land of a lost youth. But as Malcolm Cowley wrote in *Exile's Return* about American expatriates in Europe, even if they "felt homesick," that was not what brought them back. I returned largely to work in a university setting and to teach students of my flesh and blood, an imperative that I had belatedly come to acknowledge. I had outgrown Smith, not that I ever aspired to being a Mr. Chips. I was irrelevant to its students. They were neither poor nor underprivileged nor exploited. They would go on whether I taught them or not.

Yet, by returning, I exchanged a New England replete with historical tradition, some akin to Mexico's, for a California that by 1970 had, without a nod to yesterday, rushed headlong into a world I never knew. It was a time of social unrest. The Vietnam debacle had unleashed a torrent of pent-up anger among Chicanos and African Americans, as well as upset young Anglo men unwilling to risk their necks in an imperialist war. The bombing of Cambodia, mandated by Richard Nixon and his sidekick Henry Kissinger, blew the top off the kettle. On campus, there were marches and countermarches, sit-ins at administration buildings, and strident demands that professors cancel classes. Volkswagen busses full of flower children roamed the streets of La Jolla, the home of right-wing voters. Even the *San Diego Union,* a bastion of conservatism, had moved slightly leftward.

Demographically, an upheaval was taking shape. Mexicans, kin of my parents, were becoming ubiquitous: it was the reconquest of the Southwest. In keeping with national statistics that showed that Mexicans, originally rural dwellers, were now more than 90 percent urbanites, so it was in San Diego. Three decades after I first lived there, nearly one-fifth of its population was Latino, mainly of Mexican ancestry, not just in the corridor from Barrio Logan through National City to Tijuana, but also in outlying communities, even beach towns. There were more Mexicans than blacks, who now shared Imperial Avenue, once their bailiwick, with them. Mexican restaurants serving tacos, tamales, and enchiladas were found everywhere; the food was hardly Mexican, but it pleased the American palate. All groceries carried tortillas, and the big chain stores even stocked separate shelves with "Mexican foods": chile sauces, pinto beans in cans, *menudo,* and *nopalitos* (cactus pads).

San Diego had a small but thriving Mexican middle class. At the dinner of a wedding we once attended, we sat at a table with three psychiatrists of Mexican ancestry. Natalia and I have a physician of Mexican ancestry; to find a dentist or a lawyer of like background, we just need look in the telephone directory. Teachers of Mexican ancestry taught in schools, from elementary on up, and not just in the barrios. Mexicans owned plant nurseries. The Mexican food industry, in particular the making of tortillas, included a host of Mexican American–owned companies.

Nonetheless, most Mexicans still did the dirty work. Pick and shovel labor was their monopoly. They drove the trash trucks, mowed the lawns, trimmed trees, cleaned up hotel rooms, and cooked and scrubbed in private homes, but not necessarily as they did previously. Not long ago I chanced upon a Mexican trimming a hedge, but not with sheers: with a machete! A few days later I came upon a sight totally incongruous with the earlier one: a Mexican raking leaves with a rake in one hand and, with the other, holding a cellular phone to his ear. Restaurants, even the most exclusive—whether Italian, French, or American—had Mexican cooks, waiters, and busboys. Mexicans had infiltrated the building trades, once the monopoly of Anglos; most were dry wallers and roofers, but every once in a while carpenters or house painters.

Some things, however, never change or, if they do, ever so slightly. In San Diego, ethnic minorities were less segregated than in eastern cities, but more segregated than in other California cities. Racial intolerance had not disappeared, it merely had adopted new trappings: mainly learning how to hide it. When Chicano artists took over an abandoned reservoir in Balboa Park and painted murals on its walls, stalwarts of the local community wanted the murals removed because "they were ugly." This community's counterparts at the University of California at San Diego (UCSD) charged, as reported in the *San Diego Union,* that the Third College Program, which focused on minority students, "endangered the university's high standards"; it amounted "to remedial education." The demographic transformation had enraged Anglos. How else can one explain the passage of Proposition 187 by California voters, which barred "illegal aliens" (read Mexicans) from receiving health and school benefits?

Everything in Pacific Beach, meanwhile, had gone the way of the double-feature movie and ten-cents-a-gallon gas. Nothing survived of the old: the people of yore gone, the landscape altered, pepper trees uprooted, and tract houses standing where weeds and bushes had grown. The village I knew was just a memory, merely an adjunct of an overgrown, midwestern San Diego, bisected by freeways and interlacing housing tracts, one no different from another. My nostalgia was for the white, stucco house with the red-tile roof our parents built and where we grew up, which still stood on Opal Street.

I expected change, but what I encountered exceeded my worst fears. Pacific Beach, the old village, had grown by leaps and bounds. Urban sprawl was its name: gaudy neon, oversized signs, and a hodgepodge of tactless building styles. Overnight, new structures appeared, replacing others that vanished in a puff of smoke, while plate-glass windows displayed the liquidation sales of businesses gone belly up—a day before others took their place. Pacific Beach was busy day and night, especially where streets bisected Garnet, a street lined with low-scale stores, fast-food joints, and rowdy teenagers at the wheels of Jeeps and pickups, radios blaring. In describing similar, if not identical, calamitous changes in Mexico City, Carlos Monsiváis, the maverick intellectual, coined the term *coca-colificación.*

These were the years of the battle for civil rights, and the heady days of the Chicano movement, a crusade led by university students, Mexican Americans who referred to themselves as Chicanos. The Southwest—or Aztlán as they baptized it, from where their pre-Columbian ancestors supposedly came—was the ancestral home. Offspring of the militant 1960s, the Chicano movement marked the first time that people of Mexican background as a national group claimed a place for themselves. Others had done so sporadically, in labor especially. Many Mexicans of my generation were accommodationists, seeking acceptance on the terms of the Anglo establishment. *Mexican* was a pejorative term. When growing up, I knew Mexicans who changed their last names—from García to Jones, for example. Sometimes the more successful denied their Mexican ancestry, wanting to be known as "Spanish." How well I remember that when Anglos learned that I was a college student, they would invariably say, "You must be Spanish." During the heyday of Jim Crow legislation in the late nineteenth century, residents of New Mexico were so frightened of Mexican ancestry that they began calling themselves *hispanos* to differentiate themselves from Mexicans.

I was only vaguely aware of the Chicano movement until I went to Washington in 1968 to help out with the Poor People's March, where I met Corky González, the Chicano leader from Colorado, who spoke of the need to know oneself, to explore one's heritage, and to take pride in one's background. Outside of our parent's home, I had rarely heard this said by Mexican Americans. Corky so impressed me that I wrote an article about him for the *New Republic* and invited him to give a talk at Smith. He came, stayed with us, but his audience was sparse, as it was when Henry B. González, the first Mexican American in Congress, spoke. Their struggle for civil rights was not high on the agenda of Smith students and faculty.

A footnote here. I have never thought of myself as a *Chicano,* a term used rarely when I was young. Because of my parents, I consider my ancestral home to be Mexico. That acknowledged, I support the Chicano battle for equal rights. Having tasted the bitter fruit of prejudice, how could I not?

Slowly it dawned on me to ask myself what I was doing in an elite women's college when I should be helping people of my background. This nagging question came home to roost one day when I gave a lecture to the student body at California State University at Los Angeles, a school with a heavy enrollment of Chicanos. The president, who had extended the invitation, wanted to know what I thought of a separate department of Chicano studies or whether it would be best to locate Chicano faculty in traditional departments. I regret that I told him he that he should uphold the traditional academic structure and place Chicano faculty in departments, a view upheld by famous advocates, nearly all Anglos. Yet one of them was Ralph Ellison, the African American novelist, when he told a student at Southern Illinois University who had asked him for his views on black studies, "It is my opinion that disciplines such as history and literature . . . must include Negro American reality but that it cannot be taught separately, since it did not evolve separately." Well, Ellison was mistaken, as I was. Today, even Harvard has a department of African American studies. Unless they have an independent base of their own, Chicano professors are at the mercy of their Anglo-American colleagues, who seldom sympathize with them. Appointments or promotions for Chicanos come at a snail's pace, if at all.

In Los Angeles, I spoke to a large audience about the war between Mexico and the United States, a topic I knew something about since the publication of *The Mexican War: Was It Manifest Destiny?* Here and there I made out Anglos in the audience, but around them was a sea of bronze faces. This would be no cake walk:

these students had more than a war a century old on their minds. When the moment for questions arrived, a male student got up and in sarcastic tones asked why, if I felt so strongly about the unjust manner "gringos" had treated Mexicans, I stayed in New England? Why was I not in California helping people of my ancestry? The retort annoyed me, but, when I look back, it made sense. What was I doing at Smith when Chicanos badly needed teachers who spoke their language?

This was the period when Chicanos were beginning to enroll in California universities, when Anglos, suffering momentary pangs of guilt, adopted affirmative action, opening doors ever so slightly to the disenfranchised. Enough of them entered to rattle the tranquility of bureaucrats and their faculty underlings. The so-called radicals among them sometimes walked in step with Chicano demands, which, of course, reflected the loud cry for civil rights for African Americans as well as the rising anger over the senseless war in Vietnam.

No matter how strong the Chicano hunger for professors of their own, not many could be found, especially when Anglo academics raised the red flag of standards. Chicanos were not "qualified" was the hue and cry of these hypocrites, many of whom had scarcely published themselves; these naysayers scoffed at Chicano studies and believed that Chicanos were not bright enough to write books, nor did they have a history worth writing about. I remember a remark by a colleague at San Diego who voted against hiring a Chicano to teach Latin American colonial history but voted for him to teach Chicano history; the candidate was "not talented enough" to teach colonial history, "a reputable discipline," but was good enough to teach "Chicano history." The young man went on to win a McArthur grant—on my recommendation.

Clearly I was qualified: I had published books by reputable presses and taught at Smith College, a fine eastern school. So academics turned to me in their search for a minority appointment. By the fall of 1969, I had been asked if I were interested in joining the history departments at Irvine and Davis; there was a catch, however. Davis wanted me also to teach Chicano history, and Irvine asked that I work with the Chicano community. I turned down both offers. I was a historian of Spanish America, and I would teach and write about that. Yes, I wanted very much to teach Chicanos, especially to turn out Chicano Ph.D.s, but on my own terms.

That explains why I accepted an offer from UCSD. It was next door to Mexico, just miles away from Tijuana. Natalia and I would be able to establish ties with Mexicans as well as with Chicanos and thus enrich our life. We would be among persons who spoke Spanish, followed Mexican events, and enjoyed Mexican food. I would be closer to archives and libraries in Mexico and to Mexican scholars. Over the years, Natalia and I made many Mexican friends, citizens of Mexico who live among us, as well as with Chicano academics.

Before accepting, Natalia and I considered carefully the offer from San Diego; I had not forgotten the racial bigotry of the old days. "Would our daughters be victims of it?" Natalia and I asked ourselves. Neither one had lived in California. We concluded that, based on what I had seen, life had changed for the better, though clearly southern California was no racial paradise. San Diego, moreover, because of its location, was the logical campus for Mexican studies. A beginning had been made. The Spanish section of the comparative literature department was one of the best in the country, and Carlos Blanco, one of its kingpins, had been raised and educated in Mexico. A Spaniard by birth, married to a Mexican, Carlos had arrived in Mexico at the age of fourteen, one of the thousands of Spanish refugees from Francisco Franco's fascist regime. His family had settled in Mexico City, where Carlos attended public schools, the Colegio de México, and UNAM. His specialty was the Spanish novel, but he knew Mexico's literature and had a lively interest in Mexican affairs. The colonialist in the history department, a scholar of some repute, was also a Spaniard who wrote on the early days of Hispanic America. The library, too, had started to buy books on Mexico. Ironically, until I arrived on campus, neither the history department nor the administration had displayed any real interest in Mexico; one of the first scholars hired in the department wrote on the Spanish Civil War.

The campus was being organized around a system akin to the Oxford plan. There were three colleges: Revelle, for science; Muir, for humanities and social sciences; and one yet to be named. Instead of just attending the university, students enrolled in a college based on what their major might be, and professors were assigned to one, where they taught an introductory course. Revelle, for example, had a humanities sequence, the Great Books approach of the University of Chicago. The new college was to be a traditional campus, no different from any other; Armin Rappaport, formerly a professor of history at Berkeley, was its provost. Unfortunately for him, minority students, among them Angela Davis, the African American militant, took over the college, demanding that it recruit more minorities and stress Third World studies. It was soon called Third College, for want of a permanent name.

A traditional scholar, Rappaport was qualified neither by training nor temperament nor convictions to head Third College. The provost had to be a person who walked in step with minority students. If Rappaport were to keep his job, he needed help; that is why he recruited me, thinking that if I joined him as a professor in Third College, I would pull his chestnuts out of the fire. William McGill, a UCSD chancellor and the future president of Columbia University, shared similar thoughts; he hoped to quiet the student furor by appointing a provost of minority background. McGill hinted that I might be the ideal person for the job. However, the last thing on my mind was to be a campus bureaucrat. The militants in the college would have eaten me alive had I not acceded to their demands. Anglos are odd; they believe that just because you share a similar racial ancestry, militants will support you. What nonsense! Militants, whether Chicanos or African Americans, want a brother in arms. I had no wish to be caught between timid bureaucrats who wanted to keep the lid on the boiling pot and militants who wanted to blow it off.

One of the first questions I was asked at San Diego was whether I would chair the history department. That inquiry, to say the least, came out of the blue. I said no. I had no desire to chair anything, especially because I had a book under way. At Smith, I had never headed a committee of any importance, merely the graduate program in history, which only rarely conferred a master's degree. The only honor accorded me, if that be it, was a request by a campus committee that I be grand marshal of the college, which required that I march at the head of the faculty column, wearing cap and gown, at college functions. I considered all such events a terrible waste of time and had never attended one.

The UCSD offer included a sabbatical to begin in the fall of 1970. However, in reality I would start teaching in January of that year because Rappaport, still hoping that I could help save his provost's job, wanted me in La Jolla as soon as possible. I cheerfully double-crossed him, asking to be assigned to Muir College, where the provost was a former Dartmouth professor. Upon accepting the offer, I drove to San Diego in the middle of the winter of 1970, braving ice and snow. I left Natalia and our daughters behind, though I went back for visits.

At the San Diego campus, I jumped from the pot into the fire. Gentility, what I jettisoned by abandoning Smith, only now and then had a place: rancorous behavior more often than not held sway. Just more than a decade old, the university had not yet jelled. It was in more ways than one an institution in a state of emergence. I encountered a disparate faculty, lured to La Jolla from a wide range of institutions, which in the sciences included men from corporate America. There was no esprit de corps; the faculty consisted of horses of varying colors, many running on their own tracks. Yes, one came across exceptions, most certainly in literature and sociology. The science departments, huge in size, were the heart and soul of the campus; the chancellor and vice chancellor came from their ranks, so the scientists enjoyed royal treatment. The humanities, on the other hand, were poor relatives, tolerated but not necessarily respected. Physicists and biologists in Revelle College, their redoubt, knew each other, but rarely did they know their colleagues in Muir College, home to most of the humanities.

The campus was exploding, adding professors as well as buildings. Had there been a faculty club, perhaps this pervasive sense of anonymity might have been avoided, but a club did not appear until much later. It was a campus with delusions of grandeur, eager to prove itself; to listen to some of our colleagues, we stood on a par with Berkeley, particularly in the sciences. This constant striving for recognition made UCSD "hard-nosed," almost cruel; each day was a race to get ahead. It was "publish or perish" gone wild. An iron-clad rule held sway: to earn tenure in the humanities and social sciences, one needed a book; to move up to professor, two were required. At times, it seemed as though quantity and not quality wielded the upper hand.

In history, besides Rappaport, there were four full professors, three of them recent arrivals from small colleges. None of them wanted to bring in a colleague who would earn more than they did, nonsense that kept salaries down for everyone. Only Rappaport had university experience; he alone had taught graduate students. There were no associate professors. Of the seven assistant professors, all untenured, only one was a woman. Incredibly, the assistant professors ran the department. Rappaport, the acting chair, lived in Berkeley, where he had a wife and home, and arrived on campus only to teach his classes. The female administrative assistant, big and with a hearty laugh when not crossed, was the lord and master of the department office; she controlled everything.

In the meantime, I ruptured my Achilles tendon playing squash and for two months walked on crutches, one leg in a plaster cast up to my thigh. At that point, I couldn't count how many times I regretted leaving Smith. To exacerbate matters, in a foolish moment I agreed, at the urging of the junior members of the department, to become chair upon my return from the sabbatical. Meanwhile, Natalia sold our house in Williamsburg, and in June, when classes ended, we drove to Mexico City to spend a year there.

That year in Mexico City restored my spirits, but not my faith in Mexico's PRIista leaders. Our friends had lived through the massacre at the Plaza de Tlaltelolco, as yet a topic of heated debate, and on June 10, 1971, during our stay in Mexico, *halcones,* government thugs, again beat and killed student demonstrators in downtown Mexico City, a repeat of Tlaltelolco on a smaller scale. Tragic as that event was, I put it aside and every morning rode a bus to the Zócalo and the National Archives. Earlier we had rented an apartment in the Colonia Hipódromo, next door to Eva, now a widow, enrolled Olivia and Maura in Mexican schools, and renewed old ties, some from our halcyon days in Monterrey.

One of the characteristics of Mexicans from the provinces is that they stay together. In Mexico City, they keep up prior friendships, sometimes to the exclusion of forming others among *chilangos,* local natives. People from Nuevo León are notorious for this behavior. We attended dinners and get-togethers that, although in Mexico City, might just as well have been in Monterrey. They included Mari, a friend of Natalia and wife of Ario Garza Mercado, now the librarian of the Colegio de México; Hernán Garza, a psychiatrist, and his wife; the artists Jaime and Pablo Flores; and Salomón González Almazán, a colleague at the Facultad de Economía. Aside from Lucas de la Garza, Salomón, now a bureaucrat in the Ministry of Education, was the one person I had gotten to know best in Monterrey.

Whether provincials or *chilangos,* Mexicans are cliquish in other ways. One has to do with how many of them view "Mexicans" born in the United States, especially if they do not speak Spanish fluently and know little or nothing of Mexico, which is not uncommon. In my day, few Mexican Americans had ever taken the time to study either the Spanish language or the history and culture of Mexicans, although that is changing. You rarely saw Mexican American students in Spanish classes, under the supposition, I guess, that they knew the language. For these as well as other reasons, Mexicans often tend to look down on their kin in the United States, especially if there are class differences. After all, most persons of Mexican descent who live in this country belong to the working class, and Mexicans tend to be class conscious. When I was young, Mexicans displayed scant interest in their kin in this country; Manuel Gamio's studies of Mexicans in the United

States, so far as I know, stood alone. They were seen as *pochos,* traitors because they had abandoned the homeland and were bereft of Mexican cultural attributes.

For these reasons, Chicano scholars seldom feel at home in Mexico. I recall once, when we were living in Mexico City, inviting two Chicano scholars to a social gathering at the home of friends from Monterrey. It was the usual get-together: everyone knew everyone else. You drank a tequila or two, ate, and then sat around and talked. I became aware immediately that once introductions were done and polite questions about who you were and what you did were asked, the Mexicans ignored the Chicanos, who sat through the evening without saying much of anything, one reason being that they felt unsure of their Spanish. They were simply out of their cultural milieu.

I, too, have run into this attitude, although rarely, but not because of language or ignorance of Mexico but largely because of place of birth and residency or because I tend to be rather direct in my conversation, a very un-Mexican trait. In dealing with each other, Mexicans seldom are direct; to use a metaphor, they rarely enter by the front door, but go around the back and slowly make known what they think, employing an exaggerated gentility and razor-sharp innuendos. Samuel Ramos, author of the controversial *Perfil del hombre y la cultura en México,* writes that the Mexican "is ingenious in detracting from others. . . . He practices slander with the cruelty of a cannibal." Exaggerated perhaps, but not far from the truth—to that I can testify. I remember once sitting next to Moisés González Navarro, a Mexican historian whose manuscript I had just read and reviewed as a favor to him. I had known him and his wife for decades and even had dinner at his home. We were at the head table at a conference of scholars when, without any warning whatsoever, he turned to me to say: "Ramón, I know that you go around telling people that you are a Mexican, but you and I know you aren't." The accusation was untrue but also, beyond that, uncalled for, particularly because we supposedly were friends. That encounter took place some years ago, before I had acquired a Mexican passport, after Mexico made possible dual citizenship for sons and daughters of Mexican parents. His opinion is an exception; most Mexicans I meet are highly flattered by my knowledge and interest in Mexico.

In La Jolla, meanwhile, Bill McGill had left for Columbia University, and William McElroy, a biologist and once head of the National Science Foundation, became the new chancellor. That was a fortuitous turn of events because not only did he prove supportive, but he named Paul Saltman vice chancellor for academic affairs and thus my boss as the chair of history. Tall and lanky, a bit crass and crude but also kind, Paul was never at a loss for opinions peppered with eye-popping, ethnic references, which jumped about like popcorn on a hot skillet. I had known Paul when he was provost of Revelle College; he was friendly then and a big booster later on. Another stroke of luck was the appointment of Harry Scheiber, a full professor at Dartmouth at the age of thirty-one. Like Paul, Harry spoke his mind, a quality not always found among academics. I had known him since my days at Smith; both of us had interviewed for jobs at Dartmouth; he accepted, and I did not. Later we put together a student exchange between the two schools. From Mexico City, I lobbied hard to get him to come to La Jolla, and fortunately he did. That I survived five years as chair of history I owe to these two men. As I attempted to bring order out of chaos, I ran afoul of senior colleagues who came to resent me when I began to clean out their stable of weak appointments. In a fit of anger, one of them rushed into my office to shout, "Ruiz, you are finished, finished!" That day or later he and his colleagues went to ask Paul Saltman to fire me; "I told them," Paul reported to me, "that I would nail their asses to the wall if they tried that again."

The job was to clean house and hire scholars of stature. Luring Scheiber from Dartmouth was the initial step. Then it was James Scobie, a leading historian of Argentina, who left Indiana University to join us. Though also tall and slender like Paul, James was emblematic of his native Vermont, dour and taciturn. He spoke when spoken to but otherwise kept his thoughts to himself. He was a real find because he helped put our Latin American program on the map. He was spending a sabbatical in Buenos Aires when I wrote asking for names of scholars who might want to come west. To our delight, he said he himself would. We also were able to lure Stuart Hughes, a respected historian, from Harvard; Allan Mitchel, my colleague at Smith and Stuart's first doctoral student at Harvard, at my urging had come to UCSD two years earlier. Through him, I learned that Stuart was willing to leave Harvard because his wife, much younger than he, also wanted a job teaching European history. But Stuart asked that we appoint her an associate professor. This request led to the only clash I ever had with Paul Saltman because he and the Committee on Academic Personnel, which passed on appointments, rejected our recommendation for tenure for Stuart's wife. I had to go over Paul's head to get Bill McElroy to override that decision. Then Earl Pomeroy, a former colleague at Oregon, joined us; I won't forget that appointment because Earl, who could never make up his mind, ran me through the ringer, saying yes and then no before finally accepting. We began to promote the best assistants to the rank of associate professors and to recruit promising scholars. By the time I had turned things around, every one of my old antagonists had gone off to teach elsewhere. When I left the chair, the department was on its way to national ranking.

That interlude nonetheless cost me dearly both in time and research. Had I stayed at Smith, I would have completed the book on the Mexican Revolution earlier. I had a sabbatical coming and no campus politics or bureaucratic duties to handle. As chair, I had the daily grind of countless reports, preparing recommendations for appointments and promotions and service on committees. I had to put up with quarrelsome and meddlesome colleagues, among them sometimes two friends of mine. From the start, they had disliked each other. One unforgettable morning, after I had made a decision that both judged mistaken, they came separately to my office to berate me—but for diametrically opposed reasons. I remember once coming home exhausted only to have to pick up the phone and listen to a meddlesome colleague, recently denied something he wanted, tell me that he was calling to disturb my dinner. When we tried to appoint someone in his specialty, he would call the prospective candidate to tell him not to come, and then the candidate would then tell me what this man had said. And there were always scheduling problems when colleagues wanted to teach only on certain days and at certain hours. Rappaport, always unhappy, limited enrollments in his classes, on the premise that he ran a discussion course; too many students hindered the exchange of ideas. He had not published in years, yet wanted a promotion to a higher step. When Paul Saltman, to whom I relayed this message, said that Rappaport had not earned a promotion, Rappaport blamed me.

For two years, I also served as chair of the Division of Humanities and Performing Arts. Although UCSD was a young campus, Scripps Institute, the marine biology school, harked back to 1914. No deans had been appointed; the departments functioned under the supervision of Paul Saltman, the vice chancellor for academic affairs. Recommendations for appointments, which required a full-time position or engagement (FTE, or funds for an academic appointment), originated in university headquarters in Berkeley and then came through Paul and his Program Review Committee, made up of the provosts, assorted bureaucrats, and chairs of the academic divisions, of which Humanities and Performing Arts was one. It was my duty to ask the chairs of literature, philosophy, art, and drama what FTEs they wanted, then to present these requests to Paul's committee and justify them. This meant competing for FTEs with the chairs of the physical sciences and the social sciences divisions as well as with the provosts, who demanded teaching slots for special courses in their colleges. Money to fund FTEs was the mother's milk of campus politics; every department wanted one— or more. Saltman, meanwhile, counted up student enrollments of departments to determine how to award them. On a predominantly science campus, the humanities fared badly. No matter how strenuously we pleaded our case, the sciences usually triumphed. When the bad news came back to colleagues, some said it was my fault. If one of the departments fared well, and the others did not, I was in hot water again.

Campus life was a rough and rolling sea. Student unrest brought turbulence and unpredictable behavior. There were demands for ethnic history, for minority professors, and for ethnic bureaucrats. Chicanos, graduates in particular, were not forbearing with their mentors. I remember a Chicana in my seminar on the Mexican Revolution who drove an English sports car but berated me for asking her to read memoirs of blue bloods of the Old Regime, and a Chicana teaching assistant, usually quiescent, giving me the Bronx cheer because in a class lecture I had extolled the help I received from my parents. "You did not get ahead on your own" was her retort! I can call up memories of angry Chicanos, blacks, and Asians, among them one of my graduate students, stomping into my office to tell me that I must hire minority historians. When I tried to explain that I wanted to but that it would take time, they walked out in a huff.

That said, I did not neglect scholarship. Relying on research from my most recent stay in Mexico, I used a summer to write *Labor and the Ambivalent Revolutionaries* (later published in Spanish in Mexico), a book arguing that the revolutionaries of 1910, supposedly pro-labor, had not wanted an independent labor movement. They had co-opted its leadership and manipulated labor to the advantage of industry, both foreign and domestic. Working men and women, promised benefits by the Constitution of 1917, lost their right to organize and to strike.

Next came *The Great Rebellion,* enriched by documents, newspaper reports, and the memoirs of politicos and generals. In the national archives, I had uncovered a wealth of information, especially correspondence between politicos. I found letters exchanged between the colonel who murdered Emiliano Zapata, the agrarian reformer, and General Pablo González, President Venustiano Carranza's toady, who ordered the dastardly deed and rewarded the scoundrel, as well as accounts of Francisco Villa's abuse of small ranchers. For many U.S. historians, Villa is an icon of the revolution, though not to my mother's family, who in Parral witnessed his atrocities.

So I concluded that, contrary to accepted wisdom, the Revolution of 1910, the pride of leftists, had been a truncated rebellion of the bourgeoisie. Far from being radical, its leadership had capitalist goals: to destroy the old political monopoly but not to eliminate the system. How else could one explain Mexico's current plight if a social upheaval had truly taken place? The answer was that the old structure, with some modifications, survived. The revolutionaries were intent on reform rather than on radical change. This controversial thesis convinced few devotees of the myth of the revolution. Era, a publishing house in Mexico that put out the Spanish version of the book on labor, also brought out a Spanish edition of *The Great Rebellion,* but most Mexicans wanted no part of an attack on their sacred revolution. After all, it ranked along with the wars for independence and La Reforma as one of the sacred icons of Mexican history.

When Olivia, our daughter, spent a year in Hermosillo, Sonora, writing her doctoral thesis in anthropology, and Natalia and I went back and forth on visits, getting to know Hermosillenses, I decided to do a book about the ancestors of our new friends. *The People of Sonora and Yankee Capitalists* was the result, a study based almost entirely on archival material, which confirmed the thesis that Mexico enjoyed a rebellion but not a social revolution. Sonora, after all, was a cradle of the upheaval of 1910. However, the Sonorenses who captained the rebellion were neither poor nor radical; Alvaro Obregón, their leader, was in fact a planter. The last thing on his mind was to break up the haciendas, a principal demand of landless campesinos in central Mexico. Obregón and his cohorts simply wanted a larger piece of the capitalist pie.

Next came the book about *mis padres,* their forefathers, and the ancestors before them: *Triumphs and Tragedy: A History of the Mexican People.* I tried to write with the eye of an insider, to interpret the trials and tribulations of Mexicans as a Mexican might, but never blind to their sins. I wrote it with a passionate obsession for the subject. One inspiration was Justo Sierra, a Mexican intellectual who in the late nineteenth century wrote a history of Mexico around heroes in the belief that you build a sense of nation with them. Taking my cue from Sierra, I, too, wrote about them, portraying their contributions, but adding artists and writers, among them Hermenegildo Bustos, a portrait painter of the

Primitive School; José María Velasco, a landscape artist; and the muralists José Clemente Orozco, Diego Rivera, and David Siqueiros. There were writers, too, from the days of Joaquín Fernández de Lizardi's *Periquillo Sarniento,* a caustic look at *criollos* at the close of the colonial era, to Mariano Azuela's *Los de abajo,* to the literary boom of the 1950s—the novels of Juan Rulfo *(Pedro Páramo)* and Carlos Fuentes *(La muerte de Artemio Cruz).*

My book juxtaposed Mexico's accomplishments and failures. Why distorted development, the *atraso mexicano?* Like an old script, the failures of Mexicans were the same year in and year out. There was never a rewrite. Distorted development dated from late colonial times, a malady exacerbated by independence when Mexicans linked up, on grossly unequal terms, with the capitalist economies of Europe and the United States. Production and trade were geared more to the needs of the rich abroad than to the needs of Mexicans, especially workers and campesinos who still today are the beasts of burden. In 1992, *Triumphs and Tragedy* was a History Book Club selection; the Commonwealth Club of California awarded it a gold medal; and the *Los Angeles Times* named it one of the five best history books.

Ironically, despite pessimistic views on the recent course of Mexican history expressed in everything I had written, PRI officials in 1982 asked me to attend the inauguration of Miguel de la Madrid, the first of the neoliberal chiefs of state. From the moment I boarded the Mexican airliner in Tijuana, everything had been arranged. At the airport in Mexico City, a government official escorted me to a luxury hotel, and from then on it was one function after another, including the impressive ceremony in the Chamber of Deputies, where, amid pomp and stateliness, de la Madrid took the red, green, and white tricolor sash from José López Portillo, the outgoing president, and then marched out as an army band struck up the national anthem to the thunderous applause of senators and congressmen. At a reception later that evening, I stood in line with others to shake the hand of the new leader of Mexico, but even though this encounter quickly passed, I left with the distinct impression that I had met a mediocre technocrat, *simpático* perhaps but ineffective.

By chance, after de la Madrid was no longer president, I had breakfast with him in Tijuana, and, to my surprise, he was relaxed and eager to talk. I remember telling him that Televisa's fondness for using only European types as actors hardly reflected the true face of Mexico; aside from the Spanish spoken, Mexican viewers might just as well watch American television. By shunting aside the swarthy, Televisa's chieftains revealed not only their disdain for the Mexican majority but their own sense of racial inferiority. De la Madrid agreed and added that he had conveyed his views to Emilio Azcárraga Milmo, Televisa's owner. White faces continue to monopolize the Mexican television screen, so I can only assume that Azcárraga gave scant heed to de la Madrid's opinion.

When I first set foot on the UCSD campus, there were only a handful of Chicanos, everyone an untenured professor. So as a campus politico I used what clout I had, terribly little I confess, to cajole the vice chancellor and the departments of literature and drama to hire Chicano professors. In order to try to remedy this catastrophic state of affairs, my Chicano colleagues and I met once a quarter to discuss how to hire more Chicanos, bestow tenure on them, and promote Chicano enrollments. Now and then we tasted victory, but defeats occurred regularly and left a bitter taste. When I retired twenty years later, there were only fifteen Chicanos, largely junior faculty. Progress? Perhaps, but to put it bluntly, it was largely tokenism. From this uphill battle, one truth, written in ineffaceable ink, emerged: we of Mexican ancestry must stand up for ourselves; if we want the gates of the academy opened for students of our flesh and blood, we must do it ourselves. It is sheer folly to believe that we can reach our goal by any other means.

What victories we enjoyed, moreover, were helped along by the popular uproar over the war in Vietnam and the struggle for civil rights; both opened the door just a bit for Chicanos and African Americans, long pushed to the back of the proverbial bus. An offshoot was affirmative action, which on university campuses meant efforts to enroll minority students and the chance to hire professors of like ancestry. In San Diego, in an increasingly Mexican heartland, that implied enrolling and hiring Mexican Americans. Whatever its merits, affirmative action did not put an end to the shameful neglect of Chicano education. It was a "fig leaf," as Stanley Aronowitz argues cogently in *The Nation,* to cover "the downsizing of the welfare state": though it opened university doors to a handful of students, rarely from the lowest class, it was accompanied by bloated military budgets and whopping spending cuts in housing, public health, and schooling, widening the gap between rich and poor. Worse still, globalization, the brainchild of international capitalism, began to shift manufacturing jobs, the bread and butter of African Americans and Mexicans, from the United States to the Third World, stranding millions of minority workers. In the absence of anything better, affirmative action was a good idea.

Federal policy guidelines, moreover, were one thing, but practice another. It was as the sociologist Charles Moskos wrote: "Today, one is more likely to hear racial jokes at the university faculty club than in the [army] officers' club. And in the officers' club, one will surely see more blacks." This rings true for persons of Mexican descent, although not quite in the same manner: few are officers in the military, and fewer still are university professors.

One could find professors sympathetic to affirmative action when it first appeared on the scene, but as time marched on, fewer and fewer of them. That nonetheless did not prevent Anglo and Jewish professors from twisting its goals. Before long, some of my colleagues were proposing that we use affirmative action FTES— meant to help only certain categories of minorities in California, such as African Americans, Mexican Americans, Filipinos, and Native Americans—to hire Spaniards, Argentine and Columbian Jews, Asians from China, and natives of India—all proposed with a straight face. Affirmative action was turning into a farce. How many times did I not hear someone trumpet, "Ramón, if you made it, why can't others?" At meetings of department chairs, Saltman, both poignantly and pathetically human, talked a good game but never failed to remind us that it was federal policy, not his. If we did not comply, the federal wrath would be upon us. More and more the hiring of minorities became a paper exercise; according to the files, so many minority professors were screened, but none met our litmus test. Once in a blue moon, one or two were hired, and then the hiring stopped. It was the hold of times past over time present.

When I first arrived there, only one other minority, a Japanese American woman, an instructor, taught in the history department. Because she never completed her doctorate, she was let go. No plans were afoot to hire any minority professors. When the department brought in a colonial historian of Hispanic America, he was a Spaniard who, as it turned out, looked down on Chicanos. When there was talk of adding an Asianist or an Africanist, nothing was said about the possibility of hiring an African American, a Chinese American, or a Japanese American, though these fields were beginning to attract them.

Just white faces were visible among the graduate students. This was unacceptable. I had not traveled west to teach just Anglos. So a few of us began to do something to remedy this abysmal picture. Despite myriad obstacles, one being some of my colleagues, a remedy was available because of affirmative action. The university had set up a special fund reserved for minority graduate students: the San Diego Fellowships. These funds were not departmental; my colleagues could not vote to award them to someone else. That was why they mattered so much. Standard practice was to award student stipends to departments, whose members decided how to distribute them. I had only one vote, and the majority always voted for students of their own ethnic group, rarely a minority applicant. Given this situation, it would have been virtually impossible to award a minority applicant a fellowship, supposedly given out on the basis of graduate record exams (GREs), grade point average, as well as recommendations from professors who had taught the student as an undergraduate.

For understandable reasons, minority students usually tested lower than their Anglo-American counterparts. From the start, they were at a disadvantage, but not because they were less intelligent. Ambition to get ahead was never taken into account. Mario García, now a respected scholar in the field of Chicano history, was the first of these remarkable students to receive a San Diego Fellowship. Alex Saragoza, who arrived from Fresno as the son of a farm laborer, is a professor at UC Berkeley, and Miguel Tinker Salas, a former shipyard worker and husband of a Chicana Ph.D., teaches at Pomona College. All have excellent books to their credit. They are only three of the many I taught at UCSD. Their GREs may have been slightly lower than those of Anglo-American students from prestigious institutions, but, for their scholarly accomplishments, as a group they tower over those other students.

At the undergraduate level, meanwhile, as enrollments climbed, so did the number of students in my course on the history of Mexico. By the late 1980s, there were as many as 150 in the class. From the podium, when I looked out at the sea of young faces, there was always a big block, usually on my right, of bronze ones. Nearly all of these Chicanos, the first in their families to attend a university, were curious to know who I was and to hear what I had to say. I tried hard not to disappoint them, interpreting as best I could Mexican culture and life and, when possible, relating the Mexican experience of exploitation and failure to their uphill battle to get ahead. I believe that I succeeded, at least partially. In 1992, MECHA, the Chicano student organization on campus, presented me with its annual award "for distinguished service," a plaque that hangs on one wall of my study.

The faculty void was not fixed so easily. As chair, I might have dreamed of being a caudillo (dictator), but that was not possible, even with Harry Scheiber at my side. I had one other ally: Joseph Watson, an African American who became provost of Third College. A native of New York City and a graduate of City College, Joe had a Ph.D. in chemistry from UCLA and had been on campus since 1966. I had known Joe since my first visit to UCSD; he was the sole professor in a group of Chicano and black students who wanted to know how I stood on issues they felt important to them. Tall and shy, he said nothing, but I recall his eyes looking intently at me. Equally committed to adding diversity to the faculty, Joe would invariably support a request to Paul Saltman for a minority FTE. The goal was to build a department where minority professors would be among the colleagues. We made progress, but not enough. Miguel Monteón, a Mexican American from Mason City, Iowa, a town of thirty thousand inhabitants, three hundred of them Mexicans, came to teach South American history; he had a doctorate from Harvard. After two years of searching, Harry and I found Ricardo Romo, a native of Texas, to teach Chicano history; Edward Reynolds, an African from Ghana, for African history, arrived a year after I did. All went on to become published scholars, and Romo to the presidency of the University of Texas, San Antonio. Later, although no longer chair of history, I helped add Ramón Gutiérrez, the noted Chicano scholar who replaced Romo, as well as David Gutiérrez, an up-and-coming Chicano historian.

During my final year as chair of history, my father died in Mazatlán, the port city he loved so much. He was ninety-four years of age. I used to visit him in an apartment he rented on Calle Galeana, a block away from the harbor. As he got older, we had less and less to say to each other, and he was in the habit of repeating anecdotes over and over again. Natalia, however, says that he was always that way. He began to speak well of the PRI, earlier anathema to him. On my last visit, when I learned that he was not well, I found him standing on the balcony looking out over Mazatlán, a hat on his head and hands in his pockets, and appearing much shorter than I remembered him. It took him a moment or two before he recognized me. *"Hijo,"* he said, *"¿eres tu?"* (Is it you, son?). His legs were swollen because of poor blood circulation. The next day his wife and I took him to the Catholic hospital, where he spoke mostly to her as though I were not there, so I left for home, to take care of problems in the history department, knowing that Roberto, my brother, would arrive later that day. I never saw my father again. He died that night. At Eva and Berta's insistence, we flew his body to San Diego and buried him alongside our mother in the Catholic cemetery.

If I know my father, I am sure he is angry at us for taking his body out of Mexico. But there he lies, next to Mamá, on a slope where silence rules and where nothing disturbs the stone markers. "You of a hundred years from now," wrote Mary Austin, "when you visit where I lie, [and] you see the cupped silken wings of the argemone burst and float apart when there is no wind; or if, when all around is still, a sudden stir in the short-leaved pines, that shall be I."

II

Epilogue

——

What can I, an old codger, retired but still learning, tell you? Yes, I live comfortably, but unlike old-timers enamored of the status quo, I hold no brief for it. I am not the bridegroom of the conservative deity! If I have enjoyed a good life, it is in part because that tug of war in my head between two cultures helped me take note of who I am and gave me the strength to pry open doors in this country where Anglos wear the crown. For this I thank my parents, as well as their *consejos,* for their love and support. Time marches on, of course, and, to cite an old adage, "history has a way of cleaning itself so that, in retrospect, shameful events of the past lose their terror." However, long ago I came to accept what W. E. B. Du Bois knew by heart and explains in his *Souls of Black Folks:* "to attain his place in the world," a man "must be himself, and not another."

Sitting astride two horses that pull in opposite directions, I believe, has made me a better scholar. The writing of history, after all, is a tangled web, as we who try to make sense of it know, because it is the sum total of the human experience and, to bedevil matters, situated in diverse cultures and societies. Filling in gaps and cracks in the histories of peripheral countries, among them Mexico, requires minds free of Western taboos and, most important, language proficiency else the opportunity is denied. The challenge is to bring the past back to life. But how objectively can it be done? As Ramón del Valle Inclán, the Spanish intellectual, says, "Nothing is as it was, merely as it is remembered."

This bit of wisdom, which I deem indisputable, flies in the face of Leopold Van Ranke's hoary cry for objective history, the need simply to show "how it really was." From the hindsight of today, that aphorism looks profoundly shallow because facts are a slippery phenomenon. Empirical theory to the contrary, no complete separation exists between subject and object. Written history consists of a corpus of ascertained facts, and the historian, after he pieces them together, makes his own dish out of them, according to Edward Hallet Carr, the English historian.

History, clearly, is in the eye of the beholder. We see ourselves and our past deeds from a narrow prism, although the broader truth is always an interlace of cultural and psychological facts. The search for that truth, if such exists, is allusive at best and certainly exacerbated by the worship of nation, religious dogmatism, racist nonsense, and sundry ideologies that place blinders on one. To embrace patriotic gore, Edmund Wilson's graphic expression, encourages one to view history through parochial eyes.

The man who juggles dual versions of the elusive "truth" may come closer. Neither in one camp nor the other, he sees what others fail to perceive. The embrace of majority mythology is highly unlikely. The hyphenated man is an alienated man: peace of mind is a mirage because his peculiar cultural perspective is out of step with sundry patriots and, yes, historians. By stepping outside of the baggage of a society, he can, even though still a part of it, judge it more dispassionately, though I use that term cautiously because objectivity is a canard of myth makers.

I confess that after a lifetime of writing history I view optimism about the human race with jaundiced eyes. I have not completely disowned it, and I have yet to lose hope for individuals. But our world is truly an unjust one, where the rich and powerful rule. The Cold War is history, and capitalism, the American gospel, reigns triumphantly, yet half of the planet's inhabitants exist on leftovers. Modern globalization reminds one of the old colonialism; the same wealthy countries of yore dictate today's terms. Yet capitalism, as practiced since the nineteenth century, will never pull the poor out of the swamps of poverty, as its historical record easily verifies.

Signposts of our time are the global economy and its hallowed free trade, an economic order that, if one looks closely, largely allows the fox into the henhouse. The roots of the market system, as it is now known, date from the Industrial Revolution of the nineteenth century, when English exports of cheap woolen and cotton textiles toppled infant industries in Mexico and India. The peripheral world is still asked to provide raw materials but also cheap manufactured goods under imperial license. Through the International Monetary Fund and the World Bank, the Western powers, which run the system, impose measures that devastate domestic sectors of the peripheral economies and thwart the development of robust internal markets. The result is the creation of domestic elites beholden to the imperial masters amid poverty and desperation.

The transnationals, the lords of this global universe, constantly on the lookout for new consumers and for men and women who will work for a pittance, shift more and more of their investments overseas, bringing on a hemorrhage of manufacturing jobs at home, particularly in the steel, auto, and apparel industries. Increasingly, the United States becomes less of a manufacturing giant and more a market for overseas goods produced by U.S. companies employing cheap foreign labor. That transformation, according to John Kenneth Galbraith, has turned us into an economically "unequal society." The rich have more, and the poor less and less. One-fifth of Americans have less than they had twenty-five years ago, but the richest nearly twice as much. The average corporate executive earns four hundred times more than the average worker, and in the past two decades the real median wage of U.S. factory workers has fallen. Tens of millions of Americans live below the poverty line, a dismal picture commonplace in corrupt regimes in the Third World. African Americans and people of my ancestry sit at the bottom of this totem pole.

The masters of this global conglomerate strive to create identical values and encourage similar tastes, eager to sell the same products. Cities become identical, victims of polluting cars and smoke-stack industries, high-rises, fast-food chains, stores peddling Barbie Dolls and Nikes, and people watching American sit-coms on television and flocking to see Hollywood films. Villages in the peripheral world have Coca-Cola on billboards, Sylvester Stallone on television sets, and Levi ads in newspapers. Every place is fast becoming everywhere else. As long as the transnationals pressure countries to open up their forests, water, and land to what they euphemistically label development, and there are local *tío tacos* (Uncle Toms) willing to oblige, native peoples who live off the water and land die off, as do the animals, plants, and the biodiversity of the planet. U.S. hegemony, the linchpin of this global economy, is neither benign nor kind for its supposed beneficiaries in the Third World. The umbrella of freedom, so much on the tongue of American pundits, does not shelter everyone and rarely those of dark skin.

Neither can I take comfort from the life in Mexico, where the wages of time weigh heavily and where the rich, in the manner of their ancestors, turn a blind eye on the sufferings of the poor. Few care if their countrymen flee across the northern border because, landless and jobless, they cannot survive at home. Statistics tell the magnitude of the Mexican tragedy. Despite the embrace of the global model, referred to as *neoliberalismo* south of the border, nearly three out of four Mexicans exist in poverty, and their numbers multiply. At the bottom of the social scale are the Indians, millions of whom somehow manage to survive in extreme poverty and toil ten hours a day to earn half the paltry minimum wage. Nabobs in Mexico City, to the applause of a cold-hearted business elite, set aside less money for social expenditures than Bolivia, Colombia, and Zambia. Men and women who began their life as laborers in the early 1940s try to make ends meet on tacky pensions, which demands, as one man explains, that he and his wife dine on eggs and beans one day, the next day go without breakfast, and on the third drink just coffee. Others ration their tortillas lest they cannot pay the rent.

The heart saddens when I think of what has become of the nationalistic Mexico of yesteryear, the land of Emiliano Zapata, the agrarian chieftain; of Lázaro Cárdenas, who stood up to Standard Oil; and of the artists José Clemente Orozco, Diego Rivera, and David Siqueiros. Where are the Rafael Ramírezes, architects of the Cultural Missions and the Casa del Pueblo, monuments to the history of Mexican rural education, and the old *indigenistas* who labored mightily on behalf of Indian campesinos? Even José Vasconcelos, who urged illiterate campesinos to read Plato and Socrates, a recipe totally out of step with reality, looms tall by comparison with the bureaucrats of today.

The global economy twists radically the contours of the Mexican border society. With their low wages, *maquiladoras* (assembly plants), the kingpins of the border, portend a likely path for the future. As border tourist spots of my youth recede into memory, urbanization, the offspring of these assembly plants, takes hold, transforming hamlets into big cities, among them Tijuana and Ciudad Juárez. These mushrooming megalopolises take in hordes of the poor despite suffering from social ills typical of chaotic and unplanned growth. In this disparate society, the rich dwell in *colonias campestres* (country-club estates), and the poor in shacks. Inequalities are scandalous. In *Across the Wire: Life and Hard Times on the Mexican Border,* author Luis Alberto Urrea, who was born in Tijuana, vividly describes the borderlands as a "festering netherworld of orphanages and garbage dumps . . . where the poor . . . cling to the underside of the Third World." Yet, tragically, as one woman tells him, "She had come to Tijuana from a still poorer province" and viewed "the borderlands as a kind of promised land." *Maquiladoras,* according to the conservative *Wall Street Journal,* are helping to turn the border into "a sinkhole of abysmal living conditions and environmental degradation." Mindful of these consequences, naysayers in Mexicali dubbed the society of *maquiladoras* Maquilamex, a metaphor that assents grudgingly to the weighty role that *maquiladoras* play from Tijuana to Matamoros and captures the ambivalence of a people troubled by what they witness.

This homeland is a paradox. By U.S. standards, it fares poorly. Yet in the Republic of Mexico, incomes rise the closer one gets to the border. Tijuana, for instance, boasts one of the highest per capita incomes in Mexico. However, on the U.S. side, incomes drop as one gets closer to the border. The counties of the lower Rio Grande Valley of Texas are the poorest in the United States, yet compared to the Mexican side they are less poor.

This picture, where the almighty dollar calls the tune, I know firsthand. When the peso fell dramatically in December 1994, I was in Tijuana collecting material for *On the Rim of Mexico: Encounters of the Rich and Poor,* a book I eventually published fully aware of the inequality along the border. Even though I had anticipated the peso's pratfall, I was unprepared for its Humpty Dumpty behavior that started just days before Christmas. A few days later, Eliseo Mendoza Berrueto, until recently governor of the state of Coahuila, invited me·on a fact-finding trip to ascertain how the peso's plunge had affected key sectors of border society.

In January 1995, we set out by auto from Tijuana for Matamoros, a journey that took us more than two thousand miles. Traveling on Mexican roads whenever possible, we stopped at every city and interviewed each *presidente municipal* (mayor), newspaper editor, merchant group, business owner, and campesino leader. Even among PRIistas, notorious for their unwillingness to see, hear, or speak ill of their bedmates, we encountered anger with politicos in Mexico City, anxiety over the future, and fear of economic turmoil. The devaluation, they all agreed, was a disaster.

Mexico, I concluded long ago, endures a tragic drama on which the curtain never falls. True, in July 2000, the PRI candidate, the political boss for nearly seven decades, finally lost the presidency, a defeat hailed as a triumph for democracy and the dawn of a new day. The downfall of this corrupt, inefficient, and conservative mafia was long overdue. Yet the victors, the Partido de Acción Nacional, a conservative Catholic party, worships at the same shrine, wedded to the goddess of neoliberalism, a trickle-down formula masquerading in global clothes. The poor will go on being hungry under this regime. As the Mexican saying goes, *"es la misma gata no mas que se revolcó"* (life goes on as before).

North of the border, in the interim, the dreams of Mexicans, natives or not, of climbing the slippery American totem pole, have become like Cinderella's carriage turned pumpkin. For them, David Gutiérrez tells me, statistics suggest that rising wages, better jobs, more years in school, and other signs of upward mobility, nearly all of those trends have flattened and, in some cases, actually reversed. Even the wage gap between Mexicans and Anglos is wider now than before, while the numbers of poor Mexicans multiply alarmingly. Nor, Gutiérrez argues, is this gap owing to the huge influx of low-skilled Mexican workers; even third- and fourth-generation men and women enter the economy at the bottom rung and languish there. In our schools, children of my flesh and blood, even more than African American children, are the most-segregated students.

In the land of Lincoln, too, bigotry has risen from its ashes like the proverbial phoenix. In the UC system, professors and bureaucrats have largely turned their backs on minorities. Its regents even abolished affirmative action. Incredibly, Ward Connerly, an African American, led the stampede. As Jack London wrote in *The Sun-Dog Trail,* Sitka Charley, an Indian, had "performed that prodigy of prodigies, namely, the turning of his back upon his own people, and so far as it was possible . . . becoming a white man, even in his mental process." Sitka boasted that "he had . . . sat among us, by our fires, and become one of us." How at odds with Du Bois, who gave ground to no white man and rightly argued that accommodation merely legitimized and bolstered bigotry. Enrollments of minority students plummeted, especially at Berkeley, Los Angeles, and San Diego, where only a handful of African Americans attend. Not until the year 2000 did the regents rescind their vote, but by then a majority of California voters had abolished affirmative action.

Today even bilingual programs are derided. Yet, when recalling my youth, I think of that moment when I entered school unable to speak a word of English and how different my experience might have been if the teacher had known Spanish and had been able and willing to use it when speaking to me. I doubt if I would have fled through the french doors and—because I know that I am not unintelligent—would have moved on with classmates to the next grade. The hurt and shame of falling behind, which have long disappeared but still linger on in memory, could have been avoided. I am an advocate of bilingual education because of that unnerving episode and the knowledge acquired from years of teaching Mexican kids who now and then bear the same stigma of language deficiency. The goal, I know, is English proficiency. In this country, nobody gets ahead unless he or she speaks and writes English, as my nationalistic father recognized. How often did I not hear him lament his inability to speak and write English well? However, the sink-or-swim method advocated by the "speak American" crowd makes little sense. Not only is the bilingual method a better learning tool, but bilingual citizens enrich a country's culture, which brings to mind an old joke. "What do you call one who speaks three languages? Trilingual. What do you call one who speaks two languages? Bilingual. What do you call one who speaks only one language? A gringo."

At La Jolla, unsurprisingly perhaps, the bureaucratic bug bit me. Why should I not, that rare scholar of Mexican ancestry, aspire to a university presidency? Being chair of history had added gray hairs to my head, but in a perverse way I enjoyed the puny authority. Bill McElroy, the chancellor, as well as Paul Saltman told me that I was doing a fine job, and I kept receiving letters from universities looking for presidents. Gradually I began to dream of life as a campus bureaucrat. The letters, perhaps a majority I suspect, responded to affirmative action requirements. Whatever. I eventually received an offer to be vice president for academic affairs at the Binghamton branch of the State University of New York. Natalia and I visited the campus, met the president, whom I liked very much, and talked to the faculty, but, after a week of pondering, I said no and to this day have no regrets. A presidency, the goal of aspirants to campus jobs, was not the goal I had in mind when, at San Diego State, I chose to be a teacher and a history scholar.

My soul was not entirely cleansed of the bug, however. In 1979, Joseph Duffey, chair of the National Endowment for the Humanities, asked me to come to Washington for one year to head the Division of Public Programs. I should have realized that affirmative action drove Duffey. He did not know me, and I had never heard of him. I was not a bureaucrat and knew nothing about films and museums, the bread and butter of public programs. When I asked about him, I learned that he was a Protestant minister and Democratic Party hack who once ran for the Senate in Connecticut. When I met Duffey, he was at his presbyterial best, vowing concern for those left out of endowment largess, so I accepted the appointment, ready for a chance to see up close the workings of government. I would have the opportunity to make certain that not just established filmmakers or the Metropolitan Museum received grants.

Washington, D.C., was everything I dislike. Most days the weather was foul, hot and humid in the summer and sufficiently cold in the winter to compel one to rush from one heated building to another. It was a city, yet not really a city, more a bureaucratic hub at the service of politicos. Office gossip revolved around who got a promotion to a higher civil service step, and bureau heads walked on eggshells for fear of ruffling congressional feathers. I remember once standing in line at a cocktail hour on the Hill behind a man in a dark suit. He asked who I was, and when I asked for his name, he took it as a slight because, as it turned out, he was Jim Wright, the Speaker of the House. Rampant inequality was all around us; decaying African American ghettoes stood just behind the White House, in full view of the most powerful man in the United States. In the local universities, scholars of Latin America spent their time writing essays that justified congressional decisions but rarely questioned their objectivity or wisdom. The appeal of the capitol was the fabulous parade of museums, from the Smithsonian to the Corcoran, where one could spend days and weeks, and, thankfully, Natalia taught at Sidwell Friends, where presidents enrolled their children, and Maura graduated from the Madeira School.

At the National Endowment, meanwhile, Duffey, wise to the ways of the pulpit, talked a heavenly game; I even concluded that he was not simply a bureaucrat; I was wrong. When I arrived to assume my duties, he warned, to my astonishment, that he wanted no special care given to minority applicants. I was between a rock and a hard place because that was one reason I had accepted his invitation. At that moment, I held my tongue; I could not return to California because the department had hired someone to replace me.

Duffey notwithstanding, I moved ahead stubbornly with plans to include minority applicants among our grantees and won some victories. Among the recipients of planning grants were Moctezuma Esparza and Jesús Treviño, today major filmmakers. I got the Endowment to recognize Hispanic scholars in history and literature. With the help of Raquel Franco, secretary to the Hispanic Congressional Caucus, I prevailed on Duffey to honor a select group of distinguished men and women at a luncheon on Capitol Hill. They included Américo Paredes and Julian Samora, both pioneers in their fields. Edward Roybal, the Mexican American congressman from Los Angeles, came to the luncheon, as did the congressional delegate from Puerto Rico. Despite this effort, I was dispatched to the Johns Hopkins School for Advanced International Studies (SAIS), courtesy of Duffey.

That transfer, ironically, proved a blessing. I was back on familiar turf. Also, I would join faculty and students from SAIS on a ten-day trip to Havana by invitation of the Cubans. This was not the first time I had been to the island; back in 1975 I had gone there with a group of Mexican Americans, mostly lawyers from Los Angeles, one an appellate court judge. Since my days at Claremont, I had asked myself time and again why some countries developed economically, whereas Mexico, home of my ancestors, had not. This search explains in part why I wrote the book on the Cuban Revolution. True, Cuba was not Mexico, merely a cultural cousin, but it was nonetheless also "underdeveloped" or, to use the other term, the victim of "distorted" development, a situation Fidel Castro and his allies were trying to overcome using socialist remedies. Most American scholars who took the time to study Cuba were dubious if not hostile, especially after the Cubans joined the Soviet bloc, driven by Washington's hostility. What held my attention was the question of whether Cuba's socialist blueprint was solving problems created by capitalism. I wanted to see what was being done to uproot the island's racist heritage, in part exacerbated by American sugar barons, bigoted white tourists, and gambling czars from Las Vegas who had made the island their playground.

I had long ago come to believe that the state, particularly in poor countries such as Cuba, had to play a weighty role in economic and political affairs. The neoliberal model, which left a people's fate in the hands of the powerful individuals, was not a proper vehicle for the wretched of the earth. Sectors that begged for government ownership stood out like a sore thumb: public utilities, such as water and electricity, as well as social security, schools from day care to the university, housing for workers, and health care. To permit physicians, most trained at public expense, as well as hospitals to profit from health care or to ask wage laborers to fend for themselves in their old age was grotesque.

We left from Montreal, Canada, where a Cubana airliner flew us to Havana. Our hosts put us up in the home of a wealthy Cuban who had fled the island. We visited schools, met and talked to teachers, spent a day with physicians and nurses at a health clinic, watched workers and their foremen at a sugar *central,* and discussed law with judges of the high courts. We asked questions galore and brought up shortcomings, which the Cubans laid at the feet of the U.S. embargo of their country.

Clearly there was progress, most certainly in education and health care. In their primary schools, the Cubans had left the rest of Latin America far behind, particularly in third- and fourth-grade mathematics and language achievement; as the *New York Times* reported, "even the lowest fourth of Cuban students performed above the regional average." Despite the embargo, which made the purchase of medicine and medical equipment difficult, no country in the Western Hemisphere had a lower infant mortality rate. In Havana, we saw no homeless persons, and no child slept in a doorway. There was an explosive renaissance in popular music, basically Afro-Cuban, and Cuban films and literature also were enjoying a heyday. Cuba may not have been a classless society, but there was not, in the Mexican manner, a chasm between rich and poor. However, for my American colleagues, socialism had failed, and Fidel Castro was simply a dictator, regardless of what our hosts told us. The Americans had eyes only for the poverty that over-whelms Cuba. When I returned to Cuba a few years later, I ran into one of the students who had hosted her counterparts from the United States. "I remember you well," she volunteered, "because, unlike the others, you listened to us."

Since that visit, I have twice returned to Cuba at the invitation of the *rector* (president) of the University of Havana. On the first, Richard C. Atkinson, a psychologist and the chancellor at UCSD and the successor to Bill McElroy, joined me. He was not only a delightful companion but also an eager conversationalist at the dinner hosted by the rector, though he spoke no Spanish and had to rely on a translator. Our visit to the department of psychology was a tour de force because the Cubans thought well of Dick's stud-ies in mathematical psychology. The stop at the School of Medi-cine was a high point of our stay; its dean, a man in his late thir-ties, joined by his young wife, a professor at the medical school, escorted us on a tour of the facilities. He explained what was being done but lamented the lack of laboratory equipment and sup-plies—at times, it appeared, almost begging for Dick's help. The dean had come home from Chicago, where he had earned his medical degree, to support the revolution.

From that visit, the Cuban women keep turning up in my mind. At the medical school, not only did they enter with high grades, but they did so well on the entrance exams that an affirmative action plan for men was put in place else they be shut out. Academically they were doing amazingly well, not just at the University of Havana but in every one of the provincial campuses. They were chairs of divisions and departments—psychology and arts come to mind specifically because of the women who led them, one white, the other Afro-Cuban, the latter married to a vice rec-tor, a white man. We attended department meetings where the women did the talking, whereas the men, if they spoke at all, never had much to say. Women made up the student majorities on cam-pus, not merely in the humanities, where they usually do well, but also in physics, chemistry, and engineering—fields that are most often male prerogatives.

Before the revolution, Cuba was, as I mentioned earlier, hardly a racial paradise. Quite the contrary: *racist* and *segregated* best described its society. Urban Cuba was heavily white, and poverty was the lot of rural folk, mostly of African ancestry. In Havana, tourist hotels, the better beaches, as well as elite restaurants were off limits to *morenos,* as dark-skinned Cubans are known. In the 1970s, we came across a Cuba in the throes of a racial metamorphosis. Yes, whites still sat at the top of the social ladder, but blacks were starting to climb it, especially in the academic world. At night, as Dick and I walked about Havana, we stumbled across mixed couples, doing what teenagers do everywhere, necking and fondling each other. On the streets, interracial couples were not uncommon, and black children played with companions as white as Norman Rockwell's picket fences. Race prejudice lingered on, especially among older Cubans, who might still oppose the marriage of a son or daughter to a person of African ancestry, as a white woman explained to us.

A year later I was back in Cuba, this time with Natalia, again at the invitation of the *rector* and as Atkinson's representative. The goal was to try to establish a faculty exchange program between Havana and San Diego. A few months later the *rector* and his aide came to La Jolla at our invitation, where Atkinson had them over for dinner, and they discussed mutual concerns with invited faculty. There was interest on both sides, but unfortunately distance and a lack of funds in Cuba proved insurmountable.

At home at the close of the 1980s, I learned a lesson about Chicano colleagues. Convinced that unless we stood together, we were powerless to compel faculty and bureaucrats to heed our demands, I prevailed upon Chicano professors in the UC system to organize into an association. The goal was to hire more Chicano professors and to work for their tenure and their promotion; there was good reason for this. In the eight UC campuses, there were only 115 of us, most at the lower ranks, and the numbers were not increasing. No chancellor, vice chancellor, or dean was a Chicano; only once had a Chicano been a chancellor. The upshot of these efforts was the Chicano-Latino Faculty Association of the University of California; we added *Latino* to the title in hopes of attracting Spanish Americans teaching on the various campuses to join us; none ever did. At our initial meeting, I was elected president.

The association never got off the ground. We held meetings, usually poorly attended, the same persons present. To my dismay, I learned the obvious: Chicanos, despite ethnic affinities, were very much like their Anglo colleagues. They were ambitious and wanted to advance their careers by following the rules of the game. In theory, everyone embraced ethnic cooperation and unity, but in practice it was simply talk. Professors on the smaller campuses distrusted their brethren at UCLA, where forty Chicanos taught. Many UCLA Chicanos, for their part, expressed scant interest in fighting battles on other campuses. Exceptions there were, especially Raymund Paredes, professor of Chicano literature at UCLA, as well as Eloy Gutiérrez, a biologist at Irvine; they were good allies. The lesson? Shared raw deals do not necessarily make partners, let alone trusted allies, of the victimized.

The death blow occurred at a meeting in the UCLA faculty club, where Paredes and I had organized a program around the question of how to teach Chicano studies. Was it best to put professors in one Chicano studies department, in an ethnic studies department, or in established discipline departments? Since Paredes was on the UCLA campus and had funds to pay for the meeting, he took on the task of inviting professors to meet and talk. We would debate the merits of each system.

On the day of the meeting, the turnout was excellent. Too good, in fact. When I arrived at the faculty club, I ran into a band of militant Chicano students, placards in the air, demanding admittance to the meeting. What Paredes and I had overlooked was that his campus was not an appropriate place for such a meeting because at that time a rancorous debate was going on between proponents of a Chicano studies department, a majority of them students, and advocates of the departmental approach, mostly non-Chicano faculty. Behind the students, moreover, were a number of faculty manipulators, professors who, out of conviction or personal ambition, egged the students on. Although well meaning,

Paredes, at the behest of the administration, had blundered, in my opinion, by coming out in support of the departmental solution, thus playing into the hands of Anglo bureaucrats and faculty who opposed the establishment of a Chicano studies department.

Paredes allowed the student protestors to attend the meeting, a horrendous mistake it turned out. They were there to block any rational discussion. When a vice chancellor from UCLA, there to welcome us, attempted to speak, the students shouted him down. When I tried to get the meeting under way, I, too, had to leave the podium. Two or three of the students would not let me speak. Some were overtly obnoxious, shouting insults, anything but in keeping with the *modales* (social graces) Mamá had upheld. Meanwhile, the would-be faculty caudillos, who shared the students' views, sat in the back of hall, making no effort to calm them so that we could get on with the debate. When I asked one of them for help, his reply was, "You got yourself into this, now you get yourself out." Had he tried, I suspect, he would have ceased being a caudillo. These faculty provocateurs were leaders of the mob only if they ran ahead of it. The tumult at UCLA ended efforts to unite Chicano faculty in the UC system. When I left the presidency, the Chicano-Latino Faculty Association fell apart.

Yet, in fits and spurts, the battle goes on. Recently, Rodolfo (Rudy) Acuña, a scholar and teacher, fought one skirmish. Asked by Chicano professors to apply for a job in Chicano studies at UC Santa Barbara, he was rejected by Anglo professors who ruled him unqualified: according to them, he had published little, its quality was poor, and, they alleged, he was a troublemaker. Actually, Acuña, a professor at a California State University campus, was not just a published scholar; he was literally the father of Chicano studies. His book *Occupied America,* which had gone through three editions, was the classic text in Chicano history, and others of his books dealt with Chicanos in Los Angeles; his list of articles ran into multiple pages. As a teacher, he was legendary. Turned down, Acuña sued, and in court I testified on his behalf; when the university's lawyers, whose case had noticeable rents and tears, alleged that he had authored "just three books," I told the court that historians rarely publish more than their doctoral thesis. The jury ruled unanimously in Acuña's favor. Strangely, though the university had to pay damages, the judge, a black woman, ruled that it need not appoint him. To its discredit, it did not, at the expense of students who would have flocked to his classes. Shamefully, at least two Chicanos on the Santa Barbara faculty chose to side with the Anglos who rejected Acuña. Had my father lived to see this, I know what he would have said: *"Mancharon el pabellón"* (they dishonored the flag).

Rudy, whom I knew just slightly before the trial, is now more than just a friend; he has become an intellectual confidant. He is a scholar of strong convictions, unafraid to speak his mind; not just that, he acts on what he says. Most academics waffle. We talk on the phone to exchange ideas, and what I hear usually departs from what traditional scholars commonly write. Rudy was raised in East Los Angeles, a Mexican barrio, and, except for military service, has spent all of his life there, and I come from a small Anglo town, but he and I share anger at the injustice around us, hope for an equitable society, and the wish for a more right-minded Chicano leadership.

Older and less opinionated, Enrique (Hank) López, a Mexican from Colorado, was also a friend until he died suddenly from a heart attack. When he ran for lieutenant governor of California, he was the sole candidate on the Democratic ticket not elected. Why? Surely racial bigotry was the culprit. Intelligent and sophisticated, he was a lawyer, politico, and writer, author of *The Harvard Mystique* and other books. In part because we were identical in age, we shared a past and the customs and values of that day. From time to time, he would come by, either alone or with his wife, and our talk would drift over the map but sometimes come back to the Chicano movement, then going full steam, although he never quite understood the issue because of his background. I saw him for the last time in Mexico City in 1982, when he was writing an article on the inauguration of Miguel de la Madrid. With others I have known, Hank López has vanished, as if he temporarily had stepped out from the pages of a book and then ducked back inside.

One of the rewards that comes from being a university professor is that now and then you make friends of students you tutored who go on to become professors. The oldest of them is Mario García, whose friendship with me is more than three decades old. Born, raised, and educated in El Paso, Texas, he is the son of a Mexican American woman who was left by her Mexican husband to raise four offspring, but who put each one of them through college and then watched three of them earn Ph.D.s, two of them in history. In my last year at Smith, I had lectured at the University of Texas at El Paso, where at a luncheon the history department had brought a young student to my attention. I was told that he wanted to be a history professor. All through the lunch, he just sat and stared at me. He was Mario García, whom I mentioned earlier. When I arrived at San Diego, I thought of Mario and offered to find him a San Diego Fellowship. He came and completed his Ph.D., and today he is a senior scholar, a professor at UC Santa Barbara, and before that a professor at Yale. As a UC student, Mario went through a radical phase and not just as a Chicano militant, though he was certainly that. He became a Marxist, a left-winger as politics in this country go, eager to overturn the university status quo, so much so that he sometimes tended to put me off. Now he is a liberal of sorts.

Ten years have gone by since I abandoned teaching. I confess, I feel no desire to return to the classroom, though that is why I became a professor. However, I have kept up my writing. Proof of that is *Reflexiones sobre la identidad de los pueblos* (1995), which Olivia and I edited, wrote, and published in Mexico. The book is a collection of essays that explore the question of identity, how Mexicans and Chicanos see themselves. I also wrote some of *On the Rim of Mexico,* the book about the U.S.–Mexico border, in rural Coahuila, when Natalia and I spent a fall on the ranch of Eliseo Mendoza Berrueto, some twenty miles from Saltillo, the state capital. Thanks to Luis Villoro, the Mexican philosopher, I also am more or less a regular contributor to *Dialéctica,* a Mexican journal of leftist scholarship.

Here I add a footnote on the subject of writing and scholarship.

I want folks who don't have an advanced degree or any expertise but who have an interest in history to read what I have to say. I endeavor to write about people and agree with Jacques Barzun's belief that "the secret to writing a good history is to remember that the stuff of history is the thoughts and deeds of living beings." If that stuff doesn't catch your attention, why bother to tell it? I also agree with Mariano Azuela, the Mexican novelist, who years ago expressed a simple truth in *Cien años de novela mexicano:* "I know that one must strive to be a reputable author, but I deem it more important to be honest with oneself . . . and so I write what I think and feel without being mindful if my opinions coincide or not with commonly accepted ones."

By the 1970s, a calamity had befallen scholarly output: new schools of thought, at first propagated by the French, spent much energy teaching people to think by means of empty categories so that today academia in the United States is larded with essays replete with jargon fathomable only to the initiated. The use of jargon also may explain why commercial publishers and the reading public are deserting academic history. Unable to read what is written, fewer people seek the wisdom of professional scholars and turn instead to amateurs.

True, the field of history is no longer a monopoly of the old boys' club, where Anglo-Protestants at elite institutions trained their successors and in their books said nothing about ethnic tensions, while the racism that plagued their writing seldom, if ever, marred their eulogistic view of national events, and women were hidden from sight. Even Charles Beard, that iconoclastic scholar, worried that immigrants from eastern Europe distorted the cherished character of the United States. Now cultural history, gender, and race play important roles, whereas the revered cry for objectivity, a virtual impossibility, no longer takes precedence over common sense.

Unfortunately, intellectuals still often blindly follow what's trendy. That may include some who study cultural history, which heralds an embrace of "high theory" and "models" and encompasses sundry historians of Latin America. According to critics of cultural studies, its luminaries—in their pursuit of status, prestige, and stardom—turn progressive values on their head. Instead of a critique of hierarchy, we have, according to history scholar Barbara Epstein, "a kind of reveling in hierarchy and in the benefits that come with rising to the top of it." This shift in values, so goes her argument, reflects a broader trend, part of an era of "sharpening economic and social divisions, characterized by corporate demands for greater and greater profits and the canonizing of greed."

From time to time, colleges and universities with predominantly Chicano populations invite me to talk about contemporary Mexico before audiences of two hundred or more. Not that I don't lecture before Anglo-American audiences: among my cherished memories is a visit to Pomona College as the Ena H. Thompson Lecturer and spending a week meeting with students and faculty, and one of my most enjoyable experiences was as the Ralph Chase Lecturer at Angelo State University, a two-hour drive from Midland, the heart of the Texas petroleum country.

After retirement, I fulfilled a life's dream: to teach Mexican history at UNAM, the intellectual Mecca of the Mexican Republic. Earlier I had been a visiting scholar at the Colegio de Michoacán, which sits in the heart of Catholic Mexico, where in the 1920s diehard Catholics, called Cristeros, waged a guerrilla war against federal authority. Today former priests teach there, some of whom have married and divorced and married again. I also was at the Colegio de Sonora, in a state once home to some of Mexico's most notorious persecutors of the Catholic Church. And for two years, I was scholar in residence at the Colegio de la Frontera Norte in Tijuana.

I stay abreast of Mexican events by reading *Proceso* and *La Jornada,* popular journals, and by watching Mexican public television, usually better than ours. I return to visit colleagues and friends. When our travels take us through Chihuahua, Natalia and I stop in Parral to visit the cemetery where my maternal ancestors lie. One headstone always draws me, that of an uncle buried in 1914, under a tall monument his mother and father, my grandparents, dedicated to him.

We traveled, too, to Lima, Peru, as guests of the Mexican embassy, a city under siege by guerrillas and patrolled by soldiers in army tanks shielding a right-wing regime, and to Salvador, a city in the Province of Bahia on the hump of northern Brazil, where Olivia was doing research. For centuries, Bahia harbored sugar plantations, whose Portuguese masters imported Africans slaves to plant and harvest the crop. Salvador is a haven for desperately poor blacks and mulattos, which the tastes and smells of the local cuisine reflect. We could read street signs but rarely understood a spoken word; African tongues had given the oral Portuguese a peculiar sound, as we realized later in our travels through Portugal, a beautiful country, neither terribly poor nor terribly rich, where Natalia and I, if we listened carefully, could make out what natives were saying. We visited Portugal because Maura, who ran the University of Maryland overseas program, spent two years there with her husband, Scott; before he abandoned the navy, he was aide-de-camp to the U.S. admiral at NATO headquarters in Lisbon. Spain, of course, was another story; in Sevilla, our favorite Spanish city, we felt at home, by language, customs, food.

In the fall of 1998, I returned to Washington, D.C., to receive an unexpected but very welcomed recognition. As a military band struck up "Hail to the Chief," William Jefferson Clinton, the president of the United States, strode down the aisle where I and seven others waited to confer on us the National Medal of the Humanities for lifetime achievement. I am told that I am the only American of Mexican ancestry to be so honored. "A prodigious scholar," writes Jack Sproat—whom I have known since my Berkeley days— in a personal memoir not yet published, "Ramón Eduardo Ruiz is today one of the country's most gifted and authoritative historians of Mexico and Hispanic America."

Olivia, after graduating from Smith College, earned a doctorate in anthropology from UC Berkeley; she owns a home in Tijuana and teaches at the Colegio de la Frontera Norte. She speaks and writes Spanish and English fluently, is bicultural, and is as much at home in Mexico as in the United States. She studies Mexicans on the U.S.–Mexico border and migrants from Guatemala, who enter Mexico through Chiapas. Her specialty is women and the family, the poor driven out of their homes by poverty, exploitation, and brutality. Olivia is more than just an anthropologist; she writes poetry in two languages and publishes in respected journals.

Maura, our other daughter, is also bilingual and bicultural. As we did with Olivia, we enrolled her in schools in Mexico and, when she graduated from Pomona College, sent her to Hermosillo to study at the Universidad Autónoma de Sonora and to live with friends. Maura has spent years working with students on college and university campuses and for a time served in the office of the mayor of Albuquerque. Maura and Scott are the parents of our grandchildren, one named Andrés Ruiz and the other Diego Zacarías, both Parkinsons.

After a lifetime climbing the academic ladder, teaching and writing as a professor at a college or university, I had a difficult time reaching the decision to retire. Never had I contemplated any other career. For a while after I finally did retire, I felt adrift, cut off from decades-old ties to an academic institution; in time, however, I learned that I could function quite well without them. Rarely do I return to campus and then usually to have lunch with Patrick Ledden, provost of Muir College, a friend since I arrived on campus and someone with whom I share social values and political opinions.

Today Natalia and I live in a place locals call the "village" of Rancho Santa Fe. When we purchased the property in 1970 before I took up my position at UCSD, we were in Mexico City, determined to replicate a bit of Mexico when we reached California. The Ranch, as locals also refer to it, lies some twenty miles north of San Diego and was more rural than urban when we first moved there. One could not build on lots of less than two acres, and some homesteads were twenty acres or more. In Mexico City, Natalia and I had set about reading books on Mexican colonial architecture, visiting old homes and churches, and using what we learned to design an adobe house, the kind we had dreamed of owning. When we arrived in California, we carried a draft of the home we hoped to build. Our house has adobe walls, a red-tile roof, and floor tiles made in Tecate, Mexico.

Despite its name, Rancho Santa Fe is neither Mexican nor Spanish, but, until a decade or so ago, thoroughly Anglo, although its street names are in Spanish, many misspelled. We moved here because it offered country living, the kind I had as a young man in Pacific Beach, and was the closest place to the campus where we could own horses. When we left our home in Massachusetts, we left behind not only Olivia's childhood friends, but also Tiburcio, her horse. So we bought another horse for Olivia and taught Maura to ride.

It has been thirty years since we moved to Rancho Santa Fe, and during that time we have witnessed the tenacious decline of its way of life. The octopus of suburban sprawl entraps us in its tentacles. Expensive housing tracts, where the wealthy acquire homes, pop up in the fields around the Ranch like Bermuda grass, that loathsome weed that sucks the life out of blue-grass lawns. The rich buy older homes, tear them down, and build mansions, some with artificial waterfalls and Moorish towers, cupolas and all. Short miles away, shopping malls spawn satellite strips, the noise of auto traffic, and congested streets with flashing signal lights.

I live not far from a brother and two sisters, Roberto a few miles up the coast, and Emma, now an avocado rancher, even closer. Eva, the youngest, has a home on the hills between La Jolla and Pacific Beach, just blocks away from where I was born. Berta, the eldest, died some years ago. We are much older now and have gone our separate ways, yet from time to time we come together. When alive, Mamá held the family together; now I try to do the same, enjoying more success in this endeavor with Roberto and Emma, largely because I have more in common with them. Intellectually I am closer to Emma, but with Roberto I share a brother's life, years in the military during World War II, and memories of classmates and friends from bygone days.

Am I the same man who began this odyssey decades ago? Of course not, but not so different either; I am older, at an age when the past recedes, moving farther and farther away and with it people I had known and things I did. When I read or hear that someone I knew years ago has died, even celebrities I knew only from reading newspapers or watching movies, I pause for thought, not because I am necessarily saddened, but because death reminds me that everyone, no matter what his or her ethnicity, is mortal. I am wiser perhaps, but just as feisty, although less inclined to do battle with the forces of bigotry. Live and let live, so goes the old cliché, and to some extent I have accepted its wisdom, but not entirely. As a famous actress once said, "I'd rather be strongly wrong than weakly right."

I am still the hyphenated man. "I have never seen anyone as torn between two cultures as Ramón," writes Jack Sproat. "On the one hand, he is a proud Mexican cultural nationalist, rightfully scornful of gringo racism and imperialism," yet "irresistibly attracted to the good life in this country as epitomized in New England–Ivy League traditionalism." Lucas de la Garza, my friend from Monterrey, once said something that I never forgot: "Before he dies, a man must have his horse, *tener sus tierras* [land of his own], and write a book." I have done that.

About the Author

———

Ramón Eduardo Ruiz Urueta, the recipient of the National Medal of the Humanities, conferred by the president of the United States, is the son of Mexican parents; he was born in Sessions Ranch, some fifteen miles from San Diego, California. He is the author of many books, among them the award-winning *Triumphs and Tragedy: A History of the Mexican People* (1992), as well as *Cuba: The Making of a Revolution* (1968), *The Great Rebellion: Mexico, 1906–1923* (1980), and *On the Rim of Mexico: Encounters of the Rich and Poor* (1998). He also has published books and articles in Mexico. Before joining the history department of the University of California, San Diego, where he is professor emeritus, he taught at the University of Oregon and at Smith College. He also has taught at the Uni-versidad Nacional Autónoma de México and at the Facultad de Economía de la Universidad de Nuevo León and was scholar in residence at the Colegio de la Frontera Norte, Tijuana, Baja California Norte.